TEACHER'S MANUAL

FOCUS ON GRAMMAR

An **INTERMEDIATE** Course for Reference and Practice

TEACHER'S MANUAL

FOCUS ON GRAMMAR

An **INTERMEDIATE** Course for Reference and Practice

SECOND EDITION

Sarah Lynn

Longman

Focus on Grammar: An Intermediate Course for Reference and Practice, Teacher's Manual

Pearson Education, 10 Bank Street, White Plains, NY 10606

Vice president, director of publishing: Allen Ascher
Editorial director: Louisa Hellegers
Senior development manager: Penny Laporte
Vice president, director of design and production: Rhea Banker
Executive managing editor: Linda Moser
Production manager: Alana Zdinak
Senior production editor: Virginia Bernard
Director of manufacturing: Patrice Fraccio
Senior manufacturing buyer: David Dickey
Cover design: Rhea Banker
Text design adaptation: Wendy Wolf and Steven Greydanus
Text composition: TSI Graphics

ISBN: 0-201-34674-5

3 4 5 6 7 8 9 10–BAH–04 03 02 01

CONTENTS

INTRODUCTION

Focus on Grammar: An Intermediate Course for Reference and Practice, Second Edition helps intermediate students of English to understand and practice basic English grammar. However, teaching the rules is not the ultimate goal of the course. Rather, the aim is for students to use the language confidently and appropriately.

This Teacher's Manual provides suggestions for teaching the intermediate level Student Book.

The first part of this Teacher's Manual contains general suggestions for every unit. The next part gives practical unit-by-unit teaching suggestions as well as Background Notes and Culture Notes to accompany specific exercises and grammar content in the Student Book. The Teacher's Manual also provides ready-to-use diagnostic and final tests for each part in the Student Book. In addition, the Teacher's Manual includes answer keys for the diagnostic and final tests as well as a tapescript for all the listening activities in the Student Book.

Focus on Grammar recognizes different styles of language learning and provides a variety of activities to accommodate these different styles. Some learners prefer an analytical, or rule-learning, approach. Others, especially younger learners, respond best to exposure to the language in meaningful contexts. Indeed, the same students may adopt different styles as they learn or may use different styles at different times. To complicate things further, some students respond better to visual instruction, and some better to auditory.

As teachers, we want to help the rule-learners in our classes become more able to take risks and to plunge into communicative activities. We also want to encourage the risk-takers to focus on accuracy. To this end, the ***Focus on Grammar*** series provides the variety, including listening activities, that students need. Each unit presents a balanced approach with a variety of activities so that all learners can benefit.

GENERAL SUGGESTIONS

GRAMMAR IN CONTEXT

Each unit in *Focus on Grammar: An Intermediate Course for Reference and Practice, Second Edition* begins with a reading to present the grammar in a realistic context. Students first focus on the meaning of the reading, thereby establishing a context for the language study before they focus on the target grammatical structure.

BACKGROUND NOTE/CULTURE NOTE: This Teacher's Manual includes Background Notes and Culture Notes relevant to the topic of the reading and theme of the unit.

Before You Read: Each unit opens with several warm-up questions. This section gets students familiar with the topic of the reading.

1. Have the class look at the reading and illustrations and identify the context.
2. Read the questions aloud to the class and ask students to respond.
3. Alternatively, have pairs of students read the questions, respond, and then share their ideas with the class.
4. Alternatively, give students two or three minutes to read the questions individually and jot down their own responses. Then invite students to share their ideas with the class.

Reading: The reading text presents language in various formats, including magazine and newspaper articles, advertisements, greeting cards, Internet chat forums, instructions, questionnaires, and dialogues. All the readings are recorded on cassettes and CDs.

There are many ways to treat this text in the classroom. Here are alternative suggestions:

If you have the cassette/CD:
1. Have students listen to the cassette/CD, books closed, first. Have students answer the comprehension questions provided in the unit teaching suggestions and then read the text to confirm their answers.
2. Play the cassette/CD a second time as students read along. For pronunciation practice, have students read the passage aloud in pairs as a final review.

If you don't have the cassette/CD:
1. Have students read the text silently. Then have students take turns reading the text aloud.
2. Read the passage aloud to the class. Have students read along in their books.

Comprehension questions are provided in the unit teaching suggestions. When the text is particularly challenging, you may want to supply the questions before the reading. When the text is easier, present the comprehension questions after the reading. Write the questions on the board or dictate them to the class. Have students respond in pairs and then share their ideas with the class.

Focus on Grammar: This step has students identify the target grammatical structures embedded in the reading.

1. Elicit examples from the text of the target grammatical structures and write the examples on the board. The target structures are presented in boldface for easy identification.
2. Ask inductive questions to get students to identify the forms of the grammatical structures and key grammar points. Sample questions are supplied in the unit teaching suggestions
3. List students' responses to the questions on the board. As students continue on to the Grammar Presentation, encourage them to compare these notes with the information presented in the grammar charts and grammar notes.

GRAMMAR PRESENTATION

At this point in the lesson, students understand the structures in context and now are ready to study their forms in isolation. This section presents the target grammatical structures in a straightforward and comprehensive way. The grammar charts focus students on the forms and mechanics of the grammatical structures. The grammar notes list the grammar points as well as exceptions to help students understand variations in the meaning, use, and forms of the structures.

The language presented in *Focus on Grammar: An Intermediate Course for Reference and Practice, Second Edition,* is the English of daily life in the United States and Canada. Contractions and short answers are practiced. More formal usage is mentioned in the grammar notes.

Common grammatical terms are used throughout the book because they make grammar explanations clearer and because students have often learned them in their own language. Students need only understand the terms as they are used, not produce them.

Grammar Charts: The grammar is presented visually in grammar charts. It is important to allow ample time for this part of the lesson so that students may begin to internalize the patterns.

1. Write the key paradigms on the board and circle or underline important features, such as the third-person singular *-s* for simple present tense.
2. Give additional examples. Encourage students to supply their own examples when they are ready.
3. Use magazine pictures or other simple cues for drilling so that students become accustomed to producing the form.

Grammar Notes: These notes pull together and make explicit the information about meaning, use, and form that the students have encountered in the introductory reading and grammar charts. The grammar notes also offer information about degrees of formality to help students use the forms appropriately as well as correctly.

1. Ask students to read each note. Write the examples on the board and highlight important features.
2. Give additional examples and ask students to supply their own.
3. At each note, check students' comprehension by asking them to complete a sentence or fill in the blank of a sentence.
4. This Teacher's Manual provides additional suggestions in each unit for many of the grammar notes.

FOCUSED PRACTICE

This section gets students to practice using the target grammar structures in various contexts. The exercises in this section have straightforward and objective answers, and they serve well as homework or for individual work in class. These exercises are cross referenced to the grammar notes, making this section especially convenient for self-study.

All the exercises develop the theme of the introductory text, providing cultural information as well as grammar practice. The completed exercises can be used as readings to develop students' reading skills and cultural knowledge. Comprehension questions for the longer and more substantial exercise passages are provided in the unit teaching suggestions.

Discover the Grammar: This is the opening activity for the Focused Practice section. It gets students to identify the target grammar structures in a realistic context. This exercise may be done by the whole class, as pair work, or individually for homework. Specific teaching suggestions are provided in each unit.

Editing: Most units include an editing exercise to test students' sensitivity to incorrect usage of the target grammar structures. Students are required to identify and correct errors in a contextualized passage such as a letter, diary entry, or essay. The direction line indicates the number of errors in the passage. Remind students that the example error is included in the total number of errors.

1. Have students read through the passage quickly to understand its context and meaning.
2. Have students read the passage line by line, circling in pencil any incorrect structures and writing in their corrections.
3. To review the material, have students take turns reading the passage line by line, including all sentences, even the correct ones. Alternatively, slowly read the passage aloud to the class and have students interrupt you with their corrections. There are usually correct usages of the target structures in each editing exercise. Be sure to ask students about these usages as well—i.e., why they are not errors.

COMMUNICATION PRACTICE

This section has students practice using the target structures appropriately in realistic situations, as well as develop their listening comprehension and speaking fluency. The types of exercises in this section range from listening comprehension to information gaps and role plays. Because there are many variations in the exercise types, specific ideas and instructions are provided in the unit teaching suggestions. The following are general suggestions for the four most prevalent types of exercises you will encounter.

Listening:
1. Explain the situational context of the listening passage.
2. Before playing the cassette/CD, ask students to read over the items in the exercise so that they know what to listen for.
3. Explain any unknown vocabulary and give any necessary cultural information.
4. Ask students to listen the first time with their pencils down.
5. Play the cassette/CD, or read aloud the tapescript included in this Teacher's Manual. If you choose to read, speak with a lot of expression and at a natural pace. Change positions and tone of voice to indicate who the speaker is. You can also draw stick figures and label them with the characters' names so that you can point to the appropriate character as you change roles.
6. Tell students to listen again to complete the task. Play the cassette/CD again or read the tapescript.
7. Let the students listen as many times as they need in order to complete the task.
8. Elicit answers and write them on the board. Answer any questions the students may have.
9. Play the cassette/CD a final time for students to review the passage using the corrected answers.

Pair and Group Activities:
1. Review the task so students understand what is required.
2. Have students volunteer to demonstrate the activity for the class.
3. Divide the class into pairs or groups.
4. If writing is required, have groups assign one student to be the scribe for the group.
5. Give the class a fixed time limit for completing the task.
6. Circulate among the pairs or groups, answering students' questions and helping them with the activity.
7. When time is up, have each pair or group report its findings to the class.
8. Follow up with a class discussion. Use specific questions supplied in the unit teaching suggestions.

Role Plays:
1. Review the task so students understand what is required.
2. Create a sample role play with the class. Act it out with volunteers.
3. Have students write a script for some role plays; alternatively, have them plan the action without a script and present it extemporaneously for fluency practice.
4. Divide the class into the suggested groupings.
5. Give the class a fixed time limit for completing the task.
6. Have each group develop its own role play.
7. Circulate among the groups, answering students' questions and helping them with the activity.
8. Have the groups present their role plays to the class. If possible, tape record or videotape the role plays for students' own viewing.
9. Follow up with a class discussion. Use specific questions supplied in the unit teaching suggestions.

Information Gaps:
1. Divide the class into pairs (Students A and B) and have them position themselves so that they cannot see the content of each others' books.
2. Tell Student B what page they are to turn to, and circulate to check that they are looking at the correct page.
3. Have students read their separate instructions. Check comprehension of the task.
4. Explain how the A and B pages relate to each other, that is, how they are different or similar.
5. Refer students to the examples and any language provided.
6. Remind students not to show each other the contents of their pages.
7. Have students begin the task.
8. Circulate to answer individual questions, and help students with the activity if necessary and appropriate.
9. After sufficient time, have selected pairs share their results with the class.

Expansion:
One or two Expansion exercises can be found at the end of every Teacher's Manual unit. These exercises offer further communicative practice with the target structure of the unit.

Writing: The writing activities establish realistic contexts, such as notes, letters, and memos, for practice using the target grammatical structures. The activities originate from material covered in previous exercises so that students are well prepared to complete the writing task. Specific teaching instructions are provided in the unit teaching suggestions. The following are general suggestions for the teaching of writing.

Prewriting: Be sure students understand the requirements of the assignment. Have students brainstorm ideas for the writing assignment in pairs or small groups.

Composing and Correcting:
1. Have students compose a draft of the writing assignment as homework, then submit it to you or share it with a partner in class. You or the students may provide feedback on this draft for its meaning and accuracy. If students do peer corrections, you will still want to have them submit their writing to you for final review.
2. For longer assignments, have students compose two drafts. Review the first draft only for its meaning and overall organization and the second draft for its grammatical accuracy.
3. When correcting students' writing, circle the grammatical errors studied in the current and/or previous units and have students work with partners or in small groups to correct the errors. Have students submit the corrections to you for final review.

<u>Presentation:</u> When the drafts are final, have students share them with the class in small groups or in pairs. In some instances, you may want to post their work on the classroom bulletin board or publish it in a series of students' writings.

Expansion: Each unit in the Teacher's Manual includes one or more additional Expansion activities to use with students. The Expansion activity brings together the content, structures, and skills developed in the unit.

REVIEW OR SELFTEST

The units in the Student Book are grouped into eight parts. At the end of each part there is a *Review or SelfTest* section, a *From Grammar to Writing* section, and the *Answer Key* for the Review or SelfTest. The *Review or SelfTest* section gives students a chance to check their knowledge of the part's grammar and review any weak area before moving on to the next part. There are various ways to use this section. The following is a list of alternative suggestions:

1. Have students complete the exercises at home and check their answers in the *Answer Key*, bringing to class any remaining questions. Alternatively, have students compare answers in pairs or go over them as a class when they return.
2. Have students complete the exercises in class so that you can circulate to see how individual students are coping.
3. Use appropriate exercises as extra practice for students who need them as you progress through the units.

FROM GRAMMAR TO WRITING

The *From Grammar to Writing* section presents and practices a teaching point which applies specifically to writing. The points vary from combining sentences to writing a three-paragraph essay. Formats include a personal letter, a business letter, instructions, an informal note, and an essay. Students practice prewriting strategies such as brainstorming, word-mapping, tree-diagramming, and outlining. Each writing section concludes with peer review and editing. Some of these exercises serve well as homework or as self-study in class for students to work on individually. Others can be done in pairs or groups in class.

TEACHING SUGGESTIONS

PART I PRESENT, PAST, AND FUTURE: REVIEW AND EXPANSION

 UNIT 1 PRESENT PROGRESSIVE AND SIMPLE PRESENT TENSE

GRAMMAR **IN CONTEXT** (page 2)

See the General Suggestions for Grammar in Context on page 2.

CULTURE NOTE: IQ stands for intelligence quotient. A cross-cultural IQ measures a person's ability to recognize and accurately interpret cross-cultural misunderstandings.

Before You Read, page 2: Read the questions aloud. Give the class one minute to look at the cartoons and jot down a response to the questions. Briefly discuss students' ideas.

Reading, page 2: Ask the following questions:

Situation 1
What time does Eva expect her guests to arrive? (after 7:30)
What time does Karl think it is polite to arrive at Eva's party? (exactly at 7:00)
Why are they unhappy with each other? (because both think the other is inconsiderate)
What can Eva say to Karl now? (Answers will vary.)
How can they resolve their misunderstanding? (Answers will vary.)

Situation 2
At what distance do people usually stand in Sami's culture? (quite close)
At what distance do people usually stand in Taro's culture? (farther apart with little touching)
Why are they uncomfortable with one another? (They have different ideas about appropriate distance.)
How can they resolve their misunderstanding? (Answers will vary.)

Focus on Grammar: Write the headings *Usually* and *Right Now* on the board. Elicit examples of the highlighted structures from the reading and write them under the appropriate column headings. Elicit other sentences for the two situations. Ask the following questions:

What is happening now?
What usually happens in their cultures?

Point to the left column on the board and ask, *What verb tense is this? How is it formed?* With the class's input, write out the full conjugation of the verb *arrive* in the simple present tense.
Point to the right column on the board and ask, *What verb tense is this? How is it formed?* With the class's input, write out the full conjugation of the verb *arrive* in the present progressive tense.

GRAMMAR **PRESENTATION**: Present Progressive and Simple Present Tense (pages 3–5)

See the General Suggestions for Grammar Presentation on page 3.

NOTE 1: Draw the two timelines on the board and refer to the examples. Use the examples to contrast the meaning of the two tenses. For example:

Eva is talking to Karl (right now). Eva talks to Karl every day.
At the moment she is wearing a robe. She usually wears jeans.

NOTE 2: Draw the timeline on the board and write the words *nowadays, this month, these days, this year, this semester,* and *this week.* Have students form sentences about themselves using the time expressions. Have students share their sentences with the class.

To illustrate the placement of adverbs of frequency, write a simple sentence in scrambled order. For example:

she / calls / always / on the weekend / her parents
(She always calls her parents on the weekend.)

are / they / home / rarely / on the weekend
(They are rarely home on the weekend.)

Tell students that they will hear people use the present progressive with *always* to express strong feelings. For example:

He's always helping me with my homework.
She's always telling me what to do!

NOTE 3: Read the note in the Student Book with the class. Answer any questions.

NOTE 4: Describe the first situation on page 5 of the Student Book using non-action verbs. For example:

Eva likes Karl.
Eva hears the doorbell ring.
Eva sees Karl at the door.
Eva thinks Karl is rude to arrive early.
Karl believes he is on time.
Eva looks annoyed.
Karl appears confused.

Have students work in pairs to describe the second situation with non-action verbs. Have students share their sentences with the class.

NOTE 5: Give more examples:

Cats eat meat.
Many birds fly south in the winter.

Have students supply other examples. Write them on the board.

FOCUSED PRACTICE (pages 6–9)

See the General Suggestions for Focused Practice exercises on pages 3–4.

1. Discover the Grammar, page 6
Have students identify all the verbs that describe what is happening now before underlining the verbs that describe what generally happens. Have students compare their answers in pairs or as a class.

2. Schedule Changes, pages 6–7
Look at the schedule with the class. Ask:

What does Brian usually do in the morning? (He attends class.)
In the afternoon? (He eats lunch and takes a nap.)
In the evening? (He does homework, plays tennis, and has dinner.)
What is special about this morning's plans? (He is going on a field trip.)
What is special about this afternoon's plans? (He is working on his Web page.)
What is special about this evening's plans? (He is watching a video with Eva.)

3. Different Meanings, pages 7–8
Before beginning this exercise, point out that *this semester* is an example of extended present time (Grammar Note 1), so it requires present progressive tense.

To review answers, have pairs of students act out the conversations for the class.

4. Culture Shock!, pages 8–9

BACKGROUND NOTE: A person experiences *culture shock* when first immersed in a foreign culture.

Have students work individually to complete the exercise and check their quiz results. Then have small groups of students (from different cultural backgrounds, if possible) compare their results. Follow up with a class discussion. Ask, *What can help a person adjust quickly to a new culture?*

5. Editing, page 9
See the General Suggestions for Editing on page 4.

Check students' comprehension. Ask:

Where is she living? (in Toronto)
What does she do in the afternoons? (She usually takes a nap in the afternoon.)
What is social distance? (how close people stand to each other)
Is it acceptable to be late for class in Toronto? (No, it is not.)

COMMUNICATION PRACTICE (pages 10–11)

6. Listening, page 10
See the General Suggestions for Listening on page 4.

Check students' comprehension. Ask:

What is the most difficult part of living in a new culture for Maria? (English)
How is the pace of life different? (Everyone moves quickly.)

7. Getting to Know You, page 10
Read the items together as a class. Elicit a correct question for each item. Write the questions on the board for students' reference during the activity. Have students circulate around the room asking and answering the questions. Have students report their findings to the class using full sentences.

8. What's Happening?, page 11
See the General Suggestions for Pair and Group Activities on page 4.

Introduce the adverbs of possibility *perhaps, maybe, probably,* and *possibly*. Write them on the board.

To get pairs brainstorming, write these questions on the board:

What is he / she doing?
What is he / she saying?
What is just outside the frame of the photograph?

Have students share their ideas with the class. Encourage students to challenge each other's interpretations using evidence from the photographs.

Follow up with a comparative discussion of gestures from other cultures. Ask students, *How do you express the following in your culture?*

Hi!
Good-bye.
Come here.
Good luck!
Be quiet.
I can't hear you.
This tastes good.
It's great!

9. Questionable Questions, page 11
See the General Suggestions for Pair and Group Activities on page 4.

Have students work in groups to discuss each question. Have them identify which questions are appropriate in their own cultures and report to the class.

Ask the class to identify the questions that are appropriate in an English-speaking culture. If students are uncertain, explain that talking with an acquaintance about one's body, money, or romantic relationships is not appropriate in English-speaking cultures; talking about work, studies, weather, or personal hobbies is. With the class, brainstorm more questions. Write them on the board.

10. Writing, page 11
See the General Suggestions for Writing on page 5.

Remind students that this English class is a new experience for them. They can describe what they usually do at this hour and what they are doing now; how they usually study English and how they are studying English in this class.

EXPANSION

Student Interviews: If possible, have pairs of students interview English speakers about punctuality and social distance. Before the interview, have the partners brainstorm questions they want to ask. (For example: *What time do you arrive for a dinner invitation at a friend's home? What time do you arrive for a doctor's appointment? How close do you stand to your boss? How close do you stand to your classmates?*) Have students conduct their interviews and report their findings to the class. Ask the class if they can draw any conclusions.

UNIT 2 IMPERATIVE

GRAMMAR **IN CONTEXT** (page 12)

See the General Suggestions for Grammar in Context on page 2.

BACKGROUND NOTE: Kickboxing is a traditional martial art from Thailand. It uses the shins, knees, elbows, and wrists to form different fighting moves.

Before You Read, page 12: Have students read the questions and look at the pictures. Have students discuss their answers in pairs.

Reading, page 12: Call on students to read the instructions aloud while others perform the movements. Alternatively, act out the two moves incorrectly and have students correct you according to the directions in the reading.

Focus on Grammar: Elicit examples of the highlighted structures from the reading and write them on the board. Ask the following questions:
Is the subject pronoun (you) included in the imperative? (No, it isn't.)
How is a negative imperative formed? (It is formed with *don't*.)

GRAMMAR **PRESENTATION**: Imperative (page 13)

See the General Suggestions for Grammar Presentation on page 3.

NOTE 1: Have students read about the functions of the imperative. Give additional examples of each function, using classroom instructions as a context. For example:
a. *Hand out the papers.*
b. *Put your pencils down.*
c. *Please close the door.*
d. *Study a little bit every day.*
e. *Don't be late for class.*
f. *Come on! Work in our group!*

Elicit more examples from the class for each category. Write them on the board. Have students work in pairs giving and responding to imperatives.

Note 2: Point out that it is rude to use the subject *you* in an imperative. (For example: *You! Stand up!*) People speak like this only when they have a great deal of power over someone else, such as in the military.

FOCUSED PRACTICE (pages 14–15)

See the General Suggestions for Focused Practice exercises on pages 3–4.

1. Discover the Grammar, page 14
Have students do this exercise for homework. Go over answers in class.

Alternatively, have students do this exercise in pairs. Have Student A cover column B and Student B cover column A. Have Student A read the imperative prompt. Have Student B listen to the prompt and identify the situation. At item 5, have students switch roles.

2. Health Shake, page 14

Background Note: Health shakes are a popular tasty and nutritious snack. In health food stores, all sorts of vegetable and fruit drinks are available.

Language Note: *To slice* is to cut into uniform, flat sections. (For example, bread, bananas, and sandwich meats are sliced.) *To cut* is simply to divide something into pieces, no matter the shape.

Have students look at the illustrations first. Then have them work in pairs to match the verbs and phrases from the two columns to complete the instructions. Go over the answers as a class. Ask the following comprehension questions:

What are the ingredients? (strawberries, banana, and orange juice)
How long do you think it takes to prepare a health shake? (Answers will vary.)
Would you like it? Why or why not? (Answers will vary.)

3. Martial Arts Academy, page 15
Have students read through the entire passage before filling in the blanks. After the class has gone over the answers, ask the following comprehension questions:

What do students learn at the Martial Arts Academy? (They learn to reduce stress, improve
   concentration, and become fit.)
How long is the introductory trial? (two weeks)
How much does it cost? ($20)
Who is the teacher? (Master Lorenzo Gibbons)

4. Editing, page 15
See the General Suggestions for Editing on page 4.

Follow up with a brief discussion. Ask:

Do you agree with these three rules? Why or why not?
What other rules of life are important to you?

COMMUNICATION PRACTICE (pages 16–18)

5. Listening, page 16
See the General Suggestions for Listening on page 4.

Check students' comprehension. Ask:

What are the ingredients? (egg whites, white or whole wheat flour, regular or low-fat milk, and fruit)
What kind of pan do you use? (a frying pan)
How long do you think it takes to prepare this recipe? (Answers will vary.)

6. Recipe Exchange, page 16
See the General Suggestions for Pair and Group Activities on page 4.

Students can write their recipes at home for homework. In groups, have students read their recipes aloud and answer their classmates' questions.

To check students' comprehension of the recipes they heard, have students take five minutes at the end of the group work to write a summary of one recipe they learned. Have them submit their summaries to you or the original recipe author for correction.

7. Calm Down!, page 16
See the General Suggestions for Pair and Group Activities on page 4.

Give the groups a set time limit to brainstorm. Have them share their ideas with the class. Write their ideas on the board.

8. Information Gap: Find the Way, pages 17–18
Divide the class into pairs. Assign each partner a role (A or B). Assign Students A page 17 and Students B page 18. Have students read their separate instructions and look at their maps. Explain that the maps are of the same area, but each identifies different destinations. Have students refer to the language provided above each map as they give their partners directions. Remind students not to show each other their maps until each set of directions is given.

9. Writing, page 17
See the General Suggestions for Writing on page 5.

Have students read their written directions aloud in small groups. Tell students to withhold the name of the destination. Have the other group members listen to the reading and try to identify the destination.

EXPANSION

TPR Game: Set up a total physical response game with the students. This game is helpful when there is a lull in the class and students need to boost their energy.

Review vocabulary for doing physical exercises. Write students' ideas on the board. Have students take turns calling out instructions for various exercises. Have the class listen and perform the different movements. Make sure everyone gets one chance.

Student Speeches: Use one of the themes in this unit on good health as a springboard for student speeches. Have students tell the class about one healthy habit. (For example: drinking health shakes, exercising, taking vitamins, practicing meditation, etc.) Have each student instruct the class on this healthy habit using the imperative as much as possible. Keep presentations to two minutes each.

UNIT 3 · SIMPLE PAST TENSE

GRAMMAR IN CONTEXT (page 19)
See the General Suggestions for Grammar in Context on page 2.

CULTURE NOTE: Haiku is a traditional form of Japanese poetry, popular since the seventeenth century. It is a three-part poem of usually seventeen syllables in lines of five, seven, and five syllables each. It traditionally focuses on images of the natural world.

Before You Read, page 19: Have students read the questions, look at the picture, and respond. Write their answers on the board.

Reading, page 19: Ask the following questions:

What did Basho write about? (nature, daily life, and human emotions)
Did he stay in his native Kyoto? (No, he moved to Edo.)
Why did he travel so much? (because he was restless)
How many students did he have at the time of his death? (2,000)

Focus on Grammar: Write three headings on the board: *Be, Regular Verbs,* and *Irregular Verbs.* Elicit examples of each type of verb and write them under the appropriate headings. Elicit the base form of each verb. Ask the following questions and write students' responses on the board:

When did Basho live? (in the 1600s)
What's the name of this tense? (simple past)

Point to the first heading and ask, *What is the full conjugation of the verb* be *in the past?* With the class's input, write out the full conjugation.

Point to the second heading and ask, *How do you form regular verbs in the past tense? When do you add* -ed? *When do you add only* -d? With the class's input, write out any rules they can formulate.

Point to the third heading and ask, *What other verbs are irregular in the past tense?* With the class's input, list irregular past tense verbs and their base forms.

GRAMMAR **PRESENTATION:** Simple Past Tense *Be*; Regular and Irregular Verbs (pages 20–22)

See the General Suggestions for Grammar Presentation on page 3.

Grammar Charts: Practice negative statements by writing untrue statements about Basho on the board and having students correct them. For example:

He lived in the eighteenth century. (He didn't live in the eighteenth century. He lived in the seventeenth century.)
He wrote more than 1,000 books. (He didn't write more than 1,000 books. He wrote more than 1,000 poems.)
He was born in Edo in 1644. (He wasn't born in Edo in 1644. He was born in Kyoto in 1644.)
He traveled by train all over Japan. (He didn't travel by train all over Japan. He traveled on foot or horseback.)

NOTE 1: Draw the timeline on the board and have students put Basho's dates on it. Point out that the action must be finished to use the past tense. This finished action may have occurred three hundred years ago or ten minutes ago.

NOTE 2: When a time expression comes first in a sentence, it is usually followed by a comma. Give example sentences with time expressions:

By 1694, Basho had 2,000 students.
In 1684, he started to travel around Japan.

NOTE 3: Point out the regular -ed ending. Have students look at the pronunciation rules in Appendix 23 on page A-10 and review the pronunciation of regular past tense endings. Point out that the /t/ and /d/ end sounds do not add a syllable to the verb; /ɪd/ does. Have students practice pronouncing the verbs in pairs. Follow up with a class drill.

For further practice, give students a short list of regular verbs in the past tense. In small groups have them pronounce the verbs and sort them into the three groupings: /d/, /t/, and /ɪd/. Review their pronunciations as a class.

NOTE 4: Have students turn to the list of irregular verbs in Appendix 1 on pages A-1–A-2. Explain that the only two forms they need to study now are the base form and the simple past. For homework, have students study short segments of verb lists. In class, set aside a time for pronunciation practice of these assigned segments.

FOCUSED PRACTICE (pages 23–26)

See the General Suggestions for Focused Practice exercises on pages 3–4.

1. Discover the Grammar, page 23
Have students read through the passage once before identifying the verbs. Then have students complete the timeline according to the information in the passage. Have students compare their answers in pairs or as a class.

2. Another Poet, page 24
After reviewing the answers for the first two sections, ask:

What did Emily Dickinson write about? (love, nature, and time)
How long did she attend college? (one year)
Who did she live with? (she lived by herself)
How many poems did she write? (1,700 poems)
How many of her poems appeared in print during her lifetime? (seven)
Did she want her poems to appear in print? (No, she didn't.)

After reviewing answers for the last section, have students identify the rhymes in the poem (*saw/raw* and *grass/pass*). Have pairs of students practice reading the poem aloud together and then ask for volunteers to read sections of the poem to the class.

The two stanzas of the poem contrast two types of behavior. To lead a discussion about the poem, ask:

In the first stanza, did the bird see the poet? (No)
What did the bird do with the worm? (He bit it in half and ate it.)
What did he do with the beetle? (He moved to let it pass.)
Why didn't he eat the beetle? (Answers will vary.)

You can help students see the humor of the poem by pointing out the violence expressed in "ate the fellow raw" and contrasting it with the social nicety in "then hopped sidewise to the wall to let a beetle pass."

Encourage students to talk about their own ideas of how people act when they think they are unobserved compared to their behavior in a social situation.

3. Two Poets, page 25
Tell the class they are going to compare the lives of Basho and Emily Dickinson.

Write *did, where, what, how many,* and *when* on the board. Go over the underlined words in all the statements and ask students for the first word in each question. For example:

T: *The underlined words are* <u>in</u> <u>Japan</u>. *What is the first word in the question?*
S: *Where.*

Then have students compose questions and answers about Emily Dickinson. Review the questions and answers as a class.

To underscore the comparative nature of this exercise, write contrasting statements on the board. For example:

<u>Basho</u>   <u>Dickinson</u>
He was born in 1644.   *She was born in 1830.*
He lived in Japan.   *She lived in Massachusetts.*

4. Ana Castillo, page 26
Have students complete this exercise for homework.

Alternatively, as a listening activity, have students do this activity in pairs. Have Student A cover the statements and Student B read one statement aloud. Have Student A listen and decide whether the statement is true or false. After statement 4, have the students switch roles.

For homework, students can write out their sentences in the book.

COMMUNICATION PRACTICE (pages 27–29)

5. Listening, page 27
See the General Suggestions for Listening on page 4.

6. Information Gap: Complete the Biography, pages 27 and 29
Divide the class into pairs. Assign each partner a role (A or B). Assign Students A page 27 and Students B page 29. Have them read their assigned passages. Point out that their passages are the same text with different information missing. Have the partners ask and answer each others' questions to complete the missing information.

Alternatively, for lower-level students, divide the class into Groups A and B. Have each group make questions about the missing information in the assigned passage. Circulate between the two groups and help as needed. Pair students up from Groups A and B. Have them ask and answer each others' questions.

7. Different Lives, page 28
See the General Suggestions for Pair and Group Activities on page 4.

When students finish their discussion, elicit their ideas and put them on the board in note form. Have students write a paragraph comparing the two poets, using the ideas generated from the discussion.

8. Haiku for You, page 28
To encourage creative imagery, brainstorm with the class different images associated with nature. Call out a nature word (for example: *fall, winter, spring, summer, rain, snow, mountain, river,* etc.). Have students individually note all their associations with that word. Write their ideas on the board. Students can refer to these lists of associations as they write their haiku.

Remind students that haiku lines do not have to rhyme, but they are very brief.

9. Rhyming Pairs, page 28
After students have generated rhyming past tense verbs, work as a class to compose a few rhyming lines. Point out that rhyming lines have the same number of syllables.

Use this prompt:

I knew the moment that he spoke

Then have students return to their partners to compose their own rhymes.

10. Writing, page 29
See the General Suggestions for Writing on page 5.

Brainstorm with the class the kind of information given in autobiographies. (For example: birthplace, childhood hobbies, education, etc.) Write the topics on the board for students' reference as they write.

You may want to review students' autobiographies for errors and have them corrected before distributing them among classmates.

After students have read their assigned autobiographies, elicit questions they would like to ask and write them on the board for students' reference. Have students circulate around the room, asking and answering each others' questions until all autobiographies have been identified.

EXPANSION

Chain Story: Brainstorm some common verbs and their past forms with the class and write them on the board. Have students sit in a circle. Instruct the first student to begin a story using one of the verbs on the board (For example: *Yesterday I went to the store.*) Instruct the second student to repeat the phrase and add a new one to it (For example: *Yesterday I went to the store. I bought some strawberries.*) Continue until everyone has had a chance to contribute a sentence.

 UNIT 4 *USED TO*

GRAMMAR **IN CONTEXT** (page 30)

See the General Suggestions for Grammar in Context on page 2.

Before You Read, page 30: First ask the class, *Who is wearing jeans today?* Look around the room and identify the students wearing jeans or some article of clothing made of denim. Ask students the two questions in this section. Discuss students' responses as a class. If any questions remain unanswered by the end of the unit, have students conduct their own research on jeans using the Internet.

CULTURE NOTE: In 1848, gold was discovered in California. In the 1850s, thousands of people moved there to dig for gold and find their fortunes. This period of U.S. history is called the California Gold Rush.

Reading, page 30: After students have completed the reading, ask the following questions:

Why did Levi Strauss make pants out of tent material? (miners used to get holes in their pants, and tent material was stronger)
What is the traditional fabric used in jeans? (denim)
When did jeans become popular for everyone to wear? (in the 1950s)

Focus on Grammar: Write the headings *Then* and *Now* on the board. Elicit an example of the highlighted form from the reading and write it under the *Then* heading. Write its contrasting idea in the *Now* heading. For example:

Then	Now
Gold miners used to get holes in their pants.	*Now, workers have strong fabric for their pants.*
The fabric used to come from Genoa, Italy.	*These days, it comes from many places around the world.*
Jeans didn't use to be so popular.	*Today they are popular.*

Point out that *used to* contrasts a past habit or situation with a present one.

Ask the following questions:

Does the form used to *change when the pronouns change?* (no)
Do you keep the /d/ in used to *in questions and negative statements?* (no)

Point out that the *used* in the sentence *He used tent material to make extra-strong pants* means *employed* or *utilized.* It is a regular verb. It ends with a /zd/ sound (ju:zd) compared to the /st/ of the *used to* (ju:st).

GRAMMAR **PRESENTATION:** *Used to* (pages 13–14)

See the General Suggestions for Grammar Presentation on page 3.

NOTE 1: Draw the timeline on the board and give additional examples. For example:

California used to have large gold mines. Now it has large cities.
Women used to wear long dresses. Now women wear pants as well as skirts.

Elicit other examples from students and add them to the board.

NOTE 2: Have students practice using the time expressions by listing them on the board. (For example: *nowadays, today, these days, currently,* etc.) Give students prompts. For example:

People used to wear hats. (Nowadays, people don't usually wear hats.)
Men used to carry their watches in their pockets. (These days most men wear wristwatches.)
Women didn't use to wear pants. (Nowadays, women often wear pants.)
Children didn't use to wear backpacks. (Currently most children wear backpacks to school.)
People used to wash their clothes by hand. (These days most people use washing machines to wash their clothes.)
People used to sew many of their own clothes. (Nowadays, most people buy clothes that are already made.)

NOTE 3: Practice negative statements by writing untrue statements about fashion on the board and having students correct them. For example:

In Europe, men used to wear helmets. (In Europe, men didn't use to wear helmets. They used to wear hats.)
In Alaska, the Inuit people used to wear T-shirts and shorts to stay warm. (In Alaska, the Inuit people didn't use to wear T-shirts and shorts to stay warm. They used to wear animal skins to stay warm.)
Teenagers used to wear business suits to be different from their parents. (Teenagers didn't use to wear business suits to be different. They used to wear . . . .)

Jeans used to come in many different colors. (Jeans didn't use to come in many different colors. They used to come in only blue.)
Miners in the Gold Rush used to wear silk pants at work. (Miners in the Gold Rush didn't use to wear silk pants. They used to wear cotton pants.)

Point out that the pronunciation of *used to* and *use to* is identical. *Used* ends with a /t/ sound that blends with the *to* that follows.

NOTE 4: Give several examples:

I will get used to wearing glasses.
She is used to dressing up for dinner.
They aren't used to seeing women in shorts.
I got used to wearing high heels, but it wasn't easy at first.

FOCUSED PRACTICE (pages 33–34)

See the General Suggestions for Focused Practice exercises on pages 3–4.

1. Discover the Grammar, page 33
Tell the class that this exercise contrasts *used to* + base form of the verb (past habit) and *be used to* + gerund (be accustomed to).

2. Times Change, page 33
Have students look at all the pictures before beginning the exercise.

For further practice have students in pairs write more sentences about the pictures with *used to*.

3. Sneaker FAQ, page 34
Go over the chart. Have students identify the high-top and low-top models in the picture.

As a follow-up activity for writing practice and discussion, have students write statements about current sneaker trends to contrast with 1922. Then have students share their sentences with the class. For example:

Sneakers used to come in only black and white. Nowadays, they come in every color.
Sneakers used to come in two styles. Now they come in many different styles according to their use.

4. Editing, page 34
See the General Suggestions for Editing on page 4.

Follow up with these questions:

Why didn't she like to wear a school uniform when she was a girl? (She thought it took away freedom of choice.)
Why does she miss wearing school uniforms now? (Clothes are very expensive.)
In your opinion, what are the benefits of students wearing uniforms? (Answers will vary.)
What are the disadvantages? (Answers will vary.)

COMMUNICATION PRACTICE (pages 35–36)

5. Listening, page 35
See the General Suggestions for Listening on page 4.

Follow up with students discussing what they used to do in their younger years.

6. Then and Now, page 35
See the General Suggestions for Pair and Group Activities on page 4.

Have students work in pairs to form sentences and then read their sentences aloud or write them on the board.

If possible, bring in other pictures of famous people when they were younger. Discuss the changes in their appearance.

7. The Way I Used to Be, page 36

See the General Suggestions for Pair and Group Activities on page 4.

To set up the activity, brainstorm with the class questions to ask each other about the past. For example:

Where did you use to live?
Who did you use to live with?
Who did you use to play with?
How did you use to spend the days?
What did you use to look like?

Have students share their pictures in small groups and answer each others' questions.

For homework, have students write about one person in their group. Have them contrast how the person used to be and how the person is today.

8. This Used to Be My Playground, page 36

Dictate these discussion questions to the class:

Why did she use to run to her childhood playground? (to see her friends)
Was the playground a good place in her memory? (yes)
Does she miss her childhood days? (Yes, she does.)
Is it hard to grow up? (Answers will vary.)

Divide the class into pairs. Have the pairs first discuss the questions and then share their ideas with the class.

9. Things Change, Page 36

See the General Suggestions for Pair and Group Activities on page 4.

With the class, brainstorm topics to discuss. Write them on the board for students' reference. For example:

family life
cost of living
transportation
communications
diet
health issues

Encourage students to share their ideas with the class. Ask:

What are the advantages and disadvantages of this change?

10. Writing, page 36

See the General Suggestions for Writing on page 5.

Use samples of student writing to create an error correction exercise for *used to* and the simple past tense. Extract errors from students' writing and put them on the board. Have groups of students work together to correct them.

EXPANSION

The Way Things Used to Be: Have students plan a class presentation depicting the way things are today and the way they used to be. The presentation can be done individually or with partners. Have students begin by brainstorming some of the possible things to compare and some of the ways they could represent these changes in their presentations. For example, students could compare household conveniences, travel, clothing, or communication. Ways of representing these changes might include a poster, actual objects of today and of the past, or audio or video interviews of people describing their lives in the past compared to today.

GRAMMAR **IN CONTEXT** (page 37)

See the General Suggestions for Grammar in Context on page 2.

Before You Read, page 37: Have students look at the picture as you read the questions in this section. Discuss students' answers as a class.

Reading, page 37: Ask the following questions:

Where were they staying last Friday night? (the Cypress Ski Lodge)
What were they doing at 7:00 that night? (Sanders' wife was making a call from her cell phone. Sanders was watching TV.)
Do you believe they might be guilty? (Answers will vary.)

Focus on Grammar: Ask:

What was Sanders doing when the doorbell rang? (He was taking a shower.)
What was he doing at 7:00 on Friday night? (He was watching TV.)
Write the answers on the board. Explain that the past progressive describes what people were doing at a particular time in the past.

GRAMMAR **PRESENTATION:** Past Progressive (pages 38–40)

See the General Suggestions for Grammar Presentation on page 3.

NOTE 1: Draw the timeline on the board and point out that the husband and wife were eating dinner over a period of time and that their action was in progress at 6:00. Elicit further examples from the class by asking, *What were you doing last night at 7:00?* Write their sentences on the board.

NOTE 2: Give additional examples:

I was drinking coffee when the telephone rang.
We were taking a test when the fire alarm went off.
They were talking when someone knocked on the door.

Put cues on the board and have students make sentences to practice the pattern:

I walk the dog		it start to rain
You cross the street		the light change
She drive to work	when	she see a UFO
He read the newspaper		the telephone ring
We study English		the lights go out
They run away		the police arrive

NOTE 3: Put cues on the board and have students make sentences to practice the pattern with *while*.

I walk the dog		you take out the trash
You cross the street		the cars wait
She talk on the phone	while	she drive to work
He talk to his friend		the teacher speak
We listen to the news		we drive to work
They write in their journals		the teacher correct papers

NOTE 4: To practice this punctuation rule, have pairs of students write out several sentences, using the above prompts for Notes 2 and 3. Have students write each statement two ways: beginning with the time clause and ending with the time clause. Have each pair write one example on the board.

NOTE 5: Give additional examples to contrast the patterns. Have students write timelines for each sentence to explain the action.

He was doing his homework when she came home.
He did his homework. She came home.

The robbers were running away when the police arrived.
The robbers ran away. The police arrived.
She was writing her essay when the computer crashed.
She wrote her essay. The computer crashed.

NOTE 6: Give additional examples:

Chris was building a house last year.
Chris built a house last year.
Laura was doing her math homework.
Laura did her math homework.

FOCUSED PRACTICE (pages 41–43)

See the General Suggestions for Focused Practice exercises on pages 3–4.

1. Discover the Grammar, page 41
As students do this exercise, have them refer to Grammar Notes 1–6. The exercises correspond to the following notes:

1. Note 6
2. Note 6
3. Note 2
4. Note 3
5. Note 5

To help students contrast the different time frames, have them draw timelines for each sentence before answering the questions.

2. Describe the Suspects, page 41
Point out that some of the sentences have negative answers.

Have students work on the exercises individually and then share their answers with the class.

3. A Traffic Accident, page 42
Establish the situation: There has been a traffic accident involving a suspect in the burglary. A reporter is talking to a police officer. The officer is describing the accident.

To review answers, have students listen to the tape and/or have a pair of students act out the conversation for the class.

4. Answer Carefully, pages 42–43
After students have completed the exercise, ask:

Do you think he and his girlfriend have a good alibi?
What questions would you ask his girlfriend?

5. Blizzard, page 43
Have students draw timelines for each of the completed sentences. Go over their answers as a class.

COMMUNICATION PRACTICE (pages 44–45)

6. Listening, page 44
See the General Suggestions for Listening on page 4.

When students have identified the correct sequence, have them explain the accident in their own words to a partner.

Ask the class:

Have you ever been in a traffic accident?
What happened?

Have students share their stories with the class.

7. Role Play: The Real Story, page 44
See the General Suggestions for Role Plays on page 5.

Have the class brainstorm questions to ask the witnesses. Write their questions on the board. Divide the class into groups of four and have students choose their roles. After practicing their role play in groups, ask one group to perform their role play to the class.

8. What's Your Alibi?, page 45
See the General Suggestions for Pair and Group Activities on page 4.

After identifying the characteristics of good and bad alibis, have students play this alibi game.

Send two students out of the room and tell them to discuss their alibi. Tell them to be as detailed as possible. For example, if they decide to say they went to a movie, ask them to decide which movie theater, what movie was showing, who they were sitting next to, and so on. Have the class question the two suspects separately and try to find the discrepancies in the two alibis.

9. Are You a Good Witness?, page 45
See the General Suggestions for Pair and Group Activities on page 4.

Let students look at the picture for ten seconds. Instruct them to close their books and write down what was happening in the picture. Have them compare their answers with a partner.

Have students look at the picture for another ten seconds. Ask, *What details did you miss?* Have them write down any new details in their notes.

Call out true and false statements about the picture. In pairs, have students consult their notes and each other before answering. Have students check their answers by looking at the picture one last time.

10. Writing, page 45
See the General Suggestions for Writing on page 5.

Have students share their descriptions in small groups. Have each group choose one description to share with the class.

EXPANSION

And What Were You Doing? Ask students to think of a time when they learned of some major event of personal or world significance. Can they recall exactly where they were and what they were doing at that time? Some possible world events include the death of a public figure such as Princess Diana or John F. Kennedy, Jr., the tearing down of the Berlin Wall or the beginning of the millennium, or an earthquake or other disaster in their own home country. Students can write about what they were doing or describe it orally. Later, have students who described the same world events compare what they were doing.

 UNIT 6 FUTURE

GRAMMAR **IN CONTEXT** (page 46)

See the General Suggestions for Grammar in Context on page 2.

BACKGROUND NOTE: *Environmentally friendly* products reduce damage to the environment. They are non-polluting and/or recyclable.

Before You Read, page 46: In pairs, have students read the questions in this section and look at the picture. Have them discuss their answers.

Reading, page 46: Ask the following questions:
Is the vehicle of the future going to be environmentally friendly? (Yes, it is.)
Will the vehicle of the future use gas? (No, it won't.)

Will the vehicle of the future be safe? (Yes, it will.)
Will the vehicle of the future be fast? (Yes, it will.)
Will the vehicle of the future be smart? (Yes, it will.)

Focus on Grammar: Write the headings *Simple Future, Be going to,* and *Present Progressive* on the board. Elicit examples of the highlighted structures from the reading and write them under the appropriate column headings.

Point to the examples in the left column and ask, *What verb tense is this? How is it formed? How is it contracted?* With the class's input, write out the full conjugation of one of the verbs in the simple future tense. Practice pronouncing the *'ll* contractions.

Point to the examples in the middle column and ask, *What verb tense is this? How is it formed?* With the class's input, write out the full conjugation of one of the verbs in the *be going to* future tense.

Point to the examples in the right column and ask, *What verb tense is this? How is it formed?* With the class's input, write out the full conjugation of one of the verbs in the present progressive tense.

Explain that there are a number of ways to talk about the future. We make predictions that are not at all certain, or we talk about intended plans that are already arranged. Point to an example of a prediction (*It will probably still have four wheels*) and an intention (*One manufacturer . . . is holding a press conference next week*).

GRAMMAR **PRESENTATION:** *Be going to,* Present Progressive, *Will,* or the Simple Present Tense for the Future (page 47–50)

See the General Suggestions for Grammar Presentation on page 3.

NOTE 1: Draw the timeline on the board. Present more examples showing various ways to talk about the future.

I'm going to go to New York next week.
I'm catching a 6:00 flight.
I think I'll have fun.
I come back at 8:00 on Sunday.

NOTE 2: Elicit future predictions (about transportation, political events, the environment, and so on) from students and write them on the board.

NOTE 3: Distinguish between predictions about the future (guesses) and intentions (what someone plans to do). Elicit examples of students' intentions by asking, *What are you going to do this weekend?* For events that are already arranged, have students use the present progressive.

NOTE 4: Bring in some realia from your area such as concert notices, class schedules, and bus timetables. Make present tense sentences based on them. For example, hold up a concert notice and say, *This concert is on Wednesday night. It begins at 8:00.*

Have pairs of students look through the realia and form two sentences each about scheduled events using the simple present.

FOCUSED PRACTICE (pages 51–55)

See the General Suggestions for Focused Practice exercises on pages 3–4.

1. Discover the Grammar, page 51
To review answers, have a pair of students act out the conversation for the class, identifying the future forms as they occur. Ask the class:

What questions would you like to ask Professor Vroom?
How do you think he will answer these questions?

In pairs, have students role play a continuation of the interview. Ask several pairs to perform their role play for the class.

2. It's Going to Happen, page 52

With the class, review the vocabulary in the box and look at the pictures. Ask, *What do you think is going to happen next in each picture?* Write the affirmative and negative form of *be going to* on the board for student reference.

Have students complete the exercise in pairs or individually.

3. Professor Vroom's Schedule, page 53

Have students read the schedule before beginning the exercise. Point out that the present progressive should be used here because these are future plans that have already been arranged.

4. Radio Call-In Questions, pages 53–54

Point out that this conversation is making uncertain predictions about the future and therefore uses the simple future tense. Ask the class:

Which predictions do you believe will come true?

After completing the exercise, have students listen to the tape to check their answers.

5. All Aboard, pages 54–55

Have students read the schedule before beginning the exercise. Help orient students by asking:

Where does the train leave? (New York)
Where does the train arrive? (New Haven)
Are there more than fifty departures? (No, there aren't.)
Are there more A.M. or P.M. departures? (There are more P.M. departures.)

6. Choose the Future, page 55

As students do this exercise, have them refer to Grammar Notes 1–4. The exercises correspond to the following notes:

1. Note 2	5. Note 2
2. Note 3a	6. Note 3a
3. Note 4	7. Note 3a
4. Note 3a	8. Note 3

After completing the exercise, have students listen to the tape to check their answers.

COMMUNICATION PRACTICE (pages 56–57)

7. Listening, page 56
See the General Suggestions for Listening on page 4.

8. Fortune Cookies, page 57
See the General Suggestions for Pair and Group Activities on page 4.

Point out that fortunes are predictions about the future, so students may use the simple future (*will*) or *be going to* future (Grammar Note 2). Have students write their predictions individually. Divide the class into groups of four. Have group members put their fortunes in a pile or bag. If possible, add a couple of your own to each pile. Have students take turns picking a fortune out of the pile and discussing it with the group.

9. When Are You Free?, page 57
See the General Suggestions for Pair and Group Activities on page 4.

Have students work individually to complete their schedules for the coming weekend. Brainstorm with the class different ways to invite someone to a movie. Write their ideas on the board.

Divide the class into pairs. Tell the pairs to find a mutually agreeable time to see a movie without looking at each other's schedule. Then have the pairs move on to Exercise 10 to choose the movie and show time.

10. Choose a Time, page 57
Follow up with a brief discussion by asking each pair what movie plans they made. Use this as an opportunity to talk about movie tastes and preferences.

11. Writing, page 57
See the General Suggestions for Writing on page 5.

Encourage students to add drawings of cars of the future from science magazines or illustrations of their own and to label them or write captions.

EXPANSION

Dramatic Predictions: Distribute pictures in magazines portraying dramatic moments. Have pairs of students make up a story about the situation in the picture and then predict what will happen next. Have students share their pictures and stories with the class.

 UNIT 7 FUTURE TIME CLAUSES

GRAMMAR **IN CONTEXT** (page 58)

See the General Suggestions for Grammar in Context on page 2.

Before You Read, page 58: Have students read the question and look at the picture. Discuss students' ideas as a class.

Reading, page 58: Ask the following question:
What are the four steps to changing a dream into a reality? (Write your dreams down; list the benefits of the dream; break it into smaller goals; and act today.)

Focus on Grammar: Elicit examples of future time from the reading. Write the examples on the board. Ask the class:
What happens first? What happens next?
What is a timeline for this sentence?
Which part of the sentence is the time clause?
Which part of the sentence is the main clause?
Does the time clause always show what happens first? (no)
Does the main clause always show what happens second? (no)

Point to several examples of a time clause and ask, *What verb tense is this?* (simple present) *How is it formed?* With the class's input, write out the full conjugation of one of the verbs.

Point to several examples of a main clause and ask, *What verb tenses are these? How are they formed?* With the class's input, write out the full conjugation of a verb in the present progressive and the simple future tense.

GRAMMAR **PRESENTATION:** Future Time Clauses (pages 59–60)

See the General Suggestions for Grammar Presentation on page 3.

NOTE 1: Put cues on the board and have students make sentences to practice the pattern.

I get a job		*I graduate*
You work part time		*you be in school*
She be twenty-three		*she finish school*
He study evening	*when*	*he get a full-time job*
We not study English		*we speak fluently*
They get their diplomas		*they be eighteen*

NOTE 2: Point out that even though time clauses beginning with *before*, *until*, and *by the time* introduce the event that happens second, the tense is in the simple present.

Write these prompts on the board. Have pairs of students practice completing them:

When I get my dream job,
After I leave class today,
As soon as I get home today,
Before I turn sixty,
Until I speak English fluently,
By the time I get a new job,
While I study English,

FOCUSED PRACTICE (pages 61–62)

See the General Suggestions for Focused Practice exercises on pages 3–4.

1. Discover the Grammar, page 61
To help students contrast the different time frames, have them draw timelines for each sentence before choosing the sentence most similar in meaning.

2. What's Next?, pages 61–62
To help students identify the sequences, have them draw timelines for each sentence before filling in the blanks.

To check students' comprehension, ask:

Do Sandy and Jeff plan to have children? (Yes, they do.)
Do Sandy and Jeff plan to buy a house? (No, they don't.)
Does Sandy plan to go to school? (No, she doesn't.)

3. Looking Ahead, page 62
After the class reviews the answers, ask:

What are other benefits of having a job?
What are other small goals for finding a job?

COMMUNICATION PRACTICE (pages 63–64)

4. Listening, page 63
See the General Suggestions for Listening on page 4.

To check students' comprehension, ask:

What service does the agency provide? (It trains its clients, gives them consultations on the most suitable kind of work, and finds them jobs.)
What is the woman going to do next? (She is going to send her resume.)

5. The Next Step, page 63
See the General Suggestions for Pair and Group Activities on page 4.

Read the items together as a class. Have students complete the questionnaire individually and then share their plans in groups. Have each group report its findings to the class.

Have pairs of students work together to draft a graph (pie chart or bar graph) to illustrate the class findings.

6. Until Then, page 63
See the General Suggestions for Pair and Group Activities on page 4.

Have students complete the sentences individually and then share them in small groups. Have each group report to the class.

7. Interview, page 64
See the General Suggestions for Pair and Group Activities on page 4.

Brainstorm with the class possible questions to ask in the interview. Write the questions on the board. Divide the class into pairs. Set a time limit of ten minutes for the interview. Encourage students to take notes during the interview.

Have students write up their findings from the interview. You may want students to return to their original interviewing partner to check the accuracy of their summaries. Have students submit their summaries to you for final review.

8. Writing, page 64
See the General Suggestions for Writing on page 5.

Have students do this exercise for homework. In class, have students share their plans in small groups and then answer the following questions:

Are there any other benefits of achieving the goal?
Are there any other smaller goals?
Do you have any advice or information that can help your classmate reach the goal?

EXPANSION

Time Capsules: Explain what a time capsule is. Then ask students to predict the sequence of life events (marriage, homes, jobs, children) that they expect to experience in the next ten years. Ask students to write their predictions down. In small groups, students can discuss their predictions. Later, have students seal their predictions in an envelope and write on the front "Time Capsule: Open Ten Years from (today's date)." Suggest that they put it in a place where they will remember to look at it in ten years.

UNIT 8 — WH- QUESTIONS: SUBJECT AND PREDICATE

GRAMMAR IN CONTEXT (page 65)

See the General Suggestions for Grammar in Context on page 2.

BACKGROUND NOTE: In a criminal trial, the government makes an accusation of guilt and the accused (the defendant) defends himself or herself against the accusation. Both sides present arguments, witnesses, and evidence. During the trial, a court reporter sits near the judge and records everything that is said and done during the trial. The record is called a transcript. After both sides have presented their case, a jury decides if the defendant is guilty or not guilty of the crime.

Before You Read, page 65: Have students read the questions and look at the picture. Discuss their ideas as a class.

Reading, page 65: This trial is about a crime that occurred in the evening in the parking lot of a restaurant called Al's Grill.

Ask the following questions:

Where did the crime happen? (in the parking lot of Al's Grill)
What did the woman give Mr. Adams? (a package)
Why was Mr. Adams frightened? (The witness didn't know.)

Focus on Grammar: Write two large headings on the board: *Questions about the Subject* and *Questions about the Predicate.* Elicit the highlighted questions from the reading and write them on the board under the appropriate headings. Write down the answer that corresponds to each *wh-* question. For example:

<u>Questions about the Subject</u>
Who saw you?   *A woman saw me.*
What happened next?   *The woman gave him the package.*

<u>Questions about the Predicate</u>
Who did you see there?   *I saw one of the defendants.*
Which one did you see?   *It was that man.*

<u>Questions about the Subject</u>
Point to the answers of the questions. Ask, *What is the subject?* Underline the subject. Then ask, *What is the predicate?* Offer the class the answer. Circle the predicate.

Point to each element in the question and identify it: *wh- word* and *verb*. Point out that the *wh-* word holds the subject position.

<u>Questions about the Predicate</u>
Point to the answers of the questions. Ask, *What is the predicate?* Circle the predicate.

Point to the questions. Ask, *What is the question word?* Circle the question word. Point out that the question word corresponds to the predicate in the answer. (*Who? One of the defendants. Which one? That man.*)

Point to each element in the question and identify it: *wh- word, verb, auxiliary verb, subject,* and *verb*. Ask students to compare this pattern to the questions about the subject. Ask, *What are the differences in word order between the two types of questions?*

GRAMMAR **PRESENTATION:** *Wh-* Questions: Subject and Predicate (pages 66–67)

See the General Suggestions for Grammar Presentation on page 3.

NOTE 1: Ask pairs to close their books and list as many question words as possible.

NOTE 2: Give additional examples of this type of question:

Who gave him the package?
(<u>The woman</u> gave him the package.)

Who took the package?
(<u>Mr. Adams</u> took the package.)

Who left in a hurry?
(<u>Mr. Adams</u> left in a hurry.)

Substitute the subject in the *wh-* question word place to show the subject position. Point out that there is no change in word order when the question word refers to the subject of the sentence. Identify the word order pattern: question word + verb.

NOTE 3: Give additional examples of this type of question:

What did the woman give him?
(The woman gave him <u>the package</u>.)

What did Mr. Adams take?
(Mr. Adams took <u>the package</u>.)

Where did he go?
(Mr. Adams went <u>toward the parking lot</u>.)

When was the witness in the restaurant?
(He was in the restaurant <u>on the evening of May 12</u>.)

Identify the auxiliary verbs. Ask, *What tense is this verb in? Does this auxiliary verb come from the verb "be"?*

Identify the word order pattern: question word + auxiliary verb + subject + verb.

NOTE 4: Write on the board:

The witness saw the defendant.

Have students identify the subject (*The witness*). Have the class make a question about the subject. For example:

Who saw the defendant?   *The witness did.*

Have students identify the person in the predicate (*the defendant*). Have the class make a question about him. For example:

Whom did the witness see?   *The defendant.*

Write more sentences on the board and have pairs of students work together to make a question about the subject and predicate in each.

The defendant met the woman in the restaurant.
(*Who met the woman in the restaurant?* and *Whom did the defendant meet?*)

The witness watched the woman and the man.
(*Who watched the woman and the man?* and *Whom did the witness watch?*)

FOCUSED PRACTICE (pages 68–69)

See the General Suggestions for Focused Practice exercises on pages 3–4.

1. Discover the Grammar, page 68
Alternatively, have students do this exercise in pairs. Have Student A cover the answers and Student B cover the questions. Have Student A read the question as Student B listens and identifies the correct response.

2. Cross-Examination, pages 68–69
Explain that a cross-examination occurs when a lawyer asks a witness many detailed questions and compares the answers to the witness's other answers.

3. Q and A, page 69
To orient lower-level students, look at each statement and ask, *Is the underlined word in the predicate or subject? What question word do you need?* Have students work individually. Go over the answers as a class.

COMMUNICATION PRACTICE (pages 70–71)

4. Listening, page 70
See the General Suggestions for Listening on page 4.

Have students read the questions before listening. After playing the tape twice, check students' answers. If students disagree, play the segment in question again.

5. What Happened Next?, page 70
See the General Suggestions for Pair and Group Activities on page 4.

Divide the class into pairs. Have each pair reread the court transcript and then create a continuation of the questioning. Have pairs volunteer to perform their dialogue for the class.

6. Star Reporters, page 70
See the General Suggestions for Pair and Group Activities on page 4.

Model the format of the written interview for the students. With the class, write an introductory paragraph for the interview, using some of your students' names; for example:

Sumalee Chonging is a ten-year-old girl. In many ways, she's like any ten-year-old, but in some ways, she's very special. Sumalee is a genius. She attends medical school at (name of school). Recently, our reporter Kyung Lee interviewed Sumalee about her life.

Kyung: *When did you decide to become a doctor?*

Sumalee: *About three years ago.*

You may want to publish some of the interviews. You can type them up and distribute them or put them on a bulletin board for the class.

7. Information Gap: Police Crime Board, pages 71–72
Divide the class into pairs. Assign each partner a role (A or B). Assign Students A page 71 and
Students B page 72. Have them read their assigned charts. Point out that their charts are the same
but with different information missing. Have the partners ask and answer each other's questions to
complete the missing information.

Alternatively, for lower-level students, divide the class into Groups A and B. Have each group make
questions about the missing information in their assigned chart. Circulate between the two groups
and help as needed. Pair students from Groups A and B. Have them ask and answer each other's
questions.

8. Writing, page 71
See the General Suggestions for Writing on page 5.

Have partners tell each other their exciting or interesting story. Then have the partners work
individually to write up the interview questions. When ready, have them interview each other.

Have students write up their interviews in the format already introduced in Exercise 6, Star
Reporters.

EXPANSION

Imaginary Interview: Tell students to imagine an interview with any person in history. (For
example: Leonardo da Vinci, Moses, Joan of Arc, Lao Tzu, etc.) Have them write down ten questions
they would like to ask this person. Have students share their questions in groups. You may then
wish to have partners role play the interviews.

REVIEW OR SELFTEST

See the General Suggestions for Review or Self Test on pages 5–6.

FROM GRAMMAR TO WRITING:
COMBINING SENTENCES WITH TIME WORDS

See the General Suggestions for From Grammar to Writing on page 6.

In this section, students practice combining sentences with time words while further exploring the
theme of cross-cultural misunderstandings. After sharing their ideas with a partner, students
compose their own stories.

Introduction, page 80
Write the two example sentences on the board. Ask students, *How can I connect these two sentences
using the time word* while? Have students connect the sentences. Explain that by combining
sentences with time words, you make the text more connected and coherent.

Have students read the introductory text.

Exercise 1, page 80
After identifying all the combined sentences and time words, ask students to identify the two
component sentences in each combined statement.

Exercise 2, page 81
Answers to this exercise will vary. As students call out their answers, write them on the board so that
the class may see the various possibilities. Emphasize that many time words have the same meaning
and are equally correct.

Exercise 3, page 81
Have students think about the cross-cultural communication material covered in Unit 1. Brainstorm
with the class common misunderstandings they may have experienced. Write their ideas on the
board. For example:

giving an inappropriate gift
arriving too early or late for an event
saying the wrong thing in a delicate moment

Divide the class into pairs. Have the partners ask and answer each other's questions about their experiences.

Exercise 4, page 81
Have students write their story at home using the model in the book.

Exercise 5, page 82
Before students exchange their paragraphs, have them look at the chart. Explain that they will give each other feedback using the chart. A well-written passage gives complete information. The questions they ask will help the writer add the necessary details to tell a good story. Some paragraphs may need only one question, and others may need many.

Have students exchange paragraphs, read them, and give each other feedback using the chart in the book. Have the writers read the feedback and incorporate any new information into their final draft.

PART II PRONOUNS AND PHRASAL VERBS

 UNIT 9 REFLEXIVE AND RECIPROCAL PRONOUNS

GRAMMAR **IN CONTEXT** (page 86)

See the General Suggestions for Grammar in Context on page 2.

BACKGROUND NOTE: Recently, psychologists have been studying the effects of hope and optimism on people's lives. Studies indicate that positive attitudes have pervasive effects on many aspects of life, including physical and emotional health and success on the job. One study indicates that when college freshmen show a high degree of hopefulness, their grades are better than the grades of students who have similar ability but a more pessimistic outlook. Self-talk, one's dialogue with oneself, is an indicator of whether a person is optimistic or pessimistic. Optimists do not blame themselves, and they tell themselves that bad situations are temporary and limited. Pessimists, on the other hand, take the blame for bad outcomes and see them as permanent and pervasive. (Source: Daniel Goleman, "What hope can do for you," *Self,* June 1992, p. 112.)

Before You Read, page 86: Have students read the questions, look at the pictures, and discuss their responses with the class. Ask for additional examples of self-talk. Write them on the board.

Reading, page 86: Check students' comprehension. Ask:

What happened to both Sara and Tom last fall? (They both lost their jobs.)
According to Sara, why did she get her job back? (Her employers finally realized they needed her.)
According to Tom, why did he get his job back? (because they were really desperate)
Why is self-talk important? (Answers will vary.)

Focus on Grammar: Write *he, she, it, we,* and *they* on the board. Elicit examples of the highlighted structure from the reading and write them under the appropriate headings. Explain the meaning of the examples. For example:

Sara kept herself fit. (Sara kept Sara fit.)
Tom spent all of his time by himself. (Tom spent all of his time alone.)
Tom and Sara explained the problem to themselves. (Tom explained to Tom and Sara explained to Sara.)
They talked to each other. (Tom talked to Sara and Sara talked to Tom.)

GRAMMAR **PRESENTATION:** Reflexive and Reciprocal Pronouns (pages 87–88)

See the General Suggestions for Grammar Presentation on page 3.

NOTES 1–6: Read the notes in the Student Book with the class. Answer any questions. For additional practice, give students slips of paper with instructions. For example:

Read to yourself out loud.   *Talk to a classmate about the lesson.*
Read to a classmate out loud.   *Pat yourself on the back*
Talk to yourself about the lesson. *Pat a classmate on the back.*

Act out one instruction yourself, and ask questions. For example:

Teacher: *I'm reading to myself. Anna, what am I doing?*
   Anna: *You're reading to yourself.*
Teacher: *Van, ask Lee what I'm doing.*
    Van: *What is the teacher doing, Lee?*
    Lee: *She's reading to herself.*

Have students come to the front and act out the instructions. Ask questions to elicit the different reflexive pronouns. For example:

A: *What are you and Sabrina doing?*
B: *We're talking to each other about the lesson.*
A: *What are Chong and Sabrina doing?*
B: *They're talking to each other about the lesson.*

NOTE 3: Have students reread the passage to find the example of a reflexive pronoun used to emphasize a noun: "The situation itself can't explain Tom's problems."

FOCUSED **PRACTICE** (pages 89–91)

See the General Suggestions for Focused Practice exercises on pages 3–4.

1. Discover the Grammar, page 89
Have students come up with possible examples of an athlete's self-talk. ("Come on. You can do it. You can win this race.") Have other students report back. ("She told herself she could win this race.")

2. The Office Party, pages 89–90

CULTURE NOTE: American companies usually have a party at least once a year for all office employees. It is a chance to talk with people outside one's department and meet people on all levels of the office hierarchy.

After completing the exercise, have students listen to the tape to check their answers. Then ask them to identify the following statements as *true* or *false*.

Food is served to guests as they sit at tables. (False. It's a buffet.)
The boss always gives her a book for the holidays. (False. She always gives her boss a book for the holidays.)
They are learning how to use the computer program. (True)
Jessica didn't get promoted and she blames her boss. (False. She blames herself.)

3. We Learn from One Another, pages 90–91
Ask students, *What questions would an interviewer ask a person applying for a teaching position?* Write student responses on the board.

Have students read through the passage before filling in the blanks. After reviewing the answers, ask the following questions:

What does he like most about his work? (his freedom)
What does he like least? (the pay)

According to George Prudeau, what does a good teacher do? (helps students learn by themselves)
Does he sound like a good teacher to you? (Answers will vary.)

4. Editing, page 91
See the General Suggestions for Editing on page 4.

Follow up with a brief discussion. Ask, *Do you think it is easier to forgive a friend or forgive yourself?*

COMMUNICATION PRACTICE (pages 92–94)

5. Listening, page 92
See the General Suggestions for Listening on page 4.

Point out that both pronouns are possible in each context and that students must listen carefully to distinguish the correct pronoun.

After completing and checking the exercise, ask students to interpret the two choices for each item.

6. Cheer Yourself Up!, page 92
See the General Suggestions for Pair and Group Activities on page 4.

Divide the class into pairs. Give the pairs a set time limit to brainstorm positive self-talk for each of the situations. Have the pairs share their ideas with the class.

7. The Optimist Test, page 93
See the General Suggestions for Pair and Group Activities on page 4.

Have students work individually to complete the questionnaire and check their results. Then have groups of five students compare results. Have each group report its findings to the class.

Follow up with a class discussion. Ask:
Does your self-talk really influence how you act and feel?
Is self-talk useful when you are learning a new language?

8. The Memory Game, page 94
See the General Suggestions for Pair and Group Activities on page 4.

Divide the class into pairs. Have one student in each pair volunteer to be the scribe. Allow the class thirty seconds to look at the picture. Have the pairs shut their books and record everything they can remember. Have pairs match up to compare their lists.

Call out true and false statements about the picture. Have students look at the picture to answer you and correct the false statements. For example:
The two women are waving at themselves. (False. They are waving at each other.)
The woman is sitting by herself. (True)
The man is looking at his friend in the mirror. (False. He is looking at himself.)
The woman at the buffet is talking to her guests. (False. She is talking to herself.)

9. Writing, page 94
See the General Suggestions for Writing on page 5.

Have students share their letters in small groups.

EXPANSION

Group Project: Have small groups of students put together a five-minute presentation on how to stay positive while learning a new language and adapting to a new culture. Have them share their presentations with the class.

GRAMMAR **IN CONTEXT** (page 95)

See the General Suggestions for Grammar in Context on page 2.

Before You Read, page 95: Have students read the question, look at the photograph, and share their responses with the class.

Reading, page 95: Ask the following comprehension questions:

What values helped Eloy Rodriguez in high school? (being honest, fair, and quick-thinking)
What did his counselor try to talk him into? (a career in mechanics)
What did he major in? (science)
What area of science does he work in? (zoopharmacognosy)
How successful in school were his cousins? (Very—sixty-four of his sixty-seven cousins graduated from college.)

Focus on Grammar: Tell students phrasal verbs are extremely common in English. They consist of a verb plus a particle. The particle is usually a word such as *up, down, on,* or *over* that is used as a preposition in other contexts. However, when it is combined with a verb to make a phrasal verb, the combination often has a meaning quite different from the separate meanings of the verb and of the particle.

Elicit examples from the first two paragraphs and write them on the board. In a separate area of the board, write their synonyms. Ask students to reread the paragraphs and, guessing from the context, match the synonyms to the phrasal verbs.

picked up	(got)	*helped out*	(assisted)
takes off	(removes)	*talked into*	(persuaded)
puts on	(covers the body)	*cleaning up*	(cleaning completely)
grew up	(became an adult)	*went on*	(continued)
brought up	(raised)		

Have students identify in the reading all the transitive phrasal verbs—verbs that take a direct object. Write several examples on the board. Point out that most of these verbs may be separated by the direct object. For example:

He takes off his lab coat.   *He takes his lab coat off.*

Have students identify in the reading the two intransitive phrasal verbs—verbs that don't take objects. Write the two examples on the board (*grew up* and *get by*). Point out that these verbs are not separable.

GRAMMAR **PRESENTATION:** Phrasal Verbs (pages 96–97)

See the General Suggestions for Grammar Presentation on page 3.

NOTE 1: Provide additional examples of the change in meaning. For example:

His office window looks over the park. (His office window faces the park.)
He looks over the department reports every morning. (He reviews the department reports.)

The firefighter helped the little boy out of the hole. (The firefighter pulled the boy out of the hole.)
The teacher helps me out when I have a question. (The teacher assists me when I have a question.)

NOTE 2: Have partners match informal phrasal verbs with similar more formal one-word verbs. For example:

come back	(return)
talk over	(discuss)
find out	(discover)
go out	(exit)

NOTES 3 AND 4: Point out that the transitive phrasal verbs that are *inseparable* are not introduced in this unit. For now, the class will only study separable transitive verbs. Intransitive verbs are always inseparable.

Concentration Game: In class select fifteen phrasal verbs from Appendices 4–5. Write each verb and its definition in large print on a sheet of paper. Photocopy as necessary and cut into thirty cards, separating each verb from its definition. Have pairs or small groups lay all the cards face down on a desk. Have students take turns flipping two cards face up to look for a match. If no match is made, the cards are flipped face down. If a match is found, both cards are removed and the student takes another turn.

FOCUSED PRACTICE (pages 98–101)

See the General Suggestions for Focused Practice exercises on pages 3–4.

1. Discover the Grammar, page 98
Have students first identify and underline the phrasal verbs. Then have them identify and circle the direct objects of the transitive phrasal verbs.

As students read their answers aloud, write the words with the corresponding underlines or circles on the board for students to check.

For comprehension, ask:

How were Hispanic students discriminated against in Eloy Rodriguez's elementary school? (They weren't selected for honors class and were punished for speaking their native language.)
Why did Dr. Rodriguez feel pressure when he became a biology instructor at his university? (because people were waiting for him to slip up)
How does Dr. Rodriguez help out young minority students? (He works closely with Latino graduate students and set up KIDS for minority elementary school students.)

2. Come Along!, page 99
Point out that in several answers, two blanks are provided for a phrasal verb that is separated by its direct object.

Ask student the following questions:

Which department is setting up the trip? (the Biology Department)
What do the students plan to find out in Venezuela? (They plan to find out how local people use the plants in traditional medicine.)
In your opinion, is this a fun vacation? (Answers will vary.)

3. Food for Thought, page 100
Explain the title. Often a doctor will advise a patient to take some over-the-counter medicine (aspirin, for example) and call in the morning if the symptoms persist. The title of this reading instructs the patient to eat leaves instead of medicine!

Have students read the whole passage once before choosing the correct particles. To check comprehension, ask:

Why did the chimps swallow the Aspilia *leaves whole?* (because they hate the taste of the leaves)
Why didn't the chimps eat the sweet-tasting fruit nearby? (They weren't hungry. They were taking their medicine.)
What do Aspilia *leaves contain?* (an antibiotic)

4. In the Field, page 100
Tell students to repeat the phrasal verbs in their answers and convert each direct object into a pronoun. You may want to have students identify the direct objects before filling in the blanks.

5. In the Lab, page 101
As you go over the answers, write three headings on the board: *Transitive Phrasal Verbs, Transitive Phrasal Verbs with Direct Object Pronouns,* and *Intransitive Phrasal Verbs.* As students call out their answers, put the sentence in the correct category. Remind the class that transitive phrasal verbs with direct object pronouns may be separated.

6. Editing, page 101

See the General Suggestions for Editing on page 4.

Follow up with these questions:

Who are the Piaroa people? (people who live in the Amazon rain forest)
Why are the students careful about touching new insects or plants? (They can get skin rashes.)
Are there many insects in the rain forest? (yes)
Does bug repellent work in the rain forest? (not very well)

COMMUNICATION PRACTICE (pages 102–103)

7. Listening, page 102

See the General Suggestions for Listening on page 4.

Point out that both phrasal verbs are possible in each item and that students must listen carefully to distinguish the correct verb.

8 Let's Talk It Over, page 102

See the General Suggestions for Pair and Group Activities on page 4.

As a class, decide on some parameters for the field trip (length, cost, academic purpose). Write them on the board. Divide the class into small groups. Have each group decide on a destination and then write out the tasks involved in planning the trip. Have students share their lists with the class.

9. A New Leaf, page 103

See the General Suggestions for Pair and Group Activities on page 4.

Divide the class into pairs. Have each pair write a story based on the pictures in the Student Book. As the pairs read their stories aloud, have the class identify the sequence of pictures as they listen.

10. Writing, page 103

See the General Suggestions for Writing on page 5.

Use samples of student writing to create an error correction exercise for phrasal verbs. Extract errors from students' writing and put them on the board. Have groups of students work together to correct them.

EXPANSION

Student-Generated Practice: Have each student write one sentence using a phrasal verb from Appendix 4 or Appendix 5. Review the sentences for errors. Then have each student copy the corrected sentence onto two slips of paper, separating the phrasal verb between the verb and its particle. For example:

The students took   off their lab coats.

Have students put their two slips in a pile. Shuffle the pile and redistribute the slips of paper. Have students circulate around the room, looking for the matching half of the sentence. Be sure students don't read each other's sentences but rather speak and listen to each other.

When all the sentences are matched, have the students read their matched sentences aloud to the class.

Student Discussion: Herbal remedies have always been popular in some parts of the world. Have students describe what herbal remedies they use for the following conditions:

sore throat
skin burn
skin rash
headache
anxiety
poor sleep
depression
indigestion

REVIEW OR SELFTEST

See the General Suggestions for Review or SelfTest on pages 5–6.

FROM GRAMMAR TO WRITING:
USING PRONOUNS FOR COHERENCE

See the General Suggestions for From Grammar to Writing on page 6.

In this section, students practice using pronouns to make their writing more cohesive while giving directions and writing notes. Students then share their writing in pairs and give each other feedback using a chart.

Introduction, page 108
Write the two example sentences on the board. Ask students, *What word is repeated in these two sentences?* Circle *apartment*. Ask, *What pronoun can replace the word* apartment? Insert *it*. Explain that by using the pronoun *it,* they can reduce the repetition in the text and make the text more connected.

Have students read the introductory text.

Exercise 1, page 108
After identifying all the pronouns, have students identify the nouns that the pronouns refer to.

Exercise 2, page 109
Have students read their changes aloud.

Exercise 3, page 109
This is a warm-up activity. Encourage students to brainstorm freely as they write their lists. If students are uncertain about what responsibilities to assign, map out on the board different possibilities (*feeding pets, watering plants, taking in mail, taking out garbage, receiving calls,* and so on). Within each theme, brainstorm the instructions needed to complete that task.

Brainstorm questions partners can ask each other. Write their ideas on the board. For example:

Where are the keys kept?
How can I reach you if there is an emergency?
Where do you keep the pet food?
How often do I water the plants?
How much food do the fish need?

Have students form pairs to ask and answer each other's questions. Encourage them to take notes to add more detail to their own instructions

Exercise 4, page 109
Have students write their notes at home using the material they generated in class.

Exercise 5, page 110
Before exchanging notes, have students look at the chart. Explain that they will give each other feedback. Well-written instructions give complete information. By completing the chart, the reader can identify missing information.

Have students exchange paragraphs, read them, and give each other feedback using the chart in the book. Have the writers read the feedback and incorporate any new information into the final draft.

PART III MODALS AND RELATED VERBS AND EXPRESSIONS

 UNIT 11 ABILITY: *CAN, COULD, BE ABLE TO*

GRAMMAR **IN CONTEXT** (page 114)

See the General Suggestions for Grammar in Context on page 2.

Before You Read, page 114: Have students read the question, look at the photograph, and predict the main point of the article. Write students' predictions on the board.

Reading, page 114: Ask the following comprehension questions:

Why can't Mary Verdi-Fletcher walk? (She has a medical condition that affects her nervous system.)
How did people react when she danced in her first competition? (They applauded.)
How has she changed the definition of dancing? (Dancing does not have to be done standing up.)
What does she want to show through her dances? (that anything is possible and achievable)

Focus on Grammar: Point out that the article discusses Mary Verdi-Fletcher's abilities and achievements and her ideas about what people are and are not able to do.

Write two headings on the board: *Past* and *Present*. Elicit examples of these structures and write them under the appropriate headings.

GRAMMAR **PRESENTATION:** Ability: *Can, Could,* and *Be able to* (pages 115–117)

See the General Suggestions for Grammar Presentation on page 3.

NOTE 1: Give additional examples:

I can speak Spanish.   *We can't touch our toes.*
You can speak English.   *You can't lift this desk with one hand.*
He can ride a bicycle.   *They can't ice skate.*

Point out that in complete sentences the pronunciation of *can* is with a relaxed vowel /kən/ and is brief. The pronunciation of *can't* is with an open vowel /kænt/ and drawn out. Have students practice the pronunciation in the sentences.

Write on the board:

Can you touch your toes?   *Can you touch the ceiling?*
Can you hold your breath for ten seconds?   *Can you hold your breath for one minute?*
Can you ride a horse?   *Can you ride a bicycle?*
Can you recite the English alphabet?   *Can you recite the Greek alphabet?*
Can you speak French?   *Can you say "hello" in three different languages?*

Ask students the questions and have them respond with a complete phrase. Then have students take turns asking one another the questions on the board. For example:

Student 1: *Can you ice skate?*
Student 2: *No, I can't ice skate.* (To student 3) *Can you ride a bicycle?*
Student 3: *Yes, I can.*

Stop when all students have asked at least one question.

NOTE 2: Read the note in the Student Book with the class. Answer any questions.

NOTES 3–5: Give additional examples to establish the contrast between *could/was/were able to. Could* and *can* refer to a general ability but not a specific achievement.

I could speak Spanish when I was child.
I was able to win the first prize in our school's Spanish essay contest.

Jessica could run very fast when she was young.
Once she was able to run to the store and back in less than five minutes.

Write the following prompts on the board:

speak Latin	*tie my own shoelaces*	*cook a meal*
drive a car	*read a book*	*fasten my seat belt*
sign my name	*wash the dishes*	*get dressed*
make my bed	*use a computer*	*speak a foreign language*

Have students explain what they were or were not able to do (could or could not do) when they were five years old.

NOTE 6: Read the note in the Student Book with the class. Answer any questions.

FOCUSED PRACTICE (pages 118–120)

See the General Suggestions for Focused Practice exercises on pages 3–4.

1. Discover the Grammar, page 118
Have students read the information carefully first. Then have them evaluate the sentences and decide if they are *true, false,* or *uncertain.*

2. Now I Can, pages 118–119
Have students read the entire passage before filling in the blanks.

3. At the Dance Studio, page 119
Have students read each exercise before filling in the blanks. To review answers, have pairs of students act out the conversations for the class.

4. Achievement, page 120
As students do this exercise, have them refer to Grammar Notes 1–6. The items correspond to the following notes:

1. Note 4—a single event
2. Note 4—a single event
3. Note 1
4. Note 3
5. Note 3
6. Note 1
7. Note 6
8. Note 6
9. Note 4

5. Editing, page 120
See the General Suggestions for Editing on page 4.

Follow up with these questions:

What is a "driver" like? (can make decisions but is not able to listen to other people's ideas.)
What is an "enthusiast" like? (communicates well but is not dependable.)
Which best describes you? (Answers will vary.)

COMMUNICATION PRACTICE (pages 121–123)

6. Listening, page 121
See the General Suggestions for Listening on page 4.

Ask, *What will Karl be able to do in the near future?* (desktop publishing and dancing)

7. Information Gap: Can They Do the Tango?, pages 121 and 123
Divide the class into pairs. Assign each partner a role (A or B). Assign Students A page 121 and Students B page 123. Have everyone read the assigned schedules. Point out that all schedules are organized the same way but have different information according to the different dance classes. Have the partners ask each other questions to complete the schedules.

8. Class Presentation, page 122

After assigning roles within their groups, have students tell the class their assignments. Ask:

How did you learn to _____?
Where do you do it?
Can you teach other students in the class how to _____?

9. Writing, page 122

See the General Suggestions for Writing on page 5.

If possible, have students bring a photograph of the person they have chosen to write about. Have students share their writing in small groups. After each text, have them discuss the following questions:

What is special about this person?
What was this person's key to success?
What can you learn from a story like this?

Put several student paragraphs on the bulletin board.

EXPANSION

Student Survey: Have students survey each other about skills and abilities they developed in their childhood, possess now, or plan for the future. For example:

Can you play a musical instrument?
When you were a child, were you able to play an instrument?
When you were a child, could you read music?

Have students compose their surveys and submit them to you for correction. Then have students circulate around the room interviewing their classmates. Have students write up a report of their findings and submit it to you.

UNIT 12 PERMISSION: *MAY, COULD, CAN, DO YOU MIND IF . . . ?*

GRAMMAR **IN CONTEXT** (page 124)

See the General Suggestions for Grammar in Context on page 2.

Before You Read, page 124: Write the acronym *TOEFL*® on the board. Ask students what the acronym stands for. (Test of English as a Foreign Language) Discuss the questions in this section with the class.

Reading, page 124: Ask the following comprehension questions:

How many times can you take the TOEFL®*?* (as many times as you want, but only once a calendar month)
What happens if students feel they didn't do well on the test? (They can cancel their test scores.)

Focus on Grammar: Elicit questions and responses from the text with *may, can,* and *could*. Write them on the board. Ask the following questions:

Is it possible to contract may not*?* (no)
Is it possible to contract cannot*?* (yes)
Do the modals use -s in the third person singular? (no)

GRAMMAR **PRESENTATION:** Permission: *May, Could, Can, Do you mind if . . . ?* (pages 125–127)

See the General Suggestions for Grammar Presentation on page 3.

NOTE 1: Ask questions or elicit examples of *may, could,* and *can* for permission. For example:

May I borrow your pen?
Could I use your book?
Can we leave now?

NOTE 2: Point out that *please* may be placed just before the main verb or at the beginning or end of a question.

NOTE 3: Write on the board, *Do you mind if I leave now? Yes, I do.* Ask the class, *Was permission given? What is the long response to this question?* (I do mind if you leave now.) Replace the response with *No, I don't.* Ask again, *Was permission given? What is the long response to this question?* (No, I don't mind if you leave now.)

Have students practice responding rapidly to permission requests. Ask:

Do you mind if I smoke?
Can I smoke?
Do you mind if I leave class early tonight?
Could I leave early tonight?
Do you mind if I borrow a pen?
May I borrow a pen?
Could I use your dictionary?
Do you mind if I use your dictionary?

NOTE 4: Emphasize that we often reply to a request for permission (*May I be excused?*) with *Sure, Of course, No problem,* and so on. We use a yes/no answer with the modal (*Yes, you may*) less frequently.

NOTE 5: Offer multiple examples of how permission is refused indirectly. For example:

A: *Can I make a phone call?*
B: *I'm sorry. This phone is for employees only.*

A: *May I sit here?*
B: *I'm sorry. That seat is already taken.*

FOCUSED PRACTICE (pages 128–131)

See the General Suggestions for Focused Practice exercises on pages 3–4.

1. Discover the Grammar, page 128
Have the class read the responses and identify the location of each illustration before doing the exercise. To review answers, have pairs of students act out the conversations for the class.

2. Giving the Go-Ahead, page 129
Point out that the responses may be either affirmative or negative, depending on the context. Have students work individually or in pairs to complete the exercise. To review answers, have pairs of students act out the conversations for the class.

Ask the following comprehension questions:
Can friends and family enter the test hall? (No, they may not.)
Can students enter after the test has started? (No, they cannot.)
Can students use pens? (No, they can't.)

3. Taking the Test, page 130
Tell students this is a typical format used in the written TOEFL®. Remind them that they are looking only for the incorrect part. As the class goes over the answers, have students identify the errors and supply their corrections.

4. Celebrating, page 131
To review answers, have groups of three students act out the conversations for the class. One student is the narrator and the other two are the speakers.

After students have completed the exercise, ask the following comprehension questions:

Did Bob go to the concert with Lucy and Carl? (Yes, he did.)
Did they sit in their assigned seats? (No, they didn't. They moved up a few rows.)
Could they record the music? (No, they couldn't.)
Did they enjoy the concert? (No, they didn't.)

COMMUNICATION PRACTICE (pages 132–133)

5. Listening, page 132
See the General Suggestions for Listening on page 4.

Have students read the list of situations before listening. After playing the tape twice, check students' answers. For each conversation, ask, *Who was speaking? Was permission given?* If students disagree, play the segment in question again.

6. Asking Permission, page 132
See the General Suggestions for Pair and Group Activities on page 4.

Give the groups a time limit of ten minutes to read the situations and brainstorm their responses. Have the groups share with the class their ideas for each situation, as you take notes on the board. Ask:

What are possible responses to these requests?
How polite is each request?
How effective is each request?
In this situation, which request would you be most comfortable making?

7. Role Play, page 133
See the General Suggestions for Role Plays on page 5.

Have pairs of students (from different backgrounds, if possible) briefly role play the situations. To add a dramatic element to this exercise, have students read only their own role information, not that of their partners. Then have each pair select one role play to perform to the class.

8. Writing, page 133
See the General Suggestions for Writing on page 5.

Have students do this exercise for homework.

Once you have reviewed students' notes for accuracy, have pairs of students trade notes and write appropriate responses to each other's requests. Have students read each other's responses and give feedback on the accuracy of the language and appropriateness of the responses.

EXPANSION

Asking Permission: Have groups develop and write out their own situations relating to asking permission to do something (as in Exercise 6 on page 132). Then have the groups exchange situations and plan how *they* would respond.

 UNIT 13 REQUESTS: *WILL, WOULD, COULD, CAN, WOULD YOU MIND . . . ?*

GRAMMAR IN CONTEXT (page 134)
See the General Suggestions for Grammar in Context on page 2.

BACKGROUND NOTE: E-mail has become the prevalent form of communication in big companies. A message is composed on and sent by computer to another computer. The recipient is notified mail has arrived. The transmittal is instantaneous.

Before You Read, page 134: Ask the class, *Do you use e-mail? What does e-mail stand for?* (electronic mail) Have students read the questions, look at the text, and share their responses with the class.

Reading, page 134: Ask the following comprehension questions:

What does John Sanchez ask Marcia Jones to do? (to photocopy the monthly sales report)
What does Marcia Jones ask Ann Chen to do? (to photocopy and deliver the sales report)
What does Rhea Jones ask her daughter to do? (to pick up dessert at the bakery and drive her to the Burtons' house for dinner)
Do Marcia Jones, John Sanchez, and Ann Chen all work for the same company? (Yes. They all have dataline.com as their e-mail address.)
Who is the mother's favorite son-in-law? (Marcia Jones's husband)

Focus on Grammar: Elicit questions and responses from the text with *will, would, could, can,* and *would you mind.* Write them on the board and ask the following questions:

Which requests are more informal and direct? (Can you drive me to the Burtons after work?)
Who is making this request? (her mother)
Which requests are softer and less demanding? (Would you please photocopy the monthly sales report for me?)
Who is making this request? (her supervisor)

GRAMMAR **PRESENTATION:** Requests: *Will, Would, Could, Can, Would you mind . . . ?* (pages 135–136)

See the General Suggestions for Grammar Presentation on page 3.

NOTE 1: Caution students that they should soften their requests by using modals. The imperative form is used to give instructions and directions (see Unit 2), but when asking someone to do something, it is best to use the polite forms.

NOTE 2: Point out that *please* may be placed just before the main verb or at the beginning or end of a question.

NOTE 3: Write on the board:

Supervisor: *Would you mind photocopying this report?*
  Secretary: *Yes, I would.*

Ask the class, *Is the secretary going to photocopy the report?* (no) *What is the long response to this question?* (Yes, I would mind photocopying the report.)

Replace the secretary's response with *No, I wouldn't.* Ask again, *Is the secretary going to photocopy the report?* (Yes, she is.) *What is the long response to this question?* (No, I wouldn't mind photocopying the report.) Brainstorm with the class other possible ways to respond to this request *(Not at all. No problem.).* Write the responses on the board.

Brainstorm with the class ways to reply positively to a request *(Could you deliver this? Sure, Of course, No problem, Certainly, Right away,* and so on.) Write the responses on the board.

Have students practice responding rapidly to requests. Ask:

Would you mind closing the window?
Could you close the window, please?
Would you mind taking this to the post office?
Would you please take this to the post office?
Would you mind answering the phone for me?
Would you please answer the phone for me?
Would you mind giving me a ride home?
Could you give me a ride home?

Note 4: Point out that in English-speaking cultures, when someone cannot help with a request, an apology and brief explanation are expected. Brainstorm with the class possible excuses for saying no to the following requests:

Could you lend me a pen?
Could you stay after class today?
Would you mind giving me a ride home?
Could you pick up a class snack on the way to class tomorrow?

FOCUSED PRACTICE (pages 137–139)

See the General Suggestions for Focused Practice exercises on pages 3–4.

1. Discover the Grammar, page 137
As each request is identified, ask:

Was the request accepted or refused?
(If it was refused) *What is her excuse?*

2. Asking for Favors, pages 137–138
Have students work individually or in pairs to complete the exercise. To review answers, have pairs of students act out the conversations for the class.

3. Editing, page 138
See the General Suggestions for Editing on page 4.

Background Note: When a person e-mails a list of requests, often the recipient copies the whole letter and writes in a response to each request. Such an example is provided in this exercise.

Have students go over their corrections by reading the e-mail aloud.

4. Would You Mind?, page 139
Have students match the cues to the pictures. Then have students complete the requests. As the class goes over the answers, ask for a possible response for each request.

COMMUNICATION PRACTICE (pages 140–141)

5. Listening, page 140
See the General Suggestions for Listening on page 4.

Have students read the list of activities before listening. After playing the tape twice, check students' answers.

6. I'd Be Glad to, page 140
See the general suggestions for Pair and Group Activities on page 4.

After students have completed their schedules, brainstorm the types of requests they might ask of each other. For example:

give a ride
pick up the kids
return a book to the library
pick up some groceries
stop at the post office

Then have students work in small groups to ask each other polite requests.

7. Writing, page 141
See the General Suggestions for Writing on page 5.

Review the situations as a class. Have students write their notes for homework and, in class, compare their notes in small groups.

EXPANSION

Requests: Divide the class into groups of four. Have students make polite requests of each other. The student who receives the request must either perform the action or apologize and explain why he or she is refusing. For example:

Student 1: *Kenno, please open the door.*
Student 2: *I'm sorry. I can't get up right now. I have too many papers on my desk.*
Student 1: *Andrew, could you please open the door?*
Student 3: *No problem!*

UNIT 14 ADVICE: *SHOULD, OUGHT TO, HAD BETTER*

GRAMMAR **IN CONTEXT** (page 142)

See the General Suggestions for Grammar in Context on page 2.

BACKGROUND NOTE: Vocational schools offer training for non-professionals such as medical technicians, secretaries, and electricians. Community colleges also offer many similar courses in one- or two-year programs.

Before You Read, page 142: In pairs, have students look at the photograph, read the questions, and discuss their responses.

Reading, page 142: Ask the following comprehension questions:

Where will the best opportunities be in the next ten years? (in service jobs)
Does everyone need a college education? (No, many jobs don't require one.)
Do you need experience before you start your own business? (Yes, you do.)

Focus on Grammar: Elicit highlighted questions and statements of advice from the text and write them on the board. Ask the following questions:

Which modal is used in questions? (should)
How do you form the negative of the expression had better? (had better not)
How do you form the negative of the modal should? (should not *or* shouldn't)

GRAMMAR **PRESENTATION:** Advice: *Should, Ought to, Had better* (pages 143–144)

See the General Suggestions for Grammar Presentation on page 3.

NOTE 1: Have students write a sentence with *shouldn't* and a sentence with *ought to* describing the responsibilities of students in an English class. Have students share their ideas with the class. For example:

Students shouldn't be late to class.
Students ought to prepare their homework.

NOTE 2: Provide several more examples of the urgent nature of the expression *had better*. For example:

You'd better cancel the order now before they charge you.
She'd better get here soon, or the supervisor will notice she's late.
He'd better change his attitude at work, or he'll lose his job.

NOTE 3: Provide several more examples of *should* in questions. For example:

What time should they leave?
What suit should I wear?
Where should we park?

NOTE 4: Emphasize that it is usually impolite to offer advice to peers and those of higher status. We often make polite suggestions instead. For example:

Maybe you could talk to your boss about the problem.
Perhaps you could send another e-mail.
I think it would be a good idea to call.

FOCUSED PRACTICE (pages 145–147)

See the General Suggestions for Focused Practice exercises on pages 3–4.

1. Discover the Grammar, page 145
Have students first read the job notices and then complete the exercise. To go over the answers, have pairs of students read the conversations aloud as they identify the phrases that give advice.

2. Should's and Should Not's, page 146
If you do this exercise in class, have students cover the answer portion of each item. Have students read the question aloud. Elicit advice from students before looking at the answer in the book. Then have students circle the correct advice words.

3. Friendly Advice, page 146
Refer students to Grammar Note 4 to refresh their memory about softening advice for friends.

4. What Should I Do?, page 147
Remind students some of these items require the negative.

After correcting their answers, have students explain to the class the etiquette for a dinner invitation in their cultures. Be sure they describe appropriate dress, time of arrival, and gift giving.

5. Editing, page 147
See the General Suggestions for Editing on page 4.

After completing the exercise, ask the class:

What are the parents concerned about? (They are concerned the new job will interfere with his studies.)
Do you think college students should work at part-time jobs? (Answers will vary.)

COMMUNICATION PRACTICE (pages 148–149)

6. Listening, page 148
See the General Suggestions for Listening on page 4.

Ask students if they have any other advice for taking a test (the TOEFL®, for example). Have them brainstorm in small groups and then share their ideas with the class.

7. New Country, New Customs, page 148
See the General Suggestions for Pair and Group Activities on page 4.

Brainstorm other topics with students, such as:

dressing for work
punctuality at work
office schedules
socializing after work with colleagues

If interest in this subject is high, have groups of students (from the same culture, if possible) give brief presentations to the class about business etiquette in their cultures.

8. Problem Solving, page 149
After all groups have finished the discussion, ask each group to present one problem and their advice to the class. Invite the class to offer additional advice for each problem posed.

9. This Place Needs Work!, page 149
See the General Suggestions for Pair and Group Activities on page 4.

Have each pair assign a scribe. After two pairs have compared their lists, follow up with a class discussion. Ask:

What should Mo do first to improve the classroom? Why?
What are the three most important changes Mo should make?
What makes a school good ?

10. Writing, page 149
See the General Suggestions for Writing on page 5.

Use this assignment as an opportunity to teach the format of a formal letter. Make sure students include the date, their own address, the address of Mo's Training Institute, a closing, and a signature.

April 12, 2001
13 Apple Lane
Newtonville, MA 02166

Mr. Mo
Mo's Training Institute
10 Ferry Street
Newbury, MA 01951

Dear Mr. Mo:
(body of letter)

Sincerely,

Susanna Lee

EXPANSION

Interview Advice: Have students discuss the following questions in small groups:

Have you ever been to a job interview?
Was it a good interview? Why or why not?
What advice would you give to someone interviewing for the first time?

Follow up with a class discussion. Encourage students to add other suggestions for job interviews, such as what to wear, how to greet and say good-bye to the interviewer, what to say and not say, and how to follow up appropriately. Write students' ideas on the board.

UNIT 15 SUGGESTIONS: *LET'S, COULD, WHY DON'T . . . ?, WHY NOT . . . ?, HOW ABOUT . . . ?*

GRAMMAR **IN CONTEXT** (page 150)

See the General Suggestions for Grammar in Context on page 2.

BACKGROUND NOTE: Youth hostels are run by the International Youth Hostel Association. They offer inexpensive accommodations for travelers, and they are very popular with students. However, older people and non-students also use them.

Before You Read, page 150: Have students read the questions, look at the pictures, and share their responses with the class.

Reading, page 150: Ask the following comprehension questions:

What is one reason students don't travel? (They don't know where to go.)
What is one reason to try hosteling? (You'll meet friendly people from all over the world.)

Focus on Grammar: Write the headings *Question* and *Statement* on the board. Elicit examples of the highlighted structures from the reading and write them under the appropriate heading on the board. Ask the following questions:

Are these phrases offering suggestions or advice? (suggestions)
Where is the helping verb in these questions? (It is not included in the questions beginning with *Why not* and *How about.*)
What is a possible answer to one of these questions? (That's a great idea.)

GRAMMAR **PRESENTATION:** Suggestions: *Let's, Could, Why don't . . . ?, Why not . . . ?, How about . . . ?* (pages 151–153)

See the General Suggestions for Grammar Presentation on page 3.

NOTE 1: Point out that the intonation of the statements and the *wh-* questions is the same. Both fall at the end. Yes/no questions, in contrast, end on a high note.

NOTE 2: Provide additional examples of these suggestions. As you speak, indicate with your hand whom you are including in the suggestion:

Let's take a break.
Let's get a cup of coffee.
Let's listen to the teacher!

NOTE 3: Remind students that expressions with prepositions such as *How about* are always followed by gerunds. Point out that the gerund follows the preposition *about.*

NOTE 4: Write several suggestions without punctuation on the board and have students add it. For example:

Why don't you call her (?)
Let's leave now (.)
How about going to the movies (?)

FOCUSED PRACTICE (pages 154–155)

See the General Suggestions for Focused Practice exercises on pages 3–4.

1. Discover the Grammar, page 154
Have students do this for homework. Go over the answers in class.

Have students with advanced listening skills open to page 154 of the Student Book and read the tourist information before listening to the conversation. Then have students check off the items Megan and Emily plan to do. Play the tape twice before reviewing the answers. Have students turn to the previous section to read the conversation and underline the suggestions.

Alternatively, have students underline the suggestions first, go over their answers by acting out the conversation, and then check off the items Emily and Megan have planned for their Hong Kong vacation.

2. Making Plans, page 155
To review answers, have pairs of students act out the conversations for the class.

3. Let's . . . , page 155
To review answers, have pairs of students act out the conversations for the class.

COMMUNICATION PRACTICE (page 156)

4. Listening, page 156
See the General Suggestions for Listening on page 4.

Before listening to the tape, have students look over the map and practice pronouncing the names of the places so they can recognize the names while listening to the tape.

5. How About?, page 156
See the General Suggestions for Pair and Group Activities on page 4.

Have each pair present its plan to the class. If interest is sufficient, have the whole class follow up by planning a "field trip." Appoint a discussion leader and a discussion recorder to takes notes on the board. Let the class work out its own plans by making suggestions.

6. Things to Do, page 156
See the General Suggestions for Pair and Group Activities on page 4.

To ensure that all students don't select the same tourist sights, brainstorm different types of trips. For example:

class field trip
summer mini-vacation
winter mini-vacation
family day out
romantic weekend
athletic weekend
arts weekend

Give the groups a time limit of fifteen minutes to plan. Have them share their ideas with the class as you write their ideas on the board.

Students may be interested in learning more about these tourist sights. Have each group write up its information in a brochure and distribute it to the class.

7. Writing, page 156
See the General Suggestions for Writing on page 5.

EXPANSION

Student Speeches—My Hometown: Have students prepare brief presentations of about five minutes each about interesting tourist sights in their hometowns. Tell students to point out the location on a map, and encourage them to bring in photos and brochures if possible.

REVIEW OR SELFTEST

See the General Suggestions for Review or Self Test on pages 5–6.

FROM GRAMMAR TO WRITING: USING APPROPRIATE MODALS

See the General Suggestions for From Grammar to Writing on page 6.

In this section, students identify inappropriately direct statements and soften them using the modal forms learned in Units 11–15. Students also compose notes that seek and offer advice, make requests, and grant permission.

Introduction, page 161
Brainstorm with students the modals for permission, requests, advice, and suggestions. Write their ideas on the board. Write the example sentence from the Student Book:

I want you to call me in the morning.

Ask the class for other more polite ways to make the same request. Write students' ideas on the board.

Have students read the introductory text.

Exercise 1, page 161

Answers may vary, so go over students' ideas briefly. Point out that all the sentences in the note are grammatically correct; it is only a matter of tone. Depending on personal taste and cultural heritage, people vary widely in their tolerance of direct language.

Exercise 2, page 161

Have students read their changes aloud. Answers may vary. Emphasize that there are many correct ways to express functions.

Exercise 3, page 162

Review the ideas with the class. Have students complete this exercise as homework. In class, have pairs of students compare their letters before submitting them to you.

Exercise 4, page 162

Divide the class into pairs. Have each pair choose one situation. You may have students either write a script or act out the role play extemporaneously for fluency practice.

First model the listening portion of the activity for the class. Have students write down all the functions in list form. For example:

asking for advice
giving advice
making suggestions
making requests
asking for permission
giving permission

Have one pair perform for the class. As students listen, have them write all the modals they hear next to the appropriate functions. Go over the notes as a class.

Have pairs perform their role plays for one another, listening to each other and taking notes as modeled previously.

Exercise 5, page 162

Have students write a note from the point of view of one of the characters in the role play and submit their notes directly to you for review and feedback.

PART IV PRESENT PERFECT

PRESENT PERFECT: *SINCE* AND *FOR*

GRAMMAR IN CONTEXT (page 166)

See the General Suggestions for Grammar in Context on page 2.

BACKGROUND NOTE: Millions of people of all ages play tennis, and many people also watch the professional tournaments. Professional players such as Martina Hingis have the same kind of popularity as movie stars. The major international championships are the Australian, British, French and U.S. Opens. The British tournament, called Wimbledon, has the most prestige. The U.S. Open awards the most money, with prizes of more than $2 million.

Before You Read, page 166: Have students look at the photograph, read the questions, and share their responses with the class.

Reading, page 166: Ask the following questions:

When did Martina Hingis start playing tennis? (when she was two years old)
When did she turn professional? (in 1994)
How old was she when she stopped attending school? (She was fourteen years old.)
What major tournaments has she won? (Wimbledon, the U.S. Open, and the Australian Open)

How old was she when she won her first Wimbledon event? (She was sixteen years old.)
Do you think young star athletes should be required to attend school? (Answers will vary.)
Do you think young people should be allowed to live the life of celebrities? (Answers will vary.)
What do you think happens when young stars grow up into adults? (Answers will vary.)
Can you name other examples of famous young people? How are they now? (Answers will vary.)

Focus on Grammar: Point out that Martina Hingis still plays tennis. Present perfect is used to describe her accomplishments because we can expect her to keep achieving in her field. The information in this article is about things that began in the past but that continue into the present. Contrast the information with the information about Basho in Unit 3.

Elicit examples of the highlighted text. Write one or two examples in full sentences on the board and ask questions to illustrate how the time frame stretches from the past to the present. For example:

"Since then, she has become one of the greatest tennis players in the world."
When did her practice as a tennis player begin? (when she was two)
Is she still a great tennis player? (Yes, she is.)
How long is this period of time? (about twenty years)

"She and her mother have lived in Switzerland for many years."
Did she live in Switzerland when she was young? (Yes, she did.)
Does she still live in Switzerland? (Yes, she does.)
How long is this period of time? (many years)

GRAMMAR **PRESENTATION:** Present Perfect: *Since* and *For* (pages 167–169)

See the General Suggestions for Grammar Presentation on page 3.

Grammar Charts: Point out that the contraction for the third person singular of *have* (*has*) is the same as for *be: he's, she's, it's.* However, use of the past participle marks the present perfect.

NOTE 1: Draw out timelines for other examples of the present perfect in the text.

NOTE 2: Provide other examples of *since*. For example:

She hasn't attended school since 1994.
She has won many tournaments since 1997.
She has been very famous since 1996.

NOTE 3: Provide contrasting examples of *since* with a time clause in the simple past and *since* with a time clause in the present perfect. Draw a timeline for each example:

She has been famous since she became the outdoor Swiss champion at age nine.
She has played tennis all over the world since she won the French Open Junior title in 1993.
She has earned millions of dollars since she has become famous.
She hasn't attended school since she has been a professional tennis player.

NOTE 4: Provide other examples of *for*. For example:

She has played tennis for many years.
She has lived in Switzerland for more than ten years.

NOTE 5: Point out the difference between irregular past participles and the past tense. Have students call out the past tense form of the verbs listed in this note. Have them identify which verbs change in the transformation from the simple past to the past participle.

FOCUSED PRACTICE (pages 170–173)

See the General Suggestions for Focused Practice exercises on pages 3–4.

1. Discover the Grammar, page 170
Have students draw a timeline for each exercise before answering the question. Have students compare their answers in pairs or as a class.

2. Winners, pages 170–171

Review the chart and the names of the tennis champions before students do the exercise.

As a listening activity, have students do this activity in pairs. Have Students A cover the chart and Students B cover the questions. Have Students A ask question 2; have Students B look at the chart and answer the question. After question 4, have students switch roles.

3. Child Genius, page 171

Have students read the entire passage before they fill in the blanks.

After correcting the answers, ask the class:

How old was Ronnie when he began to love math? (four years old)
Where does Ronnie go to school? (at the local university)
Do you think he is going to be a good sports announcer? (Answers will vary.)

4. A Resume, pages 172–173

CULTURE NOTE: A resume is a summary or list, usually in chronological order with the most recent experience first, of a person's work history and education. People present resumes when they apply for jobs. During an interview, the interviewer usually asks about information in the resume.

Remind students that the responses can use either *since* or *for*. As you go over the answers, encourage students to try forming the sentence with each option.

5. Editing, page 173

See the General Suggestions for Editing on page 4.

Follow up with a discussion. Ask:

Which sports do you play now?
Which sports would you like to learn?
Are there any sports you used to play but have stopped playing? Why did you stop?
Would you like to return to that sport?

COMMUNICATION PRACTICE (pages 174–175)

6. Listening, page 174

See the General Suggestions for Listening on page 4.

Follow up with a discussion. Ask:

Why do you think he went back to school?
Do you think he gave a good interview?
What questions would you like to ask him?

7. The Best Person for the Job, page 174

See the General Suggestions for Pair and Group Activities on page 4.

Divide the class into small groups. Within a time limit of fifteen minutes, students must choose one of the applicants as the new math teacher at their business college. Point out the list of things to consider at the top of the exercise. Circulate around the class and help as needed.

Have each group present its decision and explain its choice to the class.

8. Role Play: A Job Interview, page 175

See the General Suggestions for Role Plays on page 5.

Brainstorm with the class several job openings that would interest them. Write out the details of each job: location, salary, and responsibilities. Tell the class they are going to write resumes and then interview for one of these jobs. Refer students to the resume on page 172 as a model for their own. Students can write accurate resumes of their experience and education, or they can add some fantastic details if they wish.

Before pairing students for their interviews, talk about good interviewing techniques. To get the class thinking about this topic, ask:

Should you try to look relaxed?
Should you look at the interviewer?
Should you smile at the interviewer?
Should you give as much information as possible or only answer the questions?
Should you ask any questions about the job?

Pair students for their interviews. Have them indicate the job they are applying for before they begin the interview. Refer them to the script as they conduct their interviews.

Follow up with a quick review. Ask:

How did the interviews go?
Who got a job?

9. Writing, page 175
See the General Suggestions for Writing on page 5.

With the class, brainstorm the names of people they are very proud of or impressed by. Tell students to write a paragraph describing that person's accomplishments.

Have students share their writing in small groups. If possible, have them bring along an accompanying photograph. In their groups have them ask each other for more details about the person's life. Have them incorporate the details into a second draft and then submit the paragraph to you for final review.

After students have composed their final drafts, have them display their paragraphs (and pictures) on the bulletin board.

EXPANSION

Who Is It?: Have students write three present tense statements about themselves. For example:

I live in New York.
I'm a pharmacist.
I'm married.

Then ask them to write sentences with *for* or *since* about each present tense statement. Have them write each sentence on a separate slip of paper. For example:

I've lived in New York for five years.
I've been a pharmacist since 1995.
I've been married since I graduated from college.

Collect the slips, shuffle, and redistribute them. Have students read the statements and identify the person.

 PRESENT PERFECT: *ALREADY* AND *YET*

UNIT
17

GRAMMAR **IN CONTEXT** (page 176)

See the General Suggestions for Grammar in Context on page 2.

BACKGROUND NOTE: *Flu* is short for *influenza*, a highly contagious virus that causes fever, aches, and congestion. A flu shot is a vaccine for the most common types of the flu. Usually children, the elderly, people with chronic health problems, and people in public services are advised to get an annual flu shot.

Before You Read, page 176: Have students look at the chart and the cartoon and predict the contents of the article.

Reading, page 176: Ask the following comprehension questions:

When is flu season? (from mid-December to mid-January)
When should people get their flu shots? (in October or early November)

How long does it take for the flu shot to be effective? (about one week)
When did this interview take place? (sometime between early October and mid-December)
Will the flu vaccine always be given with a needle? (No, the lab is testing bananas that can produce vaccines.)
Which would you prefer, a banana vaccine or a shot? (Answers will vary.)

Focus on Grammar: Elicit examples of *already* from the text. Write one or two examples in full sentences on the board and ask questions to illustrate how *already* describes something that has happened before now. For example:

Have we heard about a number of severe cases? (yes)

Elicit examples of *not yet* from the text. Write one or two examples in full sentences on the board and ask questions to illustrate how *not yet* describes something that has not happened before now but could happen soon. For example:

Has flu season arrived? (no)
Do we expect it to arrive soon? (yes)

Elicit examples of *yet* in question form from the text. Write one or two examples in full sentences on the board and explain that *yet* in a question asks whether something has happened before now. For example:

Has it started to work yet? (Has it started to work before now?)

GRAMMAR **PRESENTATION:** Present Perfect: *Already* and *Yet* (pages 177–178)

See the General Suggestions for Grammar Presentation on page 3.

NOTE 1: Draw timelines for other examples of the present perfect with *already* in the text.

To practice the usual placement of *already* (between *have/has* and the past participle), write simple sentences in scrambled order on the board. Have pairs of students put them in the correct order. For example:

already / has / gotten / she / the flu shot (She has already gotten the flu shot.)

they / giving flu shots / have / begun / already (They have already begun giving flu shots.)

NOTE 2: To practice the usual placement of *yet* (at the end of the clause), write simple sentences in scrambled order on the board. Have pairs of students put them in the correct order. For example:

haven't / they / their flu shots / gotten / yet (They haven't gotten their flu shots yet.)

started / haven't / they / to sell / yet / the banana vaccine (They haven't started to sell the banana vaccine yet.)

To practice the contrast between *already* and *yet*, write a daily schedule on the board. For example:

Fred Jones, Police Officer
5:00   gets up and exercises
5:45   takes a shower
6:00   gets dressed in his uniform

Make statements with *already* and *yet* and have students tell you whether they are true or false. For example:

Teacher: *It's 5:30. Fred has already gotten dressed.*
Student: *False.*

NOTE 3: Provide additional examples of *already* in questions. For example:

Have there already been cases of the flu? The flu season hasn't started yet!
Has the flu shot already started working? I thought it took at least three weeks to work!

FOCUSED PRACTICE (pages 179–180)

See the General Suggestions for Focused Practice exercises on pages 3–4.

1. Discover the Grammar, page 179

For listening practice, have students do this exercise in pairs. Have Students A cover the *Result* column and Students B cover the *Cause* column. Have Students A read the cause prompt. Have Students B listen to the cause and identify the result. At item 4, have students switch roles.

2. Ask Dr. Meier, page 179

Review the timeline before students do the exercise.

3. Medical Record, page 180

BACKGROUND NOTE: Immunizations are treatments with vaccines. They prevent serious diseases or make them less serious if they do occur. Children receive a series of immunizations starting at two months. In the United States and Canada, parents must show proof that their children have received immunization before the children enter school. This law helps prevent epidemics.

Lead a discussion about immunization practices in other countries. Ask:

Where are immunizations given? Are they free?
Do students have to show proof of immunization before entering school?

Go over the immunization chart with the class. Point out the time axis across the top of the chart and the diseases down the left side. If necessary, give students time to look up the diseases in their dictionaries.

COMMUNICATION PRACTICE (pages 181–183)

4. Listening, page 181

See the General Suggestions for Listening on page 4.

After identifying everything Dr. Meier has done, have students compose sentences about what he hasn't done yet. For example:

He hasn't had his appointment with Dr. Bellini yet.
He hasn't mailed the rent check yet.
He hasn't read the article about the banana vaccine yet.

5. Information Gap: Chores, pages 181 and 183

Divide the class into pairs. Assign each partner a role (A or B). Assign Students A page 181 and Students B page 183. Have students read their separate instructions and look at the picture and list of chores. Review the example together as a class. Have the partners ask and answer each other's questions. Remind them not to show each other their pictures. Follow up with a general review. Ask, *What does Gisela still need to do? What does Helmut still need to do?*

6. What About You?, page 182

See the General Suggestions for Pair and Group Activities on page 4.

Brainstorm with the class possible items for students to put on their lists. Have students compose their lists individually and then work with a partner.

7. Inventions and Discoveries, page 182

See the General Suggestions for Writing on page 5.

Have the pairs call out their additional inventions and discoveries. Ask the class, *Has this invention / discovery occurred yet?*

If interest in this subject is high, have groups of students review their lists, including any added items, and decide which items are discoveries and which are inventions. This can lead to a spirited debate.

8. Writing, page 183

See the General Suggestions for Writing on page 5.

Brainstorm with the students all the steps involved in preparing for a party.

Have students compose their notes in class and submit them to you for review and correction.

EXPANSION

Writing Exercise: Have students choose a field such as medicine, dentistry, ophthalmology, communications, or transportation and write a short paragraph about what has already been accomplished and what has not yet been developed. Students can refer to the information in Exercise 7, Inventions and Discoveries.

UNIT 18 PRESENT PERFECT: INDEFINITE PAST

GRAMMAR **IN CONTEXT** (page 184)

See the General Suggestions for Grammar in Context on page 2.

BACKGROUND NOTE: For centuries people have kept private journals to record daily life and thoughts. Recently a new phenomenon of online journals has boomed. People of all types now publish their journal entries on the Internet for the public to read. This passage is an example of a celebrity's journal to his fans. He discusses his major goals and past accomplishments.

CULTURE NOTES: The Emmy Awards are annual awards granted by the American Academy of Television Arts and Sciences to outstanding television programs or performers. This unit takes off on a popular television star and comedy series called *Seinfeld*. The series, which ended in 1998, was one of the greatest television hits of the 1990s.

Before You Read, page 184: Have students read the questions, look at the format of the reading, and share their responses with the class.

Reading, page 184: Ask the following comprehension questions:

What has just happened to this TV star? (He has just won the Emmy Award for Best Actor.)
What are signs of his success? (He has been on every talk show at least twice in the last few months, and his face has appeared on the cover of three major magazines.)
What's next for him? (He will continue with the TV show. He would like to try acting in the theater. He will also write a book about relationships.)

Focus on Grammar: Ask students to list Jimmy's accomplishments. For example:

He has won an Emmy Award.
He has been on talk shows.
He has appeared on magazine covers.
He has signed a contract for two more years of the TV show.

Ask the class, *Exactly when did these events take place?* (We don't know. We only know that they happened at an indefinite time in the past.) Point out that the celebrity is listing his accomplishments. The fact that he accomplished them is important; the exact date of the accomplishment is not.

GRAMMAR **PRESENTATION**: Present Perfect: Indefinite Past (pages 185–186)

See the General Suggestions for Grammar Presentation on page 3.

NOTE 1: Provide other examples of the present perfect, using celebrities as the context. For example:
Nicole Kidman has starred with her husband Tom Cruise in two movies.
Gene Hackman has played the villain as well as the hero.
New York City has become a center for independent films.

NOTE 2: Provide other examples of the repeated action with the present perfect. For example:
They have watched the movie Casablanca *ten times.*
Robert DeNiro has starred in many movies.
Liz Taylor has married and divorced many times.

NOTE 3: Brainstorm with students *ever* questions about local arts and tourist sites. Write their questions on the board. For example:

Have you ever been to Battery Park?
Have you ever taken the Staten Island Ferry?
Have you ever visited Greenwich Village?

With a few students, model the questions and have them respond with: *Yes, I have* or *No, never.* Then have students take turns asking one another the questions on the board. For example:

Student 1: *Have you ever been to Battery Park?*
Student 2: *Yes, I have.* (To student 3) *Have you ever taken the Staten Island Ferry?*
Student 3: *No, never.* (To student 4) *Have you ever visited Greenwich Village?*

Stop when all students have asked at least one question.

NOTE 4: Have students describe recent events, using the adverbs *just* or *recently* and the present perfect. Have each student share one sentence with the class as you write it on the board. For example:

My sister has just gotten married.
I have just received my first A grade on a paper!
We have recently had an election in my country.

Transform several of the sentences to the simple past. For example:

My sister has just gotten married. ˙   *My sister just got married.*

Explain that in American English, *just* and *recently* with the simple past also indicate indefinite time in the past. The two sentence forms have the same meaning.

FOCUSED PRACTICE (pages 187–191)

See the General Suggestions for Focused Practice exercises on pages 3–4.

1. Discover the Grammar, page 187
Have students work in pairs to decide whether the sentences are true or false.

2. Blind Date, pages 187–188

CULTURE NOTE: A blind date is a date between two people who haven't previously met. The date is often arranged by friends.

For listening practice, have students listen to the tape once before opening the book. Then have them fill in the blanks. To review answers, have pairs of students act out the conversation for the class.

Follow up with a discussion. Ask:

Do you think they make a good match?
What could Jimmy say in response to Ursula's invitation?
Have you ever been on a blind date? What happened?

3. Brainstorming, pages 188–189
This exercise may be done as homework. To review answers, have pairs of students act out the conversations for the class.

4. Editing, page 189
See the General Suggestions for Editing on page 4.

BACKGROUND NOTE: Most celebrity fan clubs operate through the Internet. Fans *chat* online, simultaneously sending and receiving notes from one another. This text is an example of a chat note.

5. Online with Gizmo, page 190
To review answers, have pairs of students act out the conversations for the class.

6. All in a Day's Work, page 191
Have students look at the illustrations and compose sentences about Jimmy in the present perfect, using the verbs provided in the box.

7. Listening, page 192
See the General Suggestions for Listening on page 4.

After students have identified the best package for Lynette Long, ask, *Which package would you choose? Why?*

8. Have You Ever?, page 192
See the General Suggestions for Pair and Group Activities on page 4.

With class input, compose the questions in the present perfect. Have students work individually to compose two additional questions. Divide the class into small groups (of varied backgrounds and ages, if possible). Have students take notes as they listen to each other's responses. Have each group report its findings to the class.

9. Writing, page 192
See the General Suggestions for Writing on page 5.

Brainstorm with the students about television shows they watch and like.

Have students compose their paragraphs at home and then share them in small groups in the following class.

EXPANSION

Television Survey: Have students individually compose surveys on students' television tastes (or movie tastes), using the present perfect. For example:

Have you ever watched a prime-time news show?
Have you ever watched professional wrestling?
Have you ever watched a movie on cable TV?
What has been your favorite show this year?

Have students circulate around the room to conduct their surveys and then report their findings to the class in brief three-minute presentations.

 UNIT 19 PRESENT PERFECT AND SIMPLE PAST TENSE

GRAMMAR IN CONTEXT (page 193)

See the General Suggestions for Grammar in Context on page 2.

CULTURE NOTE: Commuter marriages have become more common as women have entered professional careers.

Before You Read, page 193: Have students read the questions, look at the cartoon, and respond in pairs.

Reading, page 193: Ask the following questions:

Why did Joe move to Los Angeles? (because he got a great job offer there)
Why did Maria move to Boston? (because her company moved there)
What are some of the disadvantages to this arrangement? (infrequent visits, cost of air travel and long-distance telephone calls)
What are some of the advantages to this arrangement? (They are happy with their work, and they are much closer emotionally.)
What do you think of this kind of marriage? (Answers will vary.)

Focus on Grammar: Write the headings *Simple Past* and *Present Perfect* on the board. Elicit examples of the highlighted structures from the reading, and write them under the appropriate column headings.

Which events are finished? What tense is used? (simple past)
Which events continue until the present? What tense is used? (present perfect)
Which event happened at a specific time in the past? What tense is used? (simple past)
Which event happened at an indefinite time in the past? What tense is used? (present perfect)

GRAMMAR **PRESENTATION**: Present Perfect and Simple Past Tense (pages 194–195)

See the General Suggestions for Grammar Presentation on page 3.

NOTE 1: Use real information from students to create further examples of the contrast between the present perfect and the simple past. For example:

Svetlana has lived in Washington for four years. (She still lives here.)
Before that, she lived in St. Petersburg. (She doesn't live there anymore.)

NOTE 2: Have students complete the following statements:

Last week I . . .
Recently I have . . .

Have students share their completed sentences with the class. Write them up on the board under the contrasting headings *Specific Past* and *Indefinite Past*.

NOTE 3: Have students complete the following statements:

It is afternoon. Today I have . . .
It is nighttime. Today I . . .

Have students share their completed sentences with the class. Write them on the board under the contrasting headings *Specific Past* and *Indefinite Past*.

FOCUSED PRACTICE (pages 196–198)

See the General Suggestions for Focused Practice exercises on pages 3–4.

1. Discover the Grammar, page 196
This exercise contrasts things that continue to the present with things that happened in the past and have no connection to the present.

Have students do this exercise individually or in pairs.

2. It Hasn't Been Easy, page 196
Have students read the entire passage before circling the correct forms. Write on the board *indefinite time in the past, specific time in the past, finished in the past,* and *continues to the present.* Have students select a reason for each choice. For example:

1. continues to present
2. specific time in past
3. continues to present
4. indefinite time in the past
5. continues to present
6. specific time in past
7. specific time in past

3. Phone Conversation, page 197
Have students read the entire conversation before filling in the blanks. Write on the board: *indefinite time in the past, specific time in the past, finished in the past,* and *continues to the present.* Have students select a reason for each choice.

To review answers, have students listen to the tape and / or have pairs of students act out the conversations for the class. Then ask the class:

Does she want him to come visit? Why or why not?
Do you think this marriage can work? Why or why not?

4. An Interview, pages 197–198
Have students do this exercise individually and compare their answers in pairs.

5. Changes, page 198
Point out that the changes occurred at an unspecified time in the past, and therefore the present perfect is used. *Since* also signals the present perfect.

COMMUNICATION PRACTICE (pages 199–200)

6. Listening, page 199
See the General Suggestions for Listening on page 4.

After checking the statements that are true now, ask students to describe what happened in the past.

7. Marriage and Divorce, page 199
See the General Suggestions for Pair and Group Activities on page 4.

Go over the chart with the class and review the boxed vocabulary. Have students work in pairs to make at least five general statements about the statistics that are supported by information in the chart. Have students share their statements with the class.

Follow up with a class discussion. Ask:

Why do you think the number of marriages has decreased since 1980?
Why do you think half of the marriages end in divorce?
Why do you think people wait longer before getting married?
Why do you think women usually marry at a younger age than men?

8. A Country You Know Well, page 199
See the General Suggestions for Pair and Group Activities on page 4.

First discuss the kinds of changes students have observed in their culture, and write their topics on the board. Have students refer to this list as they speak in small groups. To follow up, have the groups share their ideas with the class. Ask, *What things have not changed in your country? What things would you like to see changed?*

9. Looking Back, page 200
See the General Suggestions for Pair and Group Activities on page 4.

Briefly go over the chart with the class. Make sure all students understand the symbols (× = time; L.A. = Los Angeles). Remind students that they should use the simple past to talk about last year and present perfect for this year so far. Divide the class into pairs. Assign one scribe for each pair. Have students read the chart and write sentences comparing Maria's past two years and then share their sentences with the class.

Have students write similar records about themselves and discuss them in small groups.

10. Writing, page 200
See the General Suggestions for Writing on page 5.

If possible, have students bring to class two photographs of their families: one from about five years ago and one more recent. Have students share their photographs and paragraphs in small groups. Urge their classmates to ask questions to clarify information. Tell the writers to incorporate clarifying details into their final draft and submit it to you.

EXPANSION

Who Is That?: If possible, have students bring to class photographs of themselves when they were young. Mix the photographs up and put them on display for a few minutes. Have students look at the display and try to identify their classmates. Then select a picture and ask the class, *Who is this?* Once the person has been identified, have that student describe him- / herself as a child and then describe how he / she has changed. Encourage the class to ask questions about the student's childhood.

GRAMMAR **IN CONTEXT** (page 201)

See the General Suggestions for Grammar in Context on page 2.

BACKGROUND NOTE: Journalists often write about a social problem by concentrating on some victims of the problem. In this article, the journalist spends time with John Tarver and describes what he is experiencing as a homeless person.

Before You Read, page 201: Have students read the questions, look at the photograph and the statistics, and share their responses with the class.

Reading, page 201: Ask the following comprehension questions:

How did John Tarver lose his job and apartment? (When he hurt his back, he lost his job, which also provided an apartment.)
Where does he live now? (He lives on the street.)
Is the problem of homelessness increasing or decreasing? (It has been climbing steadily since 1980.)

Focus on Grammar: Elicit the highlighted phrases and write them on the board. Ask questions to illustrate that the present progressive describes something that is in progress and has been in progress for some time. For example:

"John Tarver has been sitting on the same park bench for hours."
What is happening? (He is sitting on the bench.)
How long has this been happening? (for hours)

"He has been living on the street since then."
What is happening? (He is living on the street.)
How long has this been happening? (since he hurt his back)

Point out that the first paragraph of the reading describes a situation that began a few hours ago and still continues. The second paragraph describes the larger social problem, which began more than twenty years ago and still continues.

GRAMMAR **PRESENTATION**: Present Perfect Progressive (pages 202–203)

See the General Suggestions for Grammar Presentation on page 3.

NOTE 1: Use the present progressive as a basis for discussing the present perfect progressive. Ask:

What are we doing? (We are studying the present perfect progressive.)
How long have we been studying the present perfect progressive? (We have been studying the present perfect progressive for half an hour.)

Have students form more sentences about themselves using the present progressive and then form sentences using the present perfect progressive. Ask students to share their sentences with the class.

NOTE 2: Read the note in the Student Book with the class. Answer any questions.

NOTE 3: Give more examples:

You look tired. You haven't been sleeping well.
She looks happy. She's been working at a better job.
They look frustrated. They've been working too hard.

Write cues on the board (*sleepy, excited, sad, exhausted,* and so on). Have students compose their own sentences and share them with the class.

Point out that with the time expressions *since* and *for,* the action continues until the present.

FOCUSED PRACTICE (pages 204–205)

See the General Suggestions for Focused Practice exercises on pages 3–4.

1. Discover the Grammar, page 204
Have students do this exercise individually or in pairs.

2. An Interview, pages 204–205
To review answers, have students listen to the tape and / or have pairs of students act out the conversations for the class.

To check comprehension, ask:

Where has he been sleeping? (in the park)
How has he been getting food? (People sometimes give him money so he can buy sandwiches.)
What has he been planning to do? (He has been planning to find a job.)

3. What's Been Happening?, page 205
Remind students that some sentences are negative.

COMMUNICATION PRACTICE (pages 206–207)

4. Listening, page 206
See the General Suggestions for Listening on page 4.

Have students read the list before listening. After playing the tape twice, check students' answers. If students disagree, play the segment in question again.

5. Joblessness around the World, page 206
See the General Suggestions for Pair and Group Activities on page 4.

Go over the chart with the class and review the boxed vocabulary. Have students work in pairs to make at least five general statements about the statistics that are supported by the information in the chart. Have students share their statements with the class.

Follow up with a class discussion. Ask:

How high is unemployment in the country you are from?
Why do you think unemployment is at that rate now?
What do people do when they are unemployed?
How do people get jobs in the country you are from?
What kind of effect does high unemployment have on a society?
What kind of effect does low unemployment have on the economy?

6. Explanations, page 207
See the General Suggestions for Pair and Group Activities on page 4.

Model the activity several times with the class, brainstorming explanations and writing them on the board. Divide the class into pairs. Have the pairs create an explanation for each item and share it with the class.

For further practice, bring in photographs from magazines. Have pairs of students select a photograph to interpret and then share their interpretations with the class.

7. What about You?, page 207
See the General Suggestions for Pair and Group Activities on page 4.

After students have completed their forms, have the class brainstorm questions students may ask each other. Write their questions on the board. Divide the class into pairs. Have the pairs exchange forms and ask and answer each other's questions.

After finishing the exercise, have students write a short paragraph about their partners. Read selected paragraphs and have the class guess which student is being described.

8. Writing, page 207
See the General Suggestions for Writing on page 5.

In small groups, have students share their paragraphs. Encourage group members to ask questions to clarify any information. Tell the writers to incorporate the clarifying details into their final draft and submit it to you.

EXPANSION

The Homeless in Other Countries: Ask students to discuss what they know about the homeless in other countries they have lived in or visited. What sorts of programs exist to help the homeless in other countries? Are they government-sponsored programs or are they run by private groups such as church organizations? What are some of the causes of homelessness around the world? You may want to have students do research and present their findings to the class.

UNIT 21 — PRESENT PERFECT AND PRESENT PERFECT PROGRESSIVE

GRAMMAR **IN CONTEXT** (page 208)

See the General Suggestions for Grammar in Context on page 2.

Before You Read, page 208: Have students read the questions, look at the map and facts, and share their responses with the class.

Reading, page 208: Ask the following comprehension questions:

How long have elephants been living on this planet? (for 5 million years)
Why is it illegal to sell ivory? (because poachers were killing off the elephant population)
Where can elephants live protected? (in national parks)

Focus on Grammar: Write the headings *Unfinished* and *Finished* on the board. Elicit examples of the highlighted structures from the second paragraph of the reading and write them under the appropriate column headings. Point out that the present perfect is used when some thing is finished in the indefinite past and the present perfect progressive is used when the activity continues into the present (and perhaps the future).

GRAMMAR **PRESENTATION**: Present Perfect and Present Perfect Progressive (pages 209–210)

See the General Suggestions for Grammar Presentation on page 3.

NOTE 1: Give additional examples contrasting the finished and unfinished aspects of these tenses and draw accompanying timelines:

I have drunk some coffee. (I finished my cup of coffee.)
I have been drinking some coffee. (I am still drinking my cup of coffee.)

They have done the homework. (They finished the homework.)
They have been doing the homework. (They are still doing the homework.)

NOTE 2: Read the note in the Student Book with the class. Answer any questions.

NOTE 3: Give additional examples contrasting permanence with temporary actions:

I have been studying English for one year.
I have studied English my whole life.

She has talked about visiting Africa since she was a child.
She has been talking about visiting Africa since she saw a TV program on elephants.

NOTE 4: In quick succession, ask students the following questions:

How long have you been studying English?
How many years have you studied?

How long have you been studying the perfect tenses?
How much have you learned about the present perfect tense?

How long have you been reading in English?
How many books have you read in English?

How long have you been living away from home?
How many times have you gone back home to visit?

FOCUSED PRACTICE (pages 211–213)

See the General Suggestions for Focused Practice exercises on pages 3–4.

1. Discover the Grammar, page 211
For continued practice, have students compose sentences about themselves using either of the perfect tenses. Have students read their sentences aloud as the class listens and tries to identify whether the action is finished or unfinished.

2. Professor Owen's Work, pages 211–212
Have students read the entire sentence before circling the verbs. To help students understand the answers, refer them to the following grammar notes:

1. Note 1—unfinished
2. Note 1—finished
3. Note 1—finished; Note 4—number of elephants
4. Note 1— finished
5. Note 4—number of times
6. Note 1—finished
7. Note 1—unfinished; Note 3— temporary
8. Note 3—temporary
9. Note 3—temporary
10. Note 2—both are possible

3. Grandad, page 212
This exercise contrasts the permanence of Grandad's long life (paragraph 2) with the recent observations of the writer (paragraph 3). This contrast of time frames is explained in Note 3.

Have students read the complete text before filling in the blanks. After going over the answers, ask the following comprehension questions:

What do you think a "tusker" is? (an elephant with very long tusks)
How old is Grandad? (over sixty)
How has he survived? (with his experience and courage)

4. How Long and How Much?, page 213
Remind students that they need to calculate the answers, using the information in the field notes. Follow up with a brief discussion. Ask, *What fact surprised you the most? What other facts do you know about elephants?*

COMMUNICATION PRACTICE (pages 214–216)

5. Listening, pages 214–215
See the General Suggestions for Listening on page 4.

As you go over the answers, have students create sentences for the pictures they did not choose to contrast the meanings.

6. Giving Advice, page 215
See the General Suggestions for Pair and Group Activities on page 4.

Have students work individually to compose the questions. You may want to go over the questions as a class before you divide the class into pairs. Have the pairs ask and answer the questions. After agreeing on a response to each situation, have students do spontaneous (unscripted) role plays. Have each pair select one role play to perform for the class.

7. Find Out More, page 216
Have students do their research individually and then join in groups to compare notes. Have each group give a presentation to another group.

8. Writing, page 216
See the General Suggestions for Writing on page 5.

Use samples of student writing to create an error correction exercise for present perfect and present perfect progressive. Extract errors from student writing and put them on the board. Have groups of students work together to correct them.

EXPANSION

Other Endangered Species: Have students research other endangered species. Begin by having students brainstorm endangered species they have heard about. Remind them that an endangered species can be an animal, an insect, a sea creature, or a plant. Students can plan whatever type of presentation they want: an oral or written report, a poster or other type of graphic display, or a collage or other type of artwork representing the concept of endangered species.

REVIEW OR SELFTEST
See the General Suggestions for Review or SelfTest on pages 5–6.

FROM GRAMMAR TO WRITING: THE TOPIC SENTENCE AND PARAGRAPH UNITY

See the General Suggestions for From Grammar to Writing on page 6.

In this section, students identify the topic sentence and organization of a paragraph. Using a tree diagram, students organize their ideas. After sharing their ideas and developing topic sentences, students compose their own paragraphs.

Introduction, page 222
Have students read the opening paragraph about topic sentences.

Exercise 1, page 222
You may want to read this paragraph aloud and have students call out when they hear an irrelevant sentence.

In pairs, have students select the topic sentence. Compare ideas as a class.

Exercise 2, page 223
Have students work in pairs to diagram the paragraph. As you go over the answers, draw the diagram on the board.

Exercise 3, page 223
Brainstorm with the class possible writing topics. It may help students to think about the purpose of the personal statement (to get into a university, to get a job, and so on).

In small groups, have students explain their tree diagrams as group members listen and ask questions to clarify information. Tell the writers to incorporate these clarifying details into their tree diagrams. Don't let the groups disband until they have composed a topic sentence for each student's tree.

Exercise 4, page 223
Have students write their paragraphs at home and submit them to you for final review.

PART V ADJECTIVES AND ADVERBS: REVIEW AND EXPANSION

 UNIT 22 ADJECTIVES AND ADVERBS

GRAMMAR **IN CONTEXT** (page 226)

See the General Suggestions for Grammar in Context on page 2.

Before You Read, page 226: Have students read the questions, look at the circled ad, and share their responses with the class.

Reading, page 226: Ask the following questions:

Why do Luis and Maggie need a quiet apartment? (because they are both serious students)
How does the landlord describe the apartment? (It's cozy, quiet, and perfect for students.)
How does Luis describe the apartment? (It's too small and warm.)
How does Maggie describe the apartment? (It's lovely. It looks great. It's perfect.)
Do you think the owner will have a hard time renting the apartment? (Answers will vary.)
Why does the landlord ask Luis and Maggie to sit down? (Answers will vary.)
How much do you think the rent is? (Answers will vary.)
What title would you give this reading? (Answers will vary.)
Are there any other apartments listed that might be possible for Maggie and Luis? (Answers will vary.)

Focus on Grammar: Write the headings *Adjective* and *Adverb* on the board. Elicit examples of the highlighted structures and write them under the appropriate column headings.

Point to an example in the *Adjective* column. Ask, *What does this adjective describe?* Point to other examples and ask the same question.

Point to an example in the *Adverb* column and ask, *What does this adverb describe?* Point to other examples and ask the same question.

GRAMMAR **PRESENTATION:** Adjectives and Adverbs (pages 227–229)

See the General Suggestions for Grammar Presentation on page 3.

NOTE 1: Have students use adjectives to describe the classroom and its furnishings as you write their ideas on the board. Underline examples of non-action verbs in their sentences. Explain that adjectives come after non-action verbs. For example:

The room _feels_ large.
The room _is_ sunny.

NOTE 2: Use adverbs to expand some of the sentences from the above activity. For example:

The room feels _very_ large.
The room is _extremely_ sunny.

NOTES 3, 6, AND 7: Give additional examples of adverbs of manner. For example: *happily, angrily, nervously, quickly, slowly.*

Write adverbs of manner on the board. Have individual students volunteer to act out a simple activity (such as walking across the room) in a certain manner. Ask the class, *How is she walking?* Have the class select an adverb from the board to describe the manner of the action. For example:

She is walking quickly across the room.
She is walking slowly across the room.

NOTES 4 AND 5: Contrast adverbs of frequency and of manner. For example:

She _usually_ walks to school.
She walks _very slowly_.

Note 8: Point out that *well* can be a adjective to describe good health. For example:

Jane hasn't been well. We're worried about her.
I hope you're well.

Note 9: Give additional examples of participial adjectives. For example:

The book is interesting.
I am interested in the book.

The movie is boring her.
She is bored by the movie.

The smoke is annoying him.
He is annoyed by the smoke.

Point out that participial adjectives take on active and passive stances.

FOCUSED PRACTICE (pages 230–232)

See the General Suggestions for Focused Practice exercises on pages 3–4.

1. Discover the Grammar, page 230
First have students underline all the adjectives and draw arrows to the nouns they describe. Then have students go over the text again, circling the adverbs and identifying the words they describe.

2. Did You Like It?, page 230
Go over the answers aloud to check students' pronunciation of the adverbs.

3. Writing Home, page 231
Have students read the complete text before filling in the blanks. After going over the answers, ask the following comprehension questions:

How does she like life in New York? (She likes it a lot.)
How does she describe her new neighbor? (She seemed shy, but she is very nice.)

4. Student Evaluation, page 232
Have students read the complete text before filling in the blanks.

To expand students' vocabulary, have them work in pairs to compose a negative evaluation by brainstorming opposites of the adjectives and adverbs. Have students compare their versions in small groups.

5. It's Hard to Tell with Alice, page 232
Have students read the complete text before filling in the blanks. Then have students listen to the tape to check their answers.

To follow up, elicit participial adjectives and adverbs and write them on the board. Give students a time limit of five minutes to write a description of a close friend, using as many participial adjectives as possible. Have students share their writing in pairs.

COMMUNICATION PRACTICE (pages 233–234)

6. Listening, page 233
See the General Suggestions for Listening on page 4.

Before listening, have students read the advertisement and guess what the abbreviations stand for.

7. Apartment Ads, page 233
See the General Suggestions for Pair and Group Activities on page 4.

Have students brings in ads or refer to the ads on page 226. In pairs, have students discuss the ads.

Write the following features on the board: *sunny, spacious, close to transportation, close to shopping, quiet street, modern kitchen and bath, available immediately, parking, yard* or *garden, low cost,* and *central air conditioning.* In pairs, have students talk about the features they seek in an apartment and why. For example:

I like to be close to transportation because I don't have a car.

8. Where Do You Live?, page 233
See the General Suggestions for Pair and Group Activities on page 4.

Have each student report to the class about another classmate's home. Give the reports a time limit of one minute each.

9. Home Sweet Home, page 234
See the General Suggestions for Pair and Group Activities on page 4.

Have students share their descriptions of housing with the class. Compare and contrast the types of housing in different countries. If interest is sufficient, have students draw models of typical housing in their home countries. Students can describe the size of the living unit, the location of the garden or yard, the location of the kitchen and the bathroom, the areas for guests, and the areas for family only. Have students share their models in groups or with the whole class.

10. Your Ideal Roommate, page 234
Have each group discuss the following questions:

How similar are your ideal roommates?
Is there one ideal roommate for everyone?
How would you describe yourself?

11. Writing, page 234
See the General Suggestions for Writing on page 5.

Tell students that you will never see their individual evaluations. After reading and comparing evaluations, have the pairs seek another pair to compose a collective evaluation of the class, teacher, or textbook to submit to you.

EXPANSION

Picture Descriptions: Bring in pictures of all sorts of homes. Have pairs of students select one picture to describe in writing. After finishing the description, have students place all their pictures on display in the front of the room. Have students read their descriptions to the class as the class listens and tries to identify the picture being described.

Vocabulary Expansion Game: Divide the class into two teams. To alternating teams, call out an adjective or adverb and have the team come up with its opposite within fifteen seconds. If the team is unable to name an opposite, give the other team a chance to try. Each time a team successfully identifies an opposite, it wins one point. The team with the most points wins.

 UNIT 23 ADJECTIVES: COMPARATIVES AND EQUATIVES

GRAMMAR **IN CONTEXT** (page 235)

See the General Suggestions for Grammar in Context on page 2.

BACKGROUND NOTE: An *inn* is a small country hotel with a restaurant. Guests can have a meal in the restaurant and stay overnight in the hotel.

Before You Read, page 235: Have students read the question, look at the boxed information and the photograph, and share their responses with the class.

Reading, page 235: Ask the following questions:

Is the Country Inn a new restaurant? (No, it has new owners.)
Does the food cost the same? (No, it's more expensive.)
What happens when the restaurant gets crowded? (The service gets slow.)

What is a good time to eat there? (at lunch time)
Why do you think the Country Inn doesn't accept reservations? (Answers will vary.)

Focus on Grammar: Write the headings *Old Restaurant* and *New Restaurant* on the board. Fill in the following description of the old restaurant. Elicit comparative descriptions of the new restaurant and write them under the appropriate column heading:

Old Restaurant	New Restaurant
big	(bigger)
bright	(brighter)
pretty	(prettier)
good food	(as good as before)
varied menu	(less varied)
expensive	(more expensive)

Point to each comparative in the right column and ask if it means *more, the same,* or *less.*

Explain the expression *better and better* by drawing a timeline to show a change over time.

Explain *the more crowded . . . the slower* by showing how one element of the comparison depends on the other:

When the restaurant is half full, customers wait twenty minutes.
When the restaurant is three-quarters full, customers wait half an hour.
When the restaurant is full, customers wait forty-five minutes.

GRAMMAR **PRESENTATION:** Adjectives: Comparatives and Equatives (pages 236–238)

See the General Suggestions for Grammar Presentation on page 3.

NOTE 1: Read the note in the Student Book with the class. Answer any questions.

NOTE 2: Identify a local institution, such as a restaurant, park, or supermarket, that has recently undergone renovations and is known by most students in the class. Have students make comparisons using *-er* with the following adjectives: *clean, bright, large, friendly,* and *pretty.*

Then have students make comparisons using *more* with the following two- and three-syllable adjectives: *organized, spacious, accessible, varied,* and *interesting.*

NOTE 3: Read the note in the Student Book with the class. Answer any questions.

NOTE 4: Give additional examples:

Restaurants in this area have more and more varied menus.
Eating out is getting more and more expensive.
At popular restaurants, you have to wait a longer and longer time.

NOTE 5: Write sentences on the board that indicate cause and effect. Then rewrite them in the pattern *the* + comparative:

When the service gets slow, the customers get annoyed. The slower the service, the more annoyed the customers get.
When I am hungry, my stomach gets noisy! The hungrier I get, the noisier my stomach gets!
When he eats delicious food, he is very quiet. The more delicious the food, the quieter he is.

NOTE 6: Tell the class that they are going to compare the restaurant in the reading "The Country Inn" with a well-known restaurant such as McDonald's. Have students work in pairs to compose four comparative statements: two with *as* + adjective + *as* and two with *not as* + adjective + *as.* Have students share their sentences with the class.

NOTE 7: Give students an additional example:

McDonald's isn't as elegant as the Country Inn.
McDonald's is less elegant than the Country Inn.
The Country Inn is more elegant than McDonald's.

Have each student take one statement from the prior activity and expand on it, expressing it in as many ways as possible. Have students share their sentences with the class.

FOCUSED PRACTICE (pages 239–242)

See the General Suggestions for Focused Practice exercises on pages 3–4.

1. Discover the Grammar, page 239
Ask the class, *What is rice pudding? What are the ingredients? What adjectives describe it best?* Then review the charts with the class.

2. Not All Rice Is Equal, page 239
Review the chart with the students before they complete the exercise.

3. Menu, page 240
Have students read the menu before filling in the blanks. After going over the answers, ask the following questions:

Have you ever tasted dishes like these?
If so, how did you like them?
Which is your favorite dish?

For expansion, bring in menus from area restaurants and have students write their own comparative sentences using the adjectives from this exercise.

4. Editing, page 241
See the General Suggestions for Editing on page 4.

After completing the exercise, have students describe their favorite snack food from their country.

5. The More the Merrier, pages 241–242
CULTURE NOTE: Explain that the title is an old saying meaning *the more people we have together, the happier we all are.*

To review answers, have pairs of students act out the conversations for the class.

6. More and More, page 242
Before opening the book, ask students to predict some eating trends in the United States. Ask, *Do you think people in the United States are eating more and more candy? How about frozen pizza? How many pounds of ice cream do you think people in the United States eat a year?*

Have students open the book, read the chart, and check their predictions. Then have students complete the exercise.

COMMUNICATION PRACTICE (pages 243–246)

7. Listening, page 243
See the General Suggestions for Listening on page 4.

Before opening the book, ask the class, *Do you comparison shop for food? What do you compare?* Write students' ideas on the board. For example:

price
ingredients
number of servings
expiration date

Have students open the book and complete the exercise.

8. Information Gap: Thick and Chunky, pages 243 and 246
Divide the class into pairs. Assign each partner a role (A or B). Assign Students A page 243 and Students B page 246. Have students read their separate instructions, look at their charts, and locate the missing information (empty circles). Have students ask and answers questions to complete their charts. Remind students not to compare their charts until they are finished with the task.

9. Pizza around the World, page 244
See the General Suggestions for Pair and Group Activities on page 4.

Ask, *What is a popular pizza topping in your family?* or *What unusual pizza toppings have you heard of?*

10. Things Change, page 244
After students discuss these topics in pairs, have them write a paragraph about one aspect of change in their lives to submit to you.

11. The ESL Diner, page 245
If interest is sufficient, have students photocopy their menus and distribute them among classmates. Have the whole class ask questions about the items on the menu.

12. Writing, page 245
See the General Suggestions for Writing on page 5.

Have students write their comparisons for homework and share them in class in small groups.

EXPANSION

Food-Tasting Party: Have students bring in samples of their favorite snack foods, including snack foods from different cultures. Have the class sample two different foods at a time and compare their tastes and textures. Write their comparisons on the board.

Restaurant Reviews: Have students brainstorm types of restaurants. For example: *fast food, sandwich or sub shops, fine dining, pizzerias, bars,* or *ethnic restaurants.* Have pairs of students choose one type of restaurant to review. Have each partner choose a different restaurant within that category and review it according to the following criteria: *value, quality of food, service,* and *location.* Have the partners compare their reviews and then report their findings to the class.

 UNIT 24 ADJECTIVES: SUPERLATIVES

GRAMMAR **IN CONTEXT** (page 247)

See the General Suggestions for Grammar in Context on page 2.

CULTURE NOTE: Since many people in the United States do not celebrate the Christian holiday of Christmas, Americans often exchange general "holiday" cards at the end of the year.

Before You Read, page 247: Have students read the questions, look at the cards and the boxed information, and share their responses with the class.

Reading, page 247: Ask the following comprehension questions:
Which card is for a birthday?
Which card is for Valentine's Day?
Which card is for year-end holidays?

Focus on Grammar: Elicit one or two examples of a superlative from the text. Write it in a full sentence on the board and ask questions to illustrate how the superlative describes one of many. For example:
"Climb the highest mountain."
How many mountains are there in the world? (many)
What is special about this mountain? (It is the highest in the world.)

Write -*est* and *most* on the board as column heads. Elicit examples of the superlative from the text and write them under the appropriate column heading. Ask, *Why do these adjectives use the word* best? (because they have two or more syllables) *Why do these adjectives use* -est? (because they are one-syllable adjectives or two-syllable adjectives ending with -*y*) Since this is a review of the principles of the prior lesson, students should be able to answer these questions.

GRAMMAR **PRESENTATION:** Adjectives: Superlatives (pages 248–249)

See the General Suggestions for Grammar Presentation on page 3.

NOTE 1: Emphasize that the superlative compares three or more things. It should not be used to compare only two things.

NOTE 2: Point out that in this case *little/least* refer to quantity, not size:
Shekeina got only a little candy at the birthday party.
Toby got the least candy of all the children.

NOTES 3 AND 4: Read the notes in the Student Book with the class. Answer any questions.

FOCUSED PRACTICE (pages 250–252)

See the General Suggestions for Focused Practice exercises on pages 3–4.

1. Discover the Grammar, page 250
Have students read the entire text before underlining the superlative forms.

2. Valentine's Day, pages 250–251
Have students read all the sentences before they select the expressions in the box.

3. A Special Gift, page 251

CULTURE NOTE: Agatha Christie was the most widely read mystery author of the twentieth century. The doll is a Teletubby, a character from the popular children's television show *Teletubbies*, developed by the British Broadcasting System.

After answering the questions, have students suggest other adjectives.

4. What About You?, page 252
After reviewing the questions for errors, have students add two questions of their own.

5. Editing, page 252
See the General Suggestions for Editing on page 4.

After completing the exercise, ask students to describe the most important holiday of the year in their cultures.

COMMUNICATION PRACTICE (page 253)

6. Listening, page 253
See the General Suggestions for Listening on page 4.

After students have completed the exercise, ask:
What gift should he choose?
What is the best gift you have ever received?

7. The Most . . . , page 253
See the General Suggestions for Pair and Group Activities on page 4.

Have students use the questions from Exercise 4, What about You?, as well as their two additional questions. In a follow-up discussion, have each student report to the class one interesting fact about someone in their group.

8. What About Your Holidays?, page 253
See the General Suggestions for Pair and Group Activities on page 4.

Have students discuss their ideas in small groups and then report their findings to the class. This is an opportunity to explain in greater detail the traditional ways of celebrating the listed holidays in the United States.

9. Writing, page 253
See the General Suggestions for Writing on page 5.

Bring colored pens and pencils to class to encourage students to be creative with their cards. After sharing their cards in groups, have students present their cards to the class.

EXPANSION

Favorite Family Member: Have students think about how they would describe their favorite family member. Who is it? What adjectives could they use to describe this person? What makes this person special? Have students write a description and then share their writing in groups. Later, they can submit it to you for correction.

UNIT 25 ADJECTIVES: EQUATIVES, COMPARATIVES, SUPERLATIVES

GRAMMAR **IN CONTEXT** (page 254)

See the General Suggestions for Grammar in Context on page 2.

Before You Read, page 254: Have students read the questions, look at the photograph, and share their responses with the class.

Reading, page 254: Ask the following comprehension questions:

What two teams are playing? (the Chicago Bulls and the Los Angeles Lakers)
Who is winning? (the Bulls)
What team is Michael Jordan on? (the Bulls)
Who is not able to play now? (Michael Jordan of the Bulls and Shaquille O'Neal of the Lakers)
On whose team is Kukoc? (the Bulls)

Focus on Grammar: Ask, *How has Toni Kukoc been playing this season?* (He has been playing more and more aggressively.) Draw a timeline to show his change over time. Ask students, *What does* aggressively *describe?* (how he has been playing) Label *aggressively* as an adverb.

Then ask, *How does Toni Kukoc compare to his teammates?* (He's been scoring more frequently than any other player except Jordan. He's been playing the most consistently.) Ask students, *What does* more frequently *describe?* (how he has been scoring) Label *frequently* as an adverb. Ask, *What does* most consistently *describe?* (how he has been playing.) Label *consistently* as an adverb.

GRAMMAR **PRESENTATION:** Adverbs: Equatives, Comparatives, Superlatives (pages 255–257)

See the General Suggestions for Grammar Presentation on page 3.

NOTE 1: Read out the following true/false statements about Toni Kukoc of the Bulls. Have students correct any false statements.

Kukoc has not been scoring as frequently as Michael Jordan. (True)
Kukoc has been playing just as consistently as Michael Jordan. (False. He has been playing more consistently than any other team member.)
The more Kukoc plays, the worse he looks. (False. The more he plays, the better he looks.)

NOTE 2: Have pairs of students volunteer to act out simple actions at the same time. Have the class compare how the two students perform the action. For example:

Alicia ran faster than Ali.
Juan ran more noisily than Antonine.

NOTE 3: Provide additional examples with sentences from the Note 2 activity. For example:

Alicia ran faster.
Juan ran more noisily.

NOTE 4: Read the note in the Student Book with the class. Answer any questions.

NOTE 5: Point out that *fast, hard, late, far, little,* and *much* are both adjectives and adverbs.

For adverbs of manner that have two comparative and two superlative forms, refer students to Appendix 8 on pages A-4–A-5.

NOTE 6: Read the note in the Student Book with the class. Answer any questions.

NOTE 7: Write sentences on the board that indicate cause and effect. Then rewrite them in the pattern *the* + comparative:

When they practiced hard every day, they performed better on the court.
The harder they practiced, the better they performed on the court.

When she played aggressively, she scored badly.
The more aggressively she played, the worse she scored.

FOCUSED PRACTICE (pages 258–259)

See the General Suggestions for Focused Practice exercises on pages 3–4.

1. Discover the Grammar, page 258
Warn students that there are many examples of adjectives and adverbs in this passage that are not comparative, equative, or superlative.

2. Not All Bikes Are Equal, page 258
Review the chart with students before they complete the exercise.

3. Speed Reading, page 259
BACKGROUND NOTE: Speed reading is a strategy for significantly increasing reading speed by reading larger chunks of text at a time. Speed reading courses can be quite expensive, but they promise wonderful results. Elicit students' opinions and ideas about this speed reading course.

After students fill in and correct the answers, ask them to suggest other adverbs that could be used.

4. The All-Around Athlete, page 259
BACKGROUND NOTE: An *all-around athlete* is a person who is athletic in many different disciplines.

Review the chart with the students before they begin the exercise. This is an opportunity for students unaccustomed to measurements in feet and inches to estimate the lengths described in the chart.

COMMUNICATION PRACTICE (pages 260–261)

5. Listening, page 260
See the General Suggestions for Listening on page 4.

Review the names of the horses before students listen. Answer any vocabulary questions.

6. Sports Around the World, page 260
Brainstorm with the class names of famous athletes. Have students compose sentences about these celebrity athletes and then share their ideas with the class. Be prepared for heated debate!

7. A Questionnaire, page 261
See the General Suggestions for Pair and Group Activities on page 4.

First have students work individually to respond to the questionnaire and compose their additional questions. Then have students work in small groups to compare answers. Invite the groups to report their findings to the class.

8. Writing, page 261
See the General Suggestions for Writing on page 5.

Brainstorm the names of famous athletes. Have students brainstorm comparative statements about these athletes. At home, have students write their comparisons. In class, students can share their comparisons in small groups.

If your class is not interested in athletics, choose one of the following topics: *movie stars, musicians, theater performers, dancers,* or *politicians.*

EXPANSION

Comparison Shopping: Bring in consumer magazines that compare the price and value of products. Have each student choose a product type to research (for example: a type of sports equipment, a type of car, a type of food such as breakfast cereal, or a type of office equipment). Have students then make recommendations to the class based on their research.

REVIEW OR SELFTEST

See the General Suggestions for Review or Self Test on pages 5–6.

FROM GRAMMAR TO WRITING: USING DESCRIPTIVE ADJECTIVES

See the General Suggestions for From Grammar to Writing on page 6.

Students practice identifying descriptive adjectives and categorizing them. Using a word map, students organize their own writing ideas. Students then share their writing in pairs and give each other feedback using a chart.

Introduction, page 267
Write the example sentence on the board: *I live in an apartment.* Ask, *What kind of apartment is it?* Insert the adjectives *small, comfortable,* and *one-bedroom* into the sentence. Then have students read the introductory text.

Exercise 1, page 267
You may want to read this paragraph aloud and have students write down all the adjectives they hear that describe the writer's apartment. Then have students compare their lists with a partner and listen again before they actually read the passage and underline the words.

Exercise 2, page 267
Have students work in pairs to complete the word map. As you go over their answers, draw the map on the board.

Exercise 3, page 268
See the General Suggestions for Pair and Group Activities on page 4.

Before developing their own word maps, take students through a guided imagery exercise. Have students close their eyes and think about a room they like to be in. Ask:

How does the room look?
How does it feel?
What furniture is in the room?
What is on the walls?
What material is the floor made of?
What colors are in the room?
Where does the light come from?
What does the room smell like?
What sounds can you hear in this room?

Give them time to imagine the room in their minds. Have students open their eyes and list several elements in the room and then add adjectives to describe each element.

Exercise 4, page 268
Have students write their paragraphs at home.

Exercise 5, page 268
Before exchanging paragraphs, have students look at the chart. Explain that they will give each other feedback using the chart.

Have students exchange paragraphs, read them, and give each other feedback using the chart in the book. Have the writers read the feedback and incorporate any new information into their final draft.

PART VI GERUNDS AND INFINITIVES

UNIT 26 GERUNDS: SUBJECT AND OBJECT

GRAMMAR **IN CONTEXT** (page 272)

See the General Suggestions for Grammar in Context on page 2.

CULTURE NOTE: In recent years, people have become more aware of the dangers of smoking. Research has also shown that the smoke from other people's cigarettes is a danger to non-smokers. In the United States and Canada, smoking is now prohibited in many public places, including stores and government buildings. There is no smoking allowed on airplane trips within the country. Some cities have even passed no smoking ordinances in restaurants and bars. Smokers must be careful to smoke only in places where allowed.

BACKGROUND NOTE: The reading passage is based on the kind of bulletin board discussion that occurs on the Internet, where people read posted messages and then offer replies. Point out that the names on the bulletin board are aliases. This bulletin board is an anonymous forum for discussion.

Before You Read, page 272: Have students read the questions, look at the signs, and share their responses with the class.

Reading, page 272: Have volunteers read the names of the writers out loud. Discuss why people may have chosen these aliases. Then ask the following questions:

Why does Cigarman believe the government should prohibit ordering burgers and fries? (He believes junk food is worse for one's health than smoking is.)
What is Nuffsed concerned about? (the smell of secondhand smoke)
What does Swissfriend suggest? (practicing courtesy and tolerance)
What does Cleanaire say to Swissfriend? (Smoking is an addiction.)
Who do you agree with most? (Answers will vary.)

Focus on Grammar: Copy on the board two examples each from the text of gerunds as subjects and gerunds as objects. Point to a gerund and ask the class, *Is this a verb or a noun?* (It is the noun form of a verb.) Have students identify the subject, verb, and object in each sentence. Explain that gerunds can function as subjects and objects.

GRAMMAR **PRESENTATION:** Gerunds as Subjects and Objects (page 273)

See the General Suggestions for Grammar Presentation on page 3.

NOTE 1: Give more examples of gerunds as subjects by eliciting from students information about healthy habits. For example:

walk up stairs
ride a bicycle to work
avoid fatty foods

Compose sentences using these habits as gerund subjects. For example:

Walking up stairs is a convenient way to keep in shape and burn extra calories.

NOTE 2: Use the same information for additional examples of gerunds as objects. List the verbs that take gerund objects on the board (for example: *admit, dislike, enjoy, mind, suggest,* and *understand*). Compose sentences combining these verbs with the healthy habits. For example:

I dislike walking up four flights of stairs every day, but it is good for my heart.

NOTE 3: Brainstorm with students leisure activities they enjoy (for example: *shopping, swimming, visiting museums*). List their ideas on the board. Have partners look at the list and talk about what they like to do. For example:

Student 1: *I like to go shopping on the weekends.*
Student 2: *Oh! I don't. I hate it. I like to go hiking on the weekends!*

FOCUSED PRACTICE (pages 274–275)

See the General Suggestions for Focused Practice exercises on pages 3–4.

1. Discover the Grammar, page 274
Point out that some words ending in -*ing* are not gerunds but rather progressive forms of verbs.

2. Health Issues, page 274
Have students read all the sentences before filling in the blanks.

3. A Question of Health, page 275
Go over the boxed vocabulary with the class. To review answers, have pairs of students act out the conversations for the class.

COMMUNICATION PRACTICE (PAGES 276–277)

4. Listening, page 276
See the General Suggestions for Listening on page 4.

Have students predict what the doctor may say. After listening to the tape, ask the class, *What is the patient's problem?* (He is underweight. He does too many stressful sports, and he is a bit depressed.)

5. An Opinion Survey, page 276
See the General Suggestions for Pair and Group Activities on page 4.

Have students circulate around the room taking the survey. Follow up with a class discussion. As the class discusses the survey results, have students determine whether smokers and non-smokers respond to the opinions differently. For example, ask, *How many smokers agree with opinion 1? How many non-smokers?*

6. Poster Talk, page 277
See the General Suggestions for Pair and Group Activities on page 4.

Follow up with a discussion. Say, *This poster was aimed at teenagers because most people become addicted to smoking in their teenage years. Do you think this poster reaches teenagers? What kind of poster do you think would reach teenagers? How can adults get teenagers to stop smoking? How can adults get teenagers to never start smoking?*

7. No Smoking?, page 277
You may want to divide the class into groups for and against smoking. Have each group develop its argument and then conduct a debate. Give each group equal time to state its case and make rebuttals.

8. Writing, page 277
See the General Suggestions for Writing on page 5.

Refer students to Appendices 9 and 11 on page A-5 for verbs that take gerunds.

EXPANSION

Health Fair: Have pairs of students choose a healthy habit to promote to the class. Give pairs of students five minutes to explain the habit, its benefits, and any special instructions. Possible topics are:

eating five to nine servings of fruit and vegetables a day
not eating snack food while watching TV
exercising every day
drinking eight glasses of water a day

GRAMMAR **IN CONTEXT** (page 278)

See the General Suggestions for Grammar in Context on page 2.

CULTURE NOTE: A student council is a group that organizes campus events and brings students' ideas and complaints to the attention of school officials. Most colleges have student councils.

Before You Read, page 278: Have students read the questions, look at the illustration, and respond in pairs.

Reading, page 278: Ask the following comprehension questions:

What kinds of ideas does the Student Council want? (ideas about improving the school)
What are some people tired of? (hearing complaints and not finding solutions)
Where and when is the meeting? (at the Main Auditorium, on March 25, at 8:00 P.M.)
Where can international students meet new friends? (at the International Coffee Hour in the Student Commons on Friday from 8–10)
What other kinds of notices are on the bulletin board? (art exhibit, lost pet, study group, and housing notices)

Focus on Grammar: Elicit examples of the highlighted structure and write them on the board. Through questioning, show how gerunds follow prepositions. For example:

excited about living
Which word in this phrase is the gerund? (living)
Which word in this phrase is a preposition? (about)
Where is the preposition in all of these examples? (before the gerund)

Point out that only a gerund, not an infinitive, can follow a preposition.

GRAMMAR **PRESENTATION:** Gerunds after Prepositions (page 279)

See the General Suggestions for Grammar Presentation on page 3.

NOTE 1: Read the note in the Student Book with the class. Answer any questions.

NOTE 2: List some of the common expressions with prepositions from Appendices 13 and 14 on pages A-5 and A-6. Ask students to think of the typical new student in their program and to make sentences with these expressions. For example:

be afraid of   (He's afraid of making mistakes.)
be interested in   (She's interested in improving her English.)
look forward to   (He looks forward to meeting new friends.)

NOTE 3: Explain that *be used to* + gerund means *be/get accustomed to.* Give several examples:

I'm used to getting up early. I get up at 6:00 every day.
Jorge is used to speaking English at his office. No one there speaks Spanish.

Note that this expression always includes a form of *be.* For more explanation, refer students to Unit 4, Note 4, on page 32.

FOCUSED PRACTICE (pages 280–282)

See the General Suggestions for Focused Practice exercises on pages 3–4.

1. Discover the Grammar, page 280
Point out that some words ending in *-ing* are not gerunds but rather progressive forms of verbs.

Follow up with a discussion. Ask:
How do you think the president will respond?
In other countries, do students organize into councils?

What do students in other countries do if they want to change their school?
What do you think is the most effective way for students to change schools?

2. Spring Break, page 281
Refer students to Appendices 13 and 14 on pages A-5 and A-6. Follow up with a brief discussion about students' plans for their next break.

3. School Issues, page 282
Follow up with a discussion. Ask:

What are common school issues in other countries?
What are school issues in our program?
How can students help change the program?

4. Making Changes, page 282
This exercise focuses on the difference between *used to*, meaning habitual action in the past, and *be/get used to*, a phrasal verb that means *be/get accustomed to*. For further information, refer students to Unit 4, Note 4, on page 32.

COMMUNICATION PRACTICE (pages 283–284)

5. Listening, page 283
See the General Suggestions for Listening on page 4.

Have students read the list of situations before listening. After playing the tape twice, check students' answers. If students disagree, play the segment in question again.

6. Vote for Me, page 283
Set a time limit of two minutes for each speech. After each speech, encourage the class to ask the speaker questions. Then conduct an election by secret ballot. Follow up with a discussion. Ask:

Would you like to have a student council?
How can you set up a council?
What kinds of issues would you like to address on the council?

7. Stress, page 283
See the General Suggestions for Pair and Group Activities on page 4.

Have the small groups report to the class. Ask, *What do you think is the single most stressful event? Why?*

8. Writing, page 284
See the General Suggestions for Writing on page 5.

First have students read the text and mark the true/false statements. Go over their answers as a class. Have students in small groups brainstorm ideas for their letters. For homework, have students compose their letters and then submit them to you for review and correction.

EXPANSION

Student Information: Ask students to work in small groups to plan an information sheet. Ask the groups to brainstorm things they know now that would be useful to new students. What would they include? How would they organize the information?

UNIT 28 INFINITIVES AFTER CERTAIN VERBS

GRAMMAR IN CONTEXT (page 285)
See the General Suggestions for Grammar in Context on page 2.

CULTURE NOTES: Many newspapers publish advice columns. Readers write letters explaining their personal problems and seeking advice. The advice experts respond with commonsense advice and sometimes a touch of humor.

In the featured letter, the writer, Lonely in Seattle, mentions putting an ad in the newspaper. She is talking about *personal ads*, which are notices people post in newspapers, magazines, and on the Internet describing themselves in the hope of attracting a partner. The final exercise is this unit provides further examples of personal ads.

Before You Read, page 285: Have students read the questions, look at the column, and share their responses with the class.

Reading, page 285: Ask the following questions:

In what section of the newspaper is this column located? (Lifestyles)
What does Lonely in Seattle want to find? (someone to date)
What does Annie advise Lonely in Seattle to do? (to relax; to do things she likes to do anyway)
What do you think of Annie's advice? (Answers will vary.)

Focus on Grammar: Write the headings *No Object* and *Object* on the board. Elicit a few examples of the highlighted structures from the reading and write them under the appropriate column headings. Note that there is only one example of an infinitive with an object.

No Object	Object
I try hard to meet people.	*My roommate advised me to put an ad in the newspaper.*

Point to the left column and ask, *What does she try hard to do?* (to meet people) *What is the subject?* (I) *What is the main verb?* (try) *What follows the main verb?* (to meet—an infinitive)

Point to the right column and ask, *What did the roommate advise?* (to put an ad in the newspaper) *Whom did she advise?* (Lonely in Seattle) *What is the subject?* (my roommate) *What is the main verb?* (advised) *What follows the main verb?* (Me—an object) *What follows the object?* (to put—an infinitive)

GRAMMAR **PRESENTATION**: Infinitives after Certain Verbs (pages 286–287)

See the General Suggestions for Grammar Presentation on page 3.

NOTES 1–3: Read the notes in the Student Book with the class. Answer any questions.

NOTE 4: Make sure students understand the difference in meaning between the following sentences:

George would like to go away. (George wants to leave.)
George would like Martha to go away. (George wants Martha to leave.)

NOTE 5: Provide additional examples of how the placement of the negative changes the meaning in the sentences:

He didn't allow us to work yesterday. (We were not able to work.)
He allowed us not to work yesterday. (We had vacation.)

Dan asked me not to see her again. (Dan said, "Don't see her again.")
Dan didn't ask me to see her again. (Dan didn't say anything.)

FOCUSED **PRACTICE** (PAGES 288–289)

See the General Suggestions for Focused Practice exercises on pages 3–4.

1. Discover the Grammar, page 288
Have students read the entire text before underlining the infinitive forms. Follow up with these questions:

What did Annie advise her to do? (to join a club or take a class)
What did she decide to do? (to join the school's Outdoor Adventure Club)
Did she like the people she met? (yes)
What kinds of clubs are available to you? (Answers will vary.)

2. Plan to Succeed, page 288

Before beginning the exercise, write on the board, *When you fail to plan, you plan to fail.* Ask, *What does this mean?*

After students have checked their answers, ask the following questions:

What is the first step to finding true love? (Make a list describing the kind of person you wish to meet.)
What is the second step? (Make a list describing yourself.)
What is the third step? (Increase your chances by participating in activities that interest you.)
What is the fourth step? (Ask friends to introduce you to people who interest you.)
What do you think of this advice? (Answers will vary.)
Do you think it is possible to plan to meet someone to love? (Answers will vary.)

3. In Other Words, page 289

Have students read all the sentences before they do the exercise. Answers to these items will vary. As students call out their answers, write them on the board so that the class may see the various possibilities.

COMMUNICATION PRACTICE (pages 290–291)

4. Listening, page 290

See the General Suggestions for Listening on page 4.

CULTURE NOTE: A blended family results when two adults with offspring from prior marriages get married. They blend their families. The new child is a *stepdaughter* or a *stepson* and the new parent is called a *stepmother* or *stepfather*.

After students have completed the exercise, ask:

How did the daughter react at first to her mother's new husband? (She was angry.)
What do you think are common problems experienced in blended families? (Answers will vary.)

5. Describe Your Parents, page 290

See the General Suggestions for Pair and Group Activities on page 4.

Divide the class into pairs. As students discuss their parents, have them add questions to ask each other. Have students report to the class one or two interesting pieces of information about their partners' parents.

6. Socializing around the World, page 291

See the General Suggestions for Pair and Group Activities on page 4.

Additional questions for discussion:

Do the people you know date?
How long do people date before they marry in cultures you know?
How well do parents know their children's dates?
At what age do teenagers begin to date?
How strictly do parents control what happens on a date?
What is a popular activity on a date?

Have students discuss their ideas in small groups and then report their findings to the class.

7. Writing, page 291

See the General Suggestions for Writing on page 5.

Have small groups of students of the same gender read over the ads. Ask, *Who would you like to meet? What will you say in the note?*

Have students compose their notes at home and submit them directly to you.

EXPANSION

Meeting People: Have students work in small mixed groups to talk about how people meet other people around the world. Ask them to talk about meeting both friends—of the same gender and of the opposite gender—and potential spouses. What similarities are there across cultures? What differences are there? Later, you may want to have students report on their finding orally or in writing.

UNIT 29 INFINITIVES OF PURPOSE

GRAMMAR **IN CONTEXT** (page 292)

See the General Suggestions for Grammar in Context on page 2.

Before You Read, page 292: Have students read the questions, look at the illustration, and share their responses with the class.

Reading, page 292: Ask the following comprehension questions:

What can you use the Datalator for? (to organize your studies and save precious time)
How else can you use the Datalator? (You can use it to store names and phone numbers, and to add and subtract.)

Focus on Grammar: Ask, *According to the advertisement, why do you need the Datalator?* and write students' responses on the board (to organize studies, to save precious time, to make study notes, and so on). Underline the infinitive. Point out that the infinitive expresses purpose, the reason to do something.

GRAMMAR **PRESENTATION**: Infinitives of Purpose (page 293)

See the General Suggestions for Grammar Presentation on page 3.

NOTE 1: Have students provide additional examples by asking:

Why do you come to English class? (I come to English class to learn English.)
Why do you use a dictionary? (I use a dictionary to learn the meaning of new words.)
Why do you take notes in class? (I take notes to remember what we did in class.)
Why do you ask questions in class? (I ask questions to understand something better.)

NOTE 2: Repeat the Note 1 questions and have students respond with *in order to*. For example:

Why do you come to English class? (I come to English class in order to learn English.)

NOTE 3: Provide additional examples of negatives with *in order to*:

Why do you use an alarm clock? (I use an alarm clock in order not to oversleep. I don't want to oversleep.)
Why do you call the teacher when you are sick? (I call the teacher when I am sick in order not to miss a homework assignment. I don't want to miss a homework assignment.)
Why do you use a pencil when you write in your workbook? (I use a pencil when I write in my workbook in order not to mess up the pages. I don't want to mess up the pages.)

Point out that it is incorrect to split the infinitive.

NOTE 4: Give students additional practice by pointing to objects in the room and asking, *What do you use this for?* For example:

(Point to a pen.) *What do you use this for?* (I use it to write.)
(Point to a chair.) *What do you use this for?* (I use it to sit on.)

Alternatively, students could ask questions of each other in a chain game. Stop when every student has asked and answered a question.

FOCUSED PRACTICE (pages 294–295)

See the General Suggestions for Focused Practice exercises on pages 3–4.

1. Discover the Grammar, page 294
Point out that there are infinitives in the dialogue that do not express a purpose. If students are uncertain about whether the infinitive expresses a purpose, have them ask, "Why?" If the infinitive can answer that question, it expresses a purpose.

2. Tell Me Why, page 294
Have students look at all the reasons in the box before filling in the blanks.

3. The Reason Is . . . , page 295
As an alternative, have students do this exercise in pairs. Have Student A cover the purposes and Student B cover the actions. Have Student A read an action as Student B listens and identifies the purpose.

Have students work individually to combine the sentences using infinitives. Go over the answers as a class.

4. Editing, page 295
See the General Suggestions for Editing on page 4.

Have students go over their corrections by reading the journal entry aloud.

COMMUNICATION PRACTICE (pages 296–297)

5. Listening, page 296
See the General Suggestions for Listening on page 4.

BACKGROUND NOTE: Explain that many companies have this kind of automated answering system.

Before listening, have students read the list of options. After listening, ask students:
What strategies do you use when you hear one of these long automated messages?
Do you take notes?
Do you hold on for an operator?
Do you press the repeat button?

6. What's It For?, page 296
See the General Suggestions for Pair and Group Activities on page 4.

Divide the class into groups. Have one student in each group volunteer to be the scribe. Tell students that they have a time limit of ten minutes to try to imagine at least three different purposes for each object. Then have the groups share their ideas with the class.

7. The Datalator, page 297
See the General Suggestions for Pair and Group Activities on page 4.

Divide the class into pairs to discuss how they would use the Datalator. Ask, *Is the Datalator useful technology? Can you give an example of very useful technology? What do you use it for?*

Then write the following pairs of low technology / high technology items on the board:

date book vs. Datalator
paper dictionary vs. computer dictionary
paper mail vs. e-mail
bicycle vs. car
pen and paper vs. calculator
paper books vs. CD-ROM books
speaking to an operator vs. voice mail
paper newspaper vs. Internet news
not available for a phone call vs. answering machine

Ask, *Which option do you usually choose? Why?* Have students discuss their responses as a class.

8. Remote Control, page 297
See the General Suggestions for Pair and Group Activities on page 4.

Have groups share their ideas with the class. Encourage students to be creative with their options.

9. Writing, page 297
See the General Suggestions for Writing on page 5.

Bring old magazines, scissors, colored paper, and pens to class. After designing their ads, have students share them in small groups. Have each group look at the ads and nominate them to unique categories, for example, "Most Creative," "Most Colorful," "Most Useful," or "Most Humorous." Have the groups present their ads to the class along with their nomination categories.

EXPANSION

The Future: Have students think about a product of the future and design an ad for it. Students can work individually or with partners. Remind students to be creative and to use their imaginations. The ad can include both text and graphics.

 UNIT 30 INFINITIVES WITH *TOO* AND *ENOUGH*

GRAMMAR **IN CONTEXT** (page 298)

See the General Suggestions for Grammar in Context on page 2.

CULTURE NOTE: In the United States and Canada, people are considered adults for most purposes when they reach the age of eighteen. At that age, they can vote, sign contracts, and serve in the armed forces without needing permission from their parents or guardians. In the United States, young people cannot purchase alcohol until they are twenty-one. Prior to 1971, Americans had to be twenty-one to vote.

Before You Read, page 298: Have students read the questions, look at the photographs, and respond in pairs.

Reading, page 298: Ask the following questions:
Why do they want the right to vote? (because without it teenagers are too powerless for politicians to listen to)
What is an example of discrimination teenagers experience? (family divorce laws and curfew laws)
What do you think of their arguments? (Answers will vary.)
Do you think teenagers under eighteen should have the right to vote? (Answers will vary.)

Focus on Grammar: Write the headings *Too* and *Enough* on the board. Elicit examples of the highlighted structures from the reading and write them under the appropriate column headings. Explain their meanings. For example:
Teenagers are too powerless for politicians to listen to. (Teenagers have so little power that politicians don't listen to them.)
I'm responsible enough to work and pay taxes. (I am so responsible that I work and pay taxes.)

GRAMMAR **PRESENTATION:** Infinitives with *Too* and *Enough* (pages 299–300)

See the General Suggestions for Grammar Presentation on page 3.

NOTE 1: Have students give additional examples of *too*. Write adjective cues on the board (*heavy, light, big, small, short, tall*) and ask students:
Can Pablo lift this desk? (No, the desk is too heavy to lift.)
Can I touch the ceiling? (No, you are too short to touch the ceiling.)
Can I throw this bookcase? (No, the bookcase is too big to throw.)

Write their responses on the board.

NOTE 2: Using the sentences from the Note 1 activity, have students give contrasting examples with *enough*. Point to one of the answers given in the above activity and ask a contrasting question. For example:

Can Pablo lift this book? (Yes, it's light enough to lift.)
Can I touch the top of the bookcase? (Yes, you are tall enough to touch the top of the bookcase.)
Can I throw this set of keys? (Yes, they are small enough to throw.)

NOTE 3: Repeat the questions from the Note 1 and Note 2 activities and have students respond without the infinitive. For example:

Can Pablo lift this desk? (No, it's too heavy.)
Can Pablo lift this book? (Yes, it's light enough.)

NOTE 4: Ask questions to make sure students understand the subject of the infinitive. For example:

Sam is old enough to work and pay taxes. Who works and pays taxes? (Sam)
Sara is mature enough for her parents to trust her. Who trusts her? (Her parents)

FOCUSED PRACTICE (pages 301–303)

See the General Suggestions for Focused Practice exercises on pages 3–4.

1. Discover the Grammar, page 301
After correcting their answers, have students form small groups to read the first opinion of each item and say whether they agree or disagree and why. Have the groups report back to the class.

2. Can You Get By?, page 302
Have students look at all the illustrations and read all the sentences before they begin matching.

3. Curfew!, page 303
To review answers, have pairs of students act out the conversations for the class.

Follow up with a discussion by asking:

Do you know of any towns or cities with special curfews for young people?
Why do you think there are curfews?
What are the advantages and disadvantages of curfews?
Is there any other solution for teenagers?

4. Editing, page 303
See the General Suggestions for Editing on page 4.

Have students go over their corrections by reading the journal entry aloud.

COMMUNICATION PRACTICE (pages 304–305)

5. Listening, page 304
See the General Suggestions for Listening on page 4.

Before listening, have students look carefully at the illustrations. After listening twice, have students, in pairs, explain which illustration they believe is correct and why.

6. Youth Rights, page 304
Pose one question at a time to the class. Write students' opinions on the board. Have the class consider all the opinions on the board and try to identify two compelling (and opposing) opinions to vote on. Then conduct the vote by secret ballot.

7. Common Expressions, page 305
See the General Suggestions for Pair and Group Activities on page 4.

Divide the class into small groups. Have the groups report to class after five minutes of discussion.

8. What's Your Opinion?, page 305
See the General Suggestions for Pair and Group Activities on page 4.

Have students work individually to complete the sentences and then compare their ideas in small groups. Have the groups report to the class any interesting ideas that arose in their discussions.

9. Writing, page 305
See the General Suggestions for Writing on page 5.

Point out that opinions need supporting information. Have students think of at least three supporting reasons for their opinions. Have students write an outline and show it to a partner for feedback. Then have students write their letters.

Have students share their letters in small groups. Their classmates listen and ask questions to clarify any information. Tell the writers to incorporate clarifying details into their final draft and submit it you.

EXPANSION

Building for the Disabled: Have students work in small groups to brainstorm things that could be done in your school or in your town to make buildings more accessible for the disabled. How do buildings in your area compare to buildings students have seen in other countries? Are buildings more or less accessible? Interested students can follow up by designing an apartment, house, or building that would be more accessible.

UNIT 31 GERUNDS AND INFINITIVES

GRAMMAR **IN CONTEXT** (page 306)
See the General Suggestions for Grammar in Context on page 2.

Before You Read, page 306: Have students read the questions and cartoon and share their responses with the class.

Reading, page 306: Ask the following comprehension questions:
What's Marta's problem? (She can't remember people's names.)
What is the most common memory aid? (putting things in writing)
Does worrying help? (No. It makes the problem worse.)

Focus on Grammar: Write the headings *Verbs That Take Gerunds* and *Verbs That Take Infinitives* on the board. Elicit a few examples of the highlighted structures from the reading and write them under the appropriate column headings.

Explain that some verbs take gerunds, others take infinitives, and still others can take both. Tell students they will need to memorize the classification of these verbs; refer them to Appendices 9, 10, and 11 on page A-5.

GRAMMAR **PRESENTATION:** Gerunds and Infinitives (pages 307–308)
See the General Suggestions for Grammar Presentation on page 3.

NOTE 1: Have students compose one sentence each using a verb from the list and then share their sentences with the class.

NOTE 2: Have students compose one sentence each using a verb from the list and then share their sentences with the class.

Have students turn to Appendices 9, 10, and 11 on page A-5. For homework, have students study short segments of the verb lists. In class, set aside time to drill these assigned segments.

NOTES 3–5: Read the notes in the Student Book with the class. Answer any questions.

Note 6: Provide more examples of gerunds and infinitives as subjects:

Learning new names is hard.
It's hard to learn new names.

Walking to school is good for your health.
It is good for your health to walk to school.

Have students practice converting the following sentences to gerund subjects:

It's fun to study English. (Studying English is fun.)
It's interesting to learn a new language. (Learning a new language is interesting.)
It's hard to memorize all these verbs. (Memorizing all these verbs is hard.)

FOCUSED PRACTICE (pages 309–312)

See the General Suggestions for Focused Practice exercises on pages 3–4.

1. Discover the Grammar, page 309
This exercise contrasts the meaning of verbs in gerund and infinitive form. When the statements are false, ask students to change the first sentences to make them true. This will help them understand the contrast in meanings.

2. Super Memory, page 309
After students have checked their answers, ask the following questions:

Which of these memory tips do you use regularly?
Do you have any other memory tips?

3. Party Talk, page 310
Before beginning this exercise, be sure students are well acquainted with Appendices 9, 10, and 11 on page A-5. Knowledge of the verb classifications will help students complete this exercise.

4. Remember to Study, page 311
After students have checked their answers, ask the following questions:

Which of these study tips do you use regularly?
Do you have any other study tips?

5. In Other Words, page 311
To review answers, have pairs of students act out the exchanges for the class.

6. Editing, page 312
See the General Suggestions for Editing on page 4.

Have students go over their corrections by reading the letter aloud.

COMMUNICATION PRACTICE (pages 313–316)

7. Listening, page 313
See the General Suggestions for Listening on page 4.

After completing this exercise, ask, *When you go out with friends, what do you enjoy doing? What do you dislike doing?*

8. Social Situation Survey, page 313
See the General Suggestions for Pair and Group Activities on page 4.

Have students complete the sentences individually and then discuss them with a partner. Have each pair share with the class one or two sentences.

9. Information Gap: Remember the Party?, pages 314 and 316
Divide the class into pairs. Assign each partner a role (A or B). Assign Students A page 314 and Students B page 316. Have students read their separate instructions and look at their illustrations. Point out that their illustrations are the same but with different information missing. Have the partners ask and answer each other's questions to complete the missing information.

Alternatively, for lower-level students, divide the class into Groups A and B. Have each group make questions about the missing information in their illustration. Circulate between the two groups and help as needed. Pair students from Groups A and B. Have them ask and answer each other's questions.

If most pairs finish the Information Gap activity at about the same time, do the second memory activity as a timed competition. Have all pairs close their books and within two minutes write everything they can remember. Then go over the information. Which pair accurately remembered the most?

10. Stop Forgetting, page 315
See the General Suggestions for Pair and Group Activities on page 4.

After discussing the questions, have students share their ideas with the class.

11. Writing, page 315
See the General Suggestions for Writing on page 5.

Have students share their letters in small groups, as their classmates listen and ask questions to clarify any information. Tell the writers to incorporate clarifying details into their final draft and submit it to you.

EXPANSION

Memory Game: Put between fifteen and twenty items on a tray, and cover it with large cloth. Show the tray to the class for forty-five seconds. Have students write down everything they can remember. Compare lists. Then give students a memory strategy. Tell them to look at the items and categorize them into classes of objects. For example:

keys, paper clips, stapler	(metal objects)
sheet of paper, notebook, pen, pencil	(things for writing
glasses, binoculars	(thinks for seeing)
cell phone, calculator, electronic dictionary	(electronic devices)

Compare lists. Ask, *How many more objects can you remember when you use this strategy?*

Alternative: Instead of collecting items to put on a tray, you can also use magazine pictures or any of the many "look and find" children's books.

Group Discussion—Plans for the Weekend: In small groups, have students discuss these questions:

What do you expect to do this weekend?
What do you look forward to doing?
What do you need to do?
What do you feel like doing?

REVIEW OR SELFTEST

See the General Suggestions for Review or Self Test on pages 5–6.

FROM GRAMMAR TO WRITING:
COMBINING SENTENCES WITH *AND, BUT, SO, OR*

See the General Suggestions for From Grammar to Writing on page 6.

In this section, students practice combining sentences using conjunctions. As they write about social events (a theme from Unit 31), they also review the use of gerunds and infinitives.

Introduction, page 323
Write the example sentence from the Student Book: *Commuting to school is hard. I prefer to live in the dorm.* Ask the class:

Which of the following conjunctions can join the two sentences: and, but, so, or? (so)
Where do I put the comma? (before the conjunction)
Have the class open their books and read the introductory text.

Exercise 1, page 323
If students have difficulty choosing conjunctions, have them first do Exercise 2 to define the meaning of each conjunction.

Exercise 2, page 324
Go over students' answers as a class.

Exercise 3, page 324
Have students complete the sentences individually and then share them in small groups. Have each group share a few sentences with the class.

Exercise 4, page 324
Divide the class into pairs to discuss the questions listed in the Student Book.

Exercise 5, page 324
Have students write their letters at home.

Exercise 6, page 324
Pair students with new partners. Have them exchange their letters and answer them briefly with a letter of their own.

Have students submit all their letters to you for review.

PART VII MORE MODALS AND RELATED VERBS AND EXPRESSIONS

 PREFERENCES: *PREFER, WOULD PREFER, WOULD RATHER*

GRAMMAR **IN CONTEXT** (page 328)

See the General Suggestions for Grammar in Context on page 2.

BACKGROUND NOTE: Market researchers conduct surveys about groups of people to find out about their lifestyles and buying habits. Companies use this information to market products and services more effectively.

Before You Read, page 328: Have students read the questions, look at the chart, and share their responses with a partner.

Reading, page 328: In small groups, have students read the survey and then look at the chart carefully to answer these comprehension questions:

Do adults prefer listening to the radio or to recorded music? (listening to the radio)
What activities do adults prefer more than teenagers? (cooking and shopping in stores)
What activities do teenagers prefer more than adults? (listening to music, hobbies, and exercise)

Then ask students to indicate with a show of hands their preferences on a few items in the survey. Write the number of students per preference on the board. For example:

Nine students prefer seeing an action-adventure film.
Ten students would rather watch a romantic movie.

Focus on Grammar: Keep the preference expressions from the Reading activity on the board. Ask:

What follows the expressions prefer *and* would prefer? (gerunds and nouns, or even infinitives, although there is no such example here)
What follows the expression would rather? (the base form of a verb)

GRAMMAR PRESENTATION: Preferences: *Prefer, Would prefer, Would rather* (pages 329–331)

See the General Suggestions for Grammar Presentation on page 3.

NOTE 1: Point out that *would rather* and *would prefer* are used when making a specific choice in a particular moment. Give the following example of purchasing a plane ticket:

Would you prefer an aisle seat or a window seat?
Would you rather have a seat in the front or the back of the plane?

Whereas, when talking generally about preferences, *prefer* is used. For example:

I usually prefer a window seat.
They prefer sitting in first class.
I always prefer the front of the plane. It's easier to get on and off the plane.

NOTE 2: Read the note in the Student Book with the class. Answer any questions.

NOTE 3: Point out that *prefer* and *would prefer* can be followed by either a gerund or an infinitive with no change in meaning.

NOTES 4 AND 5: Have students practice making comparisons with *would prefer . . . to* and *would rather . . . than*. Write these cues on the board and have students compose sentences about their own preferences.

coffee or tea
strawberry or chocolate ice cream
Italian food or Chinese food
television or videos
McDonald's or my own homemade food

FOCUSED PRACTICE (pages 332–335)

See the General Suggestions for Focused Practice exercises on pages 3–4.

1. Discover the Grammar, page 332
For reading practice, have the class read the conversations, identify the sentences that talk about preferences, and then identify the places in the mall that the speakers visited.

Alternatively, for listening practice, have students cover the conversations and only read the mall directory as they listen to the tape. After students have identified the places the speakers visited, they can read the conversations and underline the sentences expressing preferences.

2. Mushrooms or Pepperoni?, page 333
Have students read the entire conversation before filling in the blanks. To review answers, have a pair of students act out the conversation for the class.

3. Decisions, pages 333–334
This exercise contrasts the three expressions of preference. Remind students of the salient features of each expression. *Prefer* speaks about general preferences. *Would prefer* speaks about specific choices and takes a gerund, a noun, or an infinitive. *Would rather* also speaks about specific choices, but it takes only the base form of a verb. If students need guidance, point out the following features of each set of items:

2. general preferences
3. choice, followed by a gerund
4. general preferences
5. choice followed by a base form of a verb
6. choice followed by a noun

4. Editing, page 334
See the General Suggestions for Editing on page 4.

Check students' comprehension. Ask:

Who prefers to watch adventure programs and science fiction? (Men do.)
Who prefers soap operas? (Women do.)

Who prefers game shows to sport events? (Women do.)
Who would rather read newspapers than magazines? (Men would.)
Who would rather read novels than nonfiction? (Women would.)

5. Sports Preferences, page 335
Have students read the entire passage before they fill in the blanks.

Check students' comprehension. Ask:

What is the most popular sport overall among teenagers? (basketball)
Do people prefer to watch or play a sport? (watch)
What percentage of Latin Americans prefer soccer? (70 percent)
What would Filipinos rather watch? (basketball)
What is the preferred sport in India? (cricket)

COMMUNICATION PRACTICE (pages 336–339)

6. Listening, page 336
See the General Suggestions for Listening on page 4.

Have students read the menus before listening. After playing the tape twice, check students' answers. If students disagree, play the segment in question again. Ask pairs of students to discuss what they would prefer to order.

7. What's on TV?, page 336
See the General Suggestions for Pair and Group Activities on page 4.

Divide the class into small groups. Give students a time limit of five minutes to agree on a program. Then have the groups share their decisions with the class. Ask:
What did you learn about your classmates?
Do you have similar tastes?

8. If I Had My Way, page 337
See the General Suggestions for Pair and Group Activities on page 4.

Have students form pairs to discuss the listed choices and then come up with more of their own. Invite students to share their ideas with the class.

For expansion, have students write a paragraph describing their partners' preferences.

9. Information Gap: Preferred Snacks, pages 337 and 339
Divide the class into pairs. Assign each partner a role (A or B). Assign Students A page 337 and Students B page 339. Have them read their assigned charts. Point out that their charts are the same but with different information missing. Have the partners ask and answer each other's questions to complete the missing information.

Alternatively, for lower-level students, divide the class into Groups A and B. Have each group make questions about the missing information in their assigned charts. Circulate between the two groups and help as needed. Pair students from Groups A and B. Have them ask and answer each other's questions.

10. Choices, page 338
See the General Suggestions for Pair and Group Activities on page 4.

Have students complete the questionnaire individually and then work with a partner. Encourage students to give reasons for their preferences.

11. Rank Order, page 338
See the General Suggestions for Pair and Group Activities on page 4.

Have students do the ranking individually and then join large groups to tally and analyze their preferences. Ask, *Are there any patterns in the preferences people have according to gender, age, marital status?* Have the groups report their findings to the class.

12. Writing, page 338

See the General Suggestions for Writing on page 5.

In pairs, have students take notes as they compare their preferences. At home, have students write a paragraph describing the differences in their preferences.

EXPANSION

Planning a Resort: Have students work with partners to plan the ideal resort or spa. What would it include? Where would it be? What would they call it? Ask the students to plan a brochure describing the activities offered at their resort.

UNIT 33 NECESSITY: *HAVE (GOT) TO, DON'T HAVE TO, MUST, MUST NOT, CAN'T*

GRAMMAR IN CONTEXT (page 340)

See the General Suggestions for Grammar in Context on page 2.

BACKGROUND NOTE: The state department of motor vehicles administers tests and awards driver's licenses. The department also gives special remedial driving classes for drivers who have had accidents or arrests.

Before You Read, page 340: Have students read the questions, look at the illustration, and share their responses with the class.

Reading, page 340: Ask the following comprehension questions:

Who has to pass a test to get a driver's license? (all drivers)
When you drive on an expressway, what must you know how to do? (change lanes, pass other cars)
Do you have to wear a seat belt when you drive? (Yes, you do.)

Focus on Grammar: Ask students to refer to the reading and answer this question: *What must people do to be safe drivers?* Write their ideas on the board in sentence form. Point out the various expressions that indicate necessity.

GRAMMAR PRESENTATION: Necessity: *Have (got) to, Don't have to, Must, Must not, Can't* (pages 341–343)

See the General Suggestions for Grammar Presentation on page 3.

NOTE 1: Point out that the pronunciation of *have to* and *has to* in complete sentences is reduced to *hafta* and *hasta*. Have students practice these reductions with the following sentences:

Everyone has to pass a road test.
You have to take an eye test.
Everyone has to stop at a red light.
We have to get insurance before we can drive.
All passengers have to wear seat belts.

NOTE 2: With student input, conjugate *have to* in the simple past, present perfect, and future.

NOTE 3: Point out that questions with *have to* often signal the speaker's dissatisfaction with a situation. In the first sentence, for example, the speaker doesn't want Paul to drive.

NOTE 4: Provide additional examples:

The speed limit is sixty-five miles per hour. You must not drive eighty miles an hour, but you don't have to drive sixty-five miles an hour. You can drive fifty-five miles an hour if you prefer.
You must not drive if you have been drinking alcohol, but you don't have to walk. You can call a taxi or ask a friend to drive you home.

FOCUSED PRACTICE (pages 344–348)

See the General Suggestions for Focused Practice exercises on pages 3–4.

1. Discover the Grammar, page 344
Have the class read the conversation, identify the language relating to necessity, and then complete the comprehension exercise. To review answers, have a pair of students act out the conversation for the class.

Orient students in reading a typical state driver's license. Have them look at the photograph and find the following information: *state, name and address of driver, expiration date, license number, date of birth (DOB), restrictions,* and *driver's appearance.*

2. Getting Ready, page 345
First ask students to think of all the things they needed to do before they last moved. Then have students read the lists and the examples. To review the answers, have students read their sentences aloud.

3. Car Games, page 346
Point out that *have to* and *have got to* (rather than *must*) and *can't* (rather than *must not*) are used in these conversations because the context is spoken, rather than written.

To review answers, have pairs of students act out the conversations for the class.

4. Following the Rules, page 347
Ask, *Are all these rules true in other countries?* Have students review their answers and discuss this question in groups.

5. At the Pool, page 348
Go over the chart with the class. Have students compare their answers in pairs and then compose additional sentences using the information in the chart. For example:

You must not drink from glass bottles at the pool.
You don't have to take a shower before you swim.

6. Editing, page 348
See the General Suggestions for Editing on page 4.

Ask the class, *How old do you think Jim is?*

COMMUNICATION PRACTICE (pages 349–351)

7. Listening, page 349
See the General Suggestions for Listening on page 4.

Have students look at the signs before listening. After playing the tape twice, check students' answers. If students disagree, play the segment in question again.

Have pairs of students write sentences to describe each sign. For example:

You have to stop.
You must not park here.

8. Reading the Signs, page 350
See the General Suggestions for Pair and Group Activities on page 4.

Divide the class into pairs. Give students a time limit of ten minutes to discuss the signs. Have the groups share their ideas with the class.

9. Invent a Sign, page 351
See the General Suggestions for Pair and Group Activities on page 4.

Bring colored pens and pencils and different-colored and textured paper to class. Encourage students to be creative. They can make signs for their cars, for their homes, for the classroom, or for anywhere else.

10. Driving around the World, page 351
See the General Suggestions for Pair and Group Activities on page 4.

For a class discussion, ask:
Which country would you like to drive in? Why?
Which country would you not like to drive in? Why?

11. Taking Care of Business, page 351
Have students compose their lists individually and then speak with a partner. Set a time limit of five minutes for this activity.

12. Writing, page 351
See the General Suggestions for Writing on page 5.

Brainstorm with the class possible topics for the writing exercise. Have students do the writing at home.

In class, have students read their paragraphs aloud in small groups. Their classmates listen and ask questions to clarify information. Tell the writers to incorporate clarifying details into their final draft and submit it you.

EXPANSION

Signs around Town: Have students take notes of signs they see around town. Have students draw the signs on the board and ask the class, *Where do you think this sign was located? What do you think it means?*

 UNIT 34 EXPECTATIONS: *BE SUPPOSED TO*

GRAMMAR **IN CONTEXT** (page 352)

See the General Suggestions for Grammar in Context on page 2.

BACKGROUND NOTE: There are several popular books on etiquette. A traditional favorite was written by Emily Post. Judith Foster, known as Miss Manners, has written several more recent ones. She also writes a newspaper column, answering questions about etiquette (or manners).

Before You Read, page 352: Have students read the questions, look at the photograph, and share their responses with the class.

Reading, 352: Ask the following comprehension questions and write students' answers on the board:

Who was the maid of honor in the past? (The bride's sister was supposed to serve as maid of honor.)
What do the maid of honor and the best man do before the ceremony? (They are supposed to help the couple prepare for the ceremony.)
What do they do after the ceremony? (They are supposed to sign the marriage certificate as witnesses.)

Focus on Grammar: Look at the examples elicited from the comprehension questions. Point out that *supposed to* is used to describe different kinds of expectations. These three examples describe customs, or the usual ways of conducting weddings in the United States.

GRAMMAR **PRESENTATION**: Expectations: *Be supposed to* (pages 353–354)

See the General Suggestions for Grammar Presentation on page 3.

NOTE 1: Point out that *be supposed to* is an idiomatic phrase and is distinct from the regular verb *to suppose*, which means *to consider as probable* or *to believe*. For example:
I suppose I should go home. It is late.

Note 2: Give additional examples of how *supposed to* in the past describes something that was expected to happen but didn't.

We were supposed to get married this June, but we changed the date to August.
He was supposed to pick the bride up at her house, but he went directly to the church instead!
They were supposed to have the wedding outdoors, but it rained. So they moved the ceremony indoors.

FOCUSED PRACTICE (pages 355–357)

See the General Suggestions for Focused Practice exercises on pages 3–4.

1. Discover the Grammar, page 355
Point out that the comprehension exercise helps students understand what type of expectation is being described with each example of *supposed to*:
2. *The weather was supposed to be beautiful.* (prediction)
3. *We were supposed to have fifty guests.* (plans)
4. *The ferry was supposed to leave.* (plans and arrangements)
5. *Bikers are supposed to stay fast and fit.* (hearsay)

2. Getting Ready, page 356
First ask students to brainstorm what must be done in preparation for a wedding. Then have students read the conversations and fill in the blanks. To review answers, have pairs of students act out the conversations for the class.

3. Editing, page 357
See the General Suggestions for Editing on page 4.

Ask the class, *What is Sophie supposed to do as Netta's maid of honor?*

COMMUNICATION PRACTICE (page 358)

4. Listening, page 358
See the General Suggestions for Listening on page 4.

After completing the exercise, ask students, *Which of these customs is true in other cultures?*

5. International Customs, page 358
See the General Suggestions for Pair and Group Activities on page 4.

Divide the class into small groups. Give students a time limit of fifteen minutes to discuss their customs and then share their ideas with the class.

6. Writing, page 358
See the General Suggestions for Writing on page 4.

In class, have students read their writing aloud in small groups. Their classmates listen and ask questions to clarify information. Tell the writers to incorporate clarifying details into their final draft and submit it to you.

EXPANSION

Sharing Memories: Have students bring pictures to class of an important event they celebrated in their home country, such as a birthday, wedding, anniversary, or first communion. In small groups, have students show their pictures and answer their classmates' questions. After an interval of five minutes, have students switch groups and share their pictures again.

GRAMMAR **IN CONTEXT** (page 359)

See the General Suggestions for Grammar in Context on page 2.

BACKGROUND NOTE: This unit talks about temperature in both Celsius and Fahrenheit measurements. Here is a conversion table:

Celsius	Fahrenheit
0	32
10	50
20	68
30	86
40	104

Before You Read, page 359: Have students read the questions, look at the weather map, and share their responses with the class.

Reading, page 359: Ask the following comprehension questions and write students' answers on the board:

Will it definitely snow in London tomorrow? (No, it might snow.)
How strong are the winds going to be? (They could reach 40 mph.)
Will it be stormy in France tomorrow? (Yes, stormy conditions may move into France.)
Will it definitely snow in Paris tomorrow? (No, rain could turn to snow in the evening.)
Will Rome be warm tomorrow? (Yes, it may be warm in Rome.)
Will the temperature reach the twenties? (The temperature could reach the twenties.)

Focus on Grammar: Look at the examples elicited from the comprehension questions. Point out that *may, might,* and *could* talk about future possibility.

GRAMMAR **PRESENTATION:** Future Possibility: *May, Might, Could* (pages 360–361)

See the General Suggestions for Grammar Presentation on page 3.

NOTE 1: Read the note in the Student Book with the class. Answer any questions.

NOTE 2: Give additional examples contrasting *could* with *could not*.

I don't know what to do for my vacation. I could visit my parents, but then I couldn't take the special class trip to Africa. I could go on this class trip to Africa, but then I couldn't see my parents until next vacation! It's a hard decision!

A: *Are you going to the dinner party?*
B: *I don't know. I could go, but I couldn't get there until 9:00. That could be too late to arrive.*

NOTE 3: Return to the comprehension questions about the reading. Have students respond to them with short answers. For example:

Will it definitely snow in London tomorrow? (It might.)
Will it be stormy in France tomorrow? (It may be.)

FOCUSED PRACTICE (pages 362–364)

See the General Suggestions for Focused Practice exercises on pages 3–4.

1. Discover the Grammar, page 362
Have the class read the conversation and identify the words that express possibility and then complete the comprehension exercises. To review answers, have a pair of students act out the conversation for the class.

2. Making Plans, page 363
Point out that the future tenses *going to* and *will* both indicate a degree of certainty. This exercise contrasts that certainty with the modals of possibility *may, might,* and *could.*

3. I Might, page 363
Point out that the future tense *going to* indicates a degree of certainty. This exercise contrasts that certainty with the modals of possibility *may* and *might.*

4. Storm Warning, page 364
This exercise contrasts possibility (*could*) with impossibility (*couldn't*). Point out that when a question uses the verb *be*, its answer requires the verb *be*.

5. Editing, page 364
See the General Suggestions for Editing on page 4.

To check comprehension, ask:

What is El Niño? (a change in water temperatures in the ocean near Peru)
What effects could El Niño have on the west coasts of South and North America? (It could cause heavy rains.)
What could happen in northern areas? (They could get wetter and warmer.)
What could happen in southern areas? (They could become much colder.)
What kind of effect will this have on plants and animals? (They might die.)
What is a possible cause of El Niño? (human pollution that traps warm air)

COMMUNICATION PRACTICE (page 365)

6. Listening, page 365
See the General Suggestions for Listening on page 4.

After completing the exercise, ask the class, *What will the weather be like for us tomorrow?* Write students' predictions on the board using future tenses and modals of possibility, depending on their certainty.

7. Possibilities, page 365
See the General Suggestions for Pair and Group Activities on page 4.

Divide the class into small groups. Give students a time limit of ten minutes to discuss the possible futures of the two characters and then share their ideas with the class.

Individually, have students write about their own future possibilities using the listed categories of occupations, hobbies, and achievements. Have students share their writing in groups and then submit it to you for review and correction.

8. Writing, page 365
See the General Suggestions for Writing on page 5.

Brainstorm with students about their future plans. Encourage them to think big. To help students organize their thoughts, you may want to organize the brainstorming into the following segments: *next year, in the next five years, in the next fifteen years.*

Have students complete their writing at home, share their plans in small groups, and submit it to you for final review and correction.

Are We Changing the Weather? Invite students to respond to the question "Are we changing the weather?" You may want to have students respond to this question as a debate. Explain the rules of debate. Then randomly assign students to teams that present the views that yes, we are, or no, we are not changing the weather. Remind students to present verifiable facts whenever possible. Students who are not assigned will be the audience. After the debate, they will have to decide which team presented a more effective and convincing argument.

UNIT 36 ASSUMPTIONS: *MUST, HAVE (GOT) TO, MAY, MIGHT, COULD, CAN'T*

GRAMMAR **IN CONTEXT** (page 366)

See the General Suggestions for Grammar in Context on page 2.

BACKGROUND NOTE: Sir Arthur Conan Doyle wrote the Sherlock Holmes stories at the end of the nineteenth century. Holmes, a fictional character, was one of the first detectives. He used his powers of observation to make deductions that helped him solve crimes. He was often accompanied by his friend, Dr. Watson, who was not as brilliant as Holmes. Usually Holmes had to explain his conclusions to Dr. Watson in great detail.

Before You Read, page 366: Have students read the questions, look at the illustration, and share their responses with the class. You may want to share details from the above background note.

Reading, page 366: After students have completed the reading, ask the following questions:
Who has red hair? (Jabez Wilson does.)
How does Watson know that Wilson writes a lot? (He has a hole in the sleeve of his jacket and his
   right shirt cuff is worn.)
What is the purpose of the Red-Headed League? (to help men with red hair)
What's the job at the league? (to copy the encyclopedia)
How does he copy the encyclopedia? (by hand)
Does this seem like useful work to you? (Answers will vary.)

If you have students listen to the tape, make sure they realize that the voices in this Sherlock Holmes story have a British accent. You could point out that some words are pronounced quite differently in British English and American English, e.g., clerk (*BrE* /klɑːk/; *AmE* /klɚrk/)

Focus on Grammar: Write on the top of the board *100% Certain* and at the bottom of the board *0% Certain*. Explain that Holmes and Watson are making assumptions about a situation they know little about. Some of these assumptions are more certain than others. Elicit examples of the highlighted assumptions in the text and, with students' input, place the assumptions on the continuum.

GRAMMAR **PRESENTATION**: Assumptions: *Must, Have (got) to, May, Might, Could, Can't* (pages 367–370)

See the General Suggestions for Grammar Presentation on page 3.

NOTE 1: Read the note in the Student Book with the class. Answer any questions.

NOTE 2: Provide additional examples of conclusions:
Holmes solves many mysteries. He must be very intelligent.
Holmes and Watson have worked together for years. They've got to work well together.

Bring a brown paper bag to class. Put an object in the bag without students seeing it. Allow students to touch, lift, press, and shake the bag. Elicit statements with *must* and explanations. For example:
Student 1: *It must be a be a book because it's rectangular and hard.*
Student 2: *It must be our workbook because it's thinner than our grammar book.*
Teacher: *Right. It's our workbook.*

Once students have guessed the object, replace it with another.

NOTE 3: As in the Note 2 paper bag activity, put an object in the bag without students seeing it. Do not allow students to touch the bag. You may shake the bag or otherwise demonstrate some small clue of what is inside, but do not give the class solid evidence. Elicit statements with *may, might,* or *could.* Once students have guessed the object, replace it with another.

NOTE 4: Refer students to Note 4b in Unit 33 (page 343) for further explanation of why the negative form of *have to* cannot be used to express assumptions. It negates necessity and expresses choice.

NOTE 5: As in the Notes 2 and 3 paper bag activities, put an object in the bag without students seeing it. Do not allow students to touch the bag. You may shake the bag or otherwise demonstrate some small clue of what is inside, but do not give the class solid evidence. Elicit student questions with *can* or *could.* For example:

Student 1: *Could it be a book?*
  Teacher: *Yes.*
Student 2: *Can it be a heavy book?*
  Teacher: *Yes.*
Student 3: *Could it be a heavy book like a dictionary?*
  Teacher: *Right! It's a dictionary!*

Once students have guessed the object, replace it with another.

NOTE 6: Read the note in the Student Book with the class. Answer any questions.

FOCUSED PRACTICE (pages 371–375)

See the General Suggestions for Focused Practice exercises on pages 3–4.

1. Discover the Grammar, page 371
Have students read the story and identify the appropriate phrases. Review answers as a class. Have students read the story again or listen to the tape. As students complete the comprehension exercise, encourage them to refer to the reading to support their answers.

2. Picture This, page 372
As students review their answers, encourage them to explain why they are making each assumption. For example:

It must be nighttime because it is very dark and the street lamp is on. Very few people are on the street.

If students are intrigued by the mystery, have them skip to Exercise 4 and Exercise 8.

3. Editing, page 372
See the General Suggestions for Editing on page 4.

Read the sentences in the passage aloud and have students correct you when you read an error.

4. Drawing Conclusions, page 373
This exercise provides more information to solve the mystery "The Red-Headed League." Before beginning this exercise, review what the students know so far and then ask them to think of possible conclusions using *may, might,* or *could.* Here are possible questions:

What does Wilson do? (He is a shop owner and he worked as a copier of the encyclopedia for the
  Red-Headed League.)
What is unusual about his job at the Red-Headed League? (The job is useless and pays very well. The
  criterion for employment—being red-headed—is absurd.)
Why did Wilson ask Holmes for help? (because he didn't understand the note he received)
What did the note say? (The Red-Headed League didn't exist.)
Does he have an assistant in his shop? (yes)
What is unusual about the assistant? (He works for only half pay and spends much of his time in
  the basement.)
Why would the assistant put the Red-Headed League job advertisement in the paper? (to be alone in
  the shop every day for four hours)
Why would his assistant have holes in the knees of his trousers? (He must be digging a tunnel.)
Why would the assistant dig a tunnel? (Answers will vary.)

Point out that a wanted poster is put up by the police when looking for a criminal. The map is of the neighborhood around Wilson's shop. Before beginning the exercise, have students look at the map and point out Wilson's shop.

5. It's Got to Be, page 374
Answers to these exercises will vary. As students call out their answers, write them on the board so that the class may see the various possibilities.

6. Speculations, pages 374–375
This exercise contrasts certainty (*must*) with uncertainty (*might*). Point out that when a question uses the verb *be*, its answer requires the verb *be*.

7. Maybe It's the Cat, page 375
This exercise contrasts possibility (*can / could*) with impossibility (*can't / couldn't*). After students have completed the exercise ask, *Who do you think it could be?*

COMMUNICATION PRACTICE (pages 376–378)

8. Listening, page 376
See the General Suggestions for Listening on page 4.

This exercise provides the conclusion to the mystery "The Red-Headed League." Have students read the statements before they listen. After playing the tape twice, check students' answers. If students disagree, play the segment in question again.

9. Tell-Tale Signs, pages 376–377
See the General Suggestions for Pair and Group Activities on page 4.

Point out that statements based on evidence (for example, the A+ grade) lead to a *must* conclusion. (*He must be a very good student.*) Statements based on unseen information use *may, might,* or *could*.

Have students work individually to interpret the illustrations, and then have them form small groups to compare their ideas. Have each group share its interpretations with the class.

10. Possible Explanations, page 377
See the General Suggestions for Pair and Group Activities on page 4.

Divide the class into pairs. Have each pair come to a conclusion about the situation and then share their ideas with the class.

11. What Could It Be?, page 378
See the General Suggestions for Pair and Group Activities on page 4.

Divide the class into small groups. Give a time limit of five minutes for the groups to think of at least five possibilities. Invite students to share their ideas with the class. Ask, *Is there a consensus? Can the class draw a conclusion?*

12. Writing, page 378
See the General Suggestions for Writing on page 5.

After brainstorming possibilities in small groups, have students individually write a paragraph explaining their conclusions. Have them submit their writing to you for correction.

Copy on the board examples of errors found in students' writing. Have students identify the errors and correct them.

EXPANSION

Mystery Stories: Ask students to think of a favorite mystery story. It could be one they read or one they saw in the movies or on television. Have students create a story map with the title of the story, a list of the major characters and a description of each, the setting, the major events in the story, and the conclusion. Then have students use their story maps to retell the story to classmates or to write a summary of the story.

REVIEW OR SELFTEST

See the General Suggestions for Review or Self Test on pages 5–6.

FROM GRAMMAR TO WRITING:
COMBINING SENTENCES WITH *BECAUSE, ALTHOUGH, EVEN THOUGH*

See the General Suggestions for From Grammar to Writing on page 6.

In this section, students practice combining sentences using subordinating conjunctions as they learn how to write a letter of complaint. Students then share their writing in pairs and give each other feedback using a chart.

Introduction, page 383
Write the two example sentences on the board. Ask students, *How can I connect these two sentences using the conjunction* even though? *Where do I place the comma?* Have students connect the sentences. Explain that by combining sentences with subordinating conjunctions, you make the text more connected and coherent.

Have students read the introductory text.

Exercise 1, page 383
You may want to introduce the concept of a letter of complaint. Ask the class, *Have you ever had a good reason to complain about poor service? What happened? Did you complain?*

Have students read the entire letter once before circling the correct conjunctions. Then have them reread the text and identify subordinate clauses and main clauses.

If students have difficulty choosing conjunctions, have them first look at items 1 and 2 of Exercise 2 to define the meaning of each conjunction.

Exercise 2, page 384
Go over students' answers as a class.

Exercise 3, page 384
See the General Suggestions for Role Plays on page 5.

Have the pairs report to the class as you write their ideas on the board. Have students return to their partners to develop a role play based on one of the situations. Have students act out the role play extemporaneously for fluency practice and then perform their role play for another pair. Have these groups of four brainstorm what to say in a letter of complaint.

Exercise 4, page 384
Have students write their letters at home.

Exercise 5, page 384
Before exchanging letters, have students look at the chart. Explain that they will give each other feedback using the chart.

Have students exchange letters and give each other feedback. Have the writers read the feedback and incorporate any new information into their final draft.

PART VIII NOUNS AND ARTICLES

 **UNIT 37 NOUNS AND QUANTIFIERS**

GRAMMAR **IN CONTEXT** (page 388)

See the General Suggestions for Grammar in Context on page 2.

Before You Read, page 388: Have students read the questions, look at the photograph and map, and share their responses with the class.

Reading, page 388: Ask the following comprehension questions:

Did Thor Heyerdahl believe Columbus was the first explorer to discover America? (No. He believed it's possible ancient people came first.)
What kind of boat did he build? (a reed boat as seen in ancient Egyptian paintings)
Did they take modern food supplies with them on the journey? (No. They took only traditional Egyptian food supplies)
Who sailed with him? (an international group)
Did the Ra *make it across the Atlantic?* (almost)
Did they try again? (Yes. *Ra II* successfully crossed the Atlantic in 1970.)

Focus on Grammar: Write the headings *Proper Nouns, Count Nouns,* and *Non-count Nouns* on the board. Elicit examples of the highlighted words from the reading and, with student input, write them under the appropriate column headings. Ask the following questions:

Which of these nouns are capitalized? (proper nouns)
What do these proper nouns describe? Can you classify them? (people, places, months, and nationalities)
Which nouns are only in the singular form? (non-count nouns)
What words come before the non-count nouns in the reading? (enough, some, a little)

GRAMMAR **PRESENTATION:** Nouns and Quantifiers (pages 389–392)

See the General Suggestions for Grammar Presentation on page 3.

NOTES 1 AND 2: To help students distinguish between the proper nouns and common nouns, call out a common noun and have students work in pairs to brainstorm proper nouns they associate with the noun. For example:

Continents (South America, North America, Australia, Africa, Europe, Asia, and Antarctica)

Other categories could be *holidays, nationalities, explorers, cities, countries on a particular continent, tourist destinations,* or *national parks*.

NOTE 3: Have students identify count nouns in the classroom as you write the list on the board. Point to various count nouns and ask, *How many _____ are there in our classroom?* This exercise illustrates that count nouns are indeed countable.

NOTE 4: Have students work in pairs to generate three more examples for each category of non-count nouns and have them share their lists with the class. For example:

Abstract words (love, curiosity, intelligence)
Activities (running, fishing, studying)

Have the class brainstorm countable nouns that are examples within the categories of non-count nouns listed separately in this note. Write them on the board. For example:

Advice (suggestions, recommendations, thoughts)
Furniture (chair, bed, table)

NOTE 5: Read the note in the Student Book with the class. Answer any questions.

NOTE 6: Provide additional examples contrasting *a few* with *few* and *a little* with *little*, for example:

I have a few dollars to contribute. (I don't have a lot of money, but I have enough to contribute.)
I have few dollars to contribute. (I barely have enough money to contribute.)

She has a little time to spend with her parents. (She doesn't have a lot of time, but she has enough to spend time with her parents.)
She has little time to spend with her parents. (She doesn't have enough time to spend with her parents.)

FOCUSED PRACTICE (pages 393–396)

See the General Suggestions for Focused Practice exercises on pages 3–4.

1. Discover the Grammar, page 393
Play the tape and have students write down all the adjectives they hear. Then have students compare their lists with a partner and listen again before they actually read the dialogue and underline the words. Go over students' categories of nouns by writing their answers on the board.

For a follow-up discussion, ask, *Would you like to take a trip like Tina Arbeit's? Why or why not?*

2. Making Plans, page 394
Have students listen once to the dialogue with books closed. Ask:

What kinds of food are good to bring camping?
What other items do they plan to bring?

Then have students open their books and fill in the blanks. Remind students that the verb of a non-count noun is singular. Have students listen to the tape again to check their answers.

3. Happy Campers, pages 395–396
Before beginning the exercise, ask the class, *What advice would you give to campers?* Write students' ideas on the board.

For a follow-up discussion, ask, *Do you have any interesting travel stories to tell the class?*

4. Editing, page 396
See the General Suggestions for Editing on page 4.

Have students do this for homework, or read the passage aloud and have students correct you when you read an error.

COMMUNICATION PRACTICE (page 397)

5. Listening, page 397
See the General Suggestions for Listening on page 4.

Have students read the list of ingredients before they listen. After playing the tape twice, check students' answers. Play the tape a third time so that students may complete the shopping list. If students disagree, play the segment in question again.

6. Desert Island, page 397
See the General Suggestions for Pair and Group Activities on page 4.

Give students a generous time limit of twenty minutes to work out their plans. Have all groups present their decisions and rationales to the class.

7. Writing, page 397
See the General Suggestions for Writing on page 5.

Have students submit their first draft to you. Return it with suggestions for improvements. When students have completed their final drafts, have them share their writing in groups along with photographs of their trips. Then invite them to put their stories and photos on a class bulletin board for display.

EXPANSION

Favorite Recipes: Ask students to share a favorite recipe with the class. With students, brainstorm the major categories of foods. Show students several examples of the way recipes are written. Discuss measurements and terms commonly used. Then ask students to write out their recipes, listing the ingredients and quantities first and then describing the steps in making the recipe. Tell students to note which category of food dishes the recipe belongs in. Students may want to enter the recipes into a computer and make a class recipe book.

GRAMMAR **IN CONTEXT** (page 398)

See the General Suggestions for Grammar in Context on page 2.

BACKGROUND NOTE: Video games are popular all over the world. They are so popular in Japan that the government has asked video stores not to release new games until after school has been dismissed for the day. Otherwise, some students miss school in order to buy new games. Because of this intense popularity, there is rising concern among educators and parents about the effects on children of playing these games.

Before You Read, page 398: Have students read the questions, look at the illustration, and share their responses with the class.

Reading, page 398: Ask the following comprehension questions:

What role does the player have in this game? (The player is a magician.)
What does the player have at the beginning? (The player has some gold and some weapons.)
What does music do? (It tells you when Zado is near, and it signals your new magic power.)

Focus on Grammar: Write on the board the following excerpts and ask the questions.

"*An* evil magician from a universe beyond ours . . . .
    The magician is Zado."

Are there many possible evil magicians in the world? (yes)
How do you know? (because of the indefinite article *an*, which means one of many)
Who is the specific magician the advertisement describes? (Zado)

"You have <u>some</u> gold. . . . You can use <u>the</u> gold to buy tools."
In the text, which sentence comes first? (You have some gold.)
The second time the gold is mentioned, there is a definite article. Why? (because we now know exactly which gold is being talked about)

GRAMMAR **PRESENTATION**: Articles: Indefinite and Definite (pages 399–401)

See the General Suggestions for Grammar Presentation on page 3.

NOTE 1: Collect several small classroom items and put them into categories, for example, pens, pencils, books, keys, paper clips, backpacks. With a student volunteer, secretly identify one item from each category to work with. Give instructions to the student for all the class to hear:

Juan, pick up the backpack and put it on the chair.
Put the book into the backpack.
Put the pencil on top of the backpack.

Point out to the class that both you and Juan knew which backpack, book, and pencil was meant. Therefore you used the definite article with each noun.

For contrast, choose another student and give the same instructions, but this time without conferring. Point out that the second student cannot carry out the instructions without further information. Then give the instructions with enough information to identify the objects. For example:

Pick up the red backpack. Put it on the wooden chair.
Put the smallest book in the backpack.
Put the red pen on top of the backpack.

Point out that with these descriptive phrases, both the speaker and the listener know which item is being referred to.

NOTES 2–4: Read the notes in the Student Book with the class. Answer any questions.

NOTE 5: Give additional examples of how the context determines whether the item is definite or indefinite. For example:

Please open the door. (There is only one door.)
Please open a window. (There is more than one window.)
Point to the teacher. (There is only one teacher.)
Point to a student. (There is more than one student.)

NOTE 6: Use pictures from magazines to present and practice first and second mention. Use a picture with many people or items. Introduce several people or items, and then make statements about them. For example:

There's a man standing in the corner.
There are two women in the middle of the room.
<u>*The*</u> *man is looking at* <u>*the*</u> *women.*

Elicit more examples from students. Make sure to include non-count nouns.

NOTE 7: Read the note in the Student Book with the class. Answer any questions.

NOTE 8: Play a game to demonstrate and practice classification with singular and plural count nouns. Put small objects on the desk and cover them with a piece of cloth. Have students feel the objects through the cloth and guess what they are. For example:

I think it's an apple.
They're pencils.

To practice classifying with non-count nouns, have students identify materials and substances in the classroom. Point to an object in the classroom and ask, *What is this material?* Then have students practice by asking each other in a chain game. For example:

Student 1: (Points to a paper clip.) *What is this material?*
Student 2: *I think it's metal.* (Points to the desk top.) *What is this material?*
Student 3: *I think it's plastic.*

NOTE 9: Give examples of likes and dislikes to practice generalizations. Elicit other examples from students. For example:

I like football but not baseball.
I like opera. I don't like heavy metal.

FOCUSED PRACTICE (pages 402–405)

See the General Suggestions for Focused Practice exercises on pages 3–4.

1. Discover the Grammar, page 402
As you go over the answers, have students explain their rationales.

2. Games People Play, page 402
You may want to help students identify the rationale for each answer:

1. unique noun (Note 4)
2. indefinite (Note 1)
3. indefinite (Note 1)
4. first mention (Note 6)
5. first mention (Note 6)
6. proper noun (Unit 37, Note 1)
7. second mention (Note 6)
8. first mention (Note 6)
9. second mention (Note 6)
10. clear from context (Note 5)
11. classifying statement (Note 8)
12. indefinite (Note 1)
13. defining adjective (Note 5)
14. unique noun (Note 4)

3. Fun and Games, page 403
To review answers, have pairs of students act out the conversations for the class.

4. Scary Rides, page 404
Remind students not to use *the* in general statements. You may want to help students identify the rationale for each answer:

1. general statement (Note 9)	7. not specific (Note 2)
2. specific (Note 3)	8. general statement (Note 9)
3. defining adjective (Note 5)	9. general statement (Note 9)
4. specific (Note 3)	10. specific (Note 3)
5. general statement (Note 9)	11. defining adjective (Note 5)
6. not specific (Note 2)	12. specific (Note 3)

To review answers, have a pair of students act out the conversation for the class.

5. Person, Place, or Thing?, pages 404–405
Have the class look at the illustrations and identify each one before filling in the blanks.

6. Editing, page 405
See the General Suggestions for Editing on page 4.

Have students do this exercise for homework, or read the passage aloud and have students correct you when you read an error.

Follow up with these questions:
What was unique about Donkey Kong?
How did it change the industry of video games?

COMMUNICATION PRACTICE (pages 406–409)

7. Listening, page 406
See the General Suggestions for Listening on page 4.

Have students read each exercise before they listen. After listening twice, go over students' answers. Then have students do the second half of the exercise. Go over the answers with the class.

8. Quiz Show, page 406
See the General Suggestions for Pair and Group Activities on page 4.

You may want to model this activity for the class. Ask several students to volunteer to leave the classroom for three minutes. Tell the class they are going to generate clues for _____ (an interesting or famous thing). Write their clues on the board. Invite the volunteers back into the room. Have various students give the clues. Can they guess the answer? Model several times before having groups do the activity.

9. Information Gap: Story Time, pages 407 and 409
Divide the class into pairs. Assign each partner a role (A or B). Assign Students A page 407 and Students B page 409. Have students read their separate instructions and look at their illustrations. Explain that the illustrations are the same, but each is lacking certain information. Have students refer to the language provided above each illustration as they ask and answer each other's questions to complete the missing information. Remind them not to show each other their illustrations until they are finished with the task.

Alternatively, for lower-level students, divide the class into Groups A and B. Have each group make questions about the missing information in their assigned illustration. Circulate between the two groups and help as needed. Pair students from Groups A and B. Have them ask and answer each other's questions.

10. Writing, page 408
See the General Suggestions for Writing on page 5.

In pairs, have students look at the two pictures and brainstorm possible story lines. For homework, have students write their stories. In class, have students share their stories in small groups and give each other feedback. Have students rewrite their stories, incorporating feedback from students, and submit them to you for review and correction.

Designing a Theme Park: Have students work with partners or in small groups to design a theme park. Students can prepare maps or drawings showing how they would organize the major attractions. Plan to help students with vocabulary. Suggest that students consider what types of rides they would include. Suggest that they think of names for the rides. What types of food would they sell? Where would the food stands or restaurants be located? What names would they give the restaurant(s)? What about restrooms? What about souvenirs? What would the overall theme of the park be? Later, you may want to display students' work.

REVIEW OR SELFTEST

See the General Suggestions for Review or Self Test on pages 5–6.

FROM GRAMMAR TO WRITING: THE FORM OF AN ESSAY

See the General Suggestions for From Grammar to Writing on page 6.

In this section, students read an essay and identify its title and organization. Using an outline, students develop their own ideas for an essay on an important holiday. After composing their essays, students give each other feedback in peer sessions.

Introduction, page 413
Have students read the opening paragraph about essays.

Exercise 1, page 413
Alternatively, students can take turns reading the essay aloud and then decide as a class the most appropriate title.

Exercise 2, page 414
Have students work individually to complete the outline. Wording in this exercise can vary. As students call out their answers, write them on the board so that the class may see the various possibilities.

Exercise 3, page 414
Have students compose their outlines at home and then work with a partner to share ideas. Encourage students to ask for details about the holidays.

Exercise 4, page 414
Have students write their essays at home.

Exercise 5, page 414
Before exchanging letters, have students look at the chart. Explain that they will give each other feedback using the chart. Have students exchange their letters and give each other feedback. Have the writers read the feedback and incorporate any new information into their final draft.

TAPESCRIPT

UNIT 1 EXERCISE 6, PAGE 10. LISTENING.

INTERVIEWER: Today's the end of your first week of classes here. How do you feel?

MARIA: Pretty good. Things are going well. Everyone is friendly, and I'm learning a lot.

INTERVIEWER: You're living in a new country, a new culture. What's the most difficult part?

MARIA: Well, there are many changes. The language is the biggest. Right now I'm speaking English, of course. At home I speak Spanish all the time.

INTERVIEWER: Where in Mexico do you come from?

MARIA: A very small town in Durango.

INTERVIEWER: And now you're living in a big city.

MARIA: That's right. It's very different. The pace of life, especially.

INTERVIEWER: The pace of life. What do you mean?

MARIA: When I'm in Mexico, I walk slowly. Everyone does. People never seem in a hurry. But here, everyone moves very quickly.

INTERVIEWER: And what about you?

MARIA: I find myself moving quickly, too. And I'm wearing a watch!

INTERVIEWER: You don't usually wear a watch?

MARIA: No. But people here expect you to arrive exactly on time, so I don't want to be late. Oops, speaking of late, I'd better go. My next class starts in exactly five minutes.

INTERVIEWER: What are you studying?

MARIA: Computer sciences. This is something new for me, too. Back in Mexico, I study history.

INTERVIEWER: Well, thank you very much for your time, and good luck!

MARIA: Thank you.

UNIT 2 EXERCISE 5, PAGE 16. LISTENING.

Good morning, and welcome to "Cooking Light and Easy"—where we cook healthy food that tastes delicious. I'm Danny Morgan, and today I'm going to show you an easy and healthy breakfast that everyone loves—pancakes.

To start with, beat two egg whites in a large bowl. . . . Don't overbeat. You just need to beat them a little bit . . . like this.

Now, measure one and a quarter cups of flour—you can use white flour, but I prefer to use whole wheat flour.

Add the flour to the beaten egg whites, like this. . . . OK.

Now we're going to add a cup of milk. Again, you can use regular milk, or you can use low-fat milk. I'm adding milk with 2% fat. . . .

Mix thoroughly. . . . Again, don't overmix. . . . That looks right. . . .

At this point we can add some fruit. Any kind of fruit works well. Today I have some nice fresh blueberries, so I'm going to blend those in like this. . . .

Now we're ready to heat a frying pan and melt a small piece of butter in it. You could use margarine, but I prefer the taste of real butter, and you really only need to use a little bit . . . like that. OK.

The butter is melted and the pan is nice and hot, so I'm going to gently pour some of the pancake mixture into the frying pan . . . just like this. In about two to three minutes, you'll see little bubbles forming on the outside edge of the pancakes. That means it's time to flip the pancakes over . . . like this. Good. That's nice and brown. . . .

Now wait a few minutes to allow the other side to brown, too, and then remove it from the pan. . . . These look beautiful. Top them with more fruit or yogurt, and you and your family are in for a real treat!

If you want a copy of this recipe, send a self-addressed stamped envelope to WCTV or get a free copy at our Web site at www.litecooking.com. See you tomorrow with some more recipes that are "light and easy"!

UNIT 3 EXERCISE 5, PAGE 27. LISTENING.

JANA: Good morning. You're listening to "Literary Notes." With us in the studio today is prize-winning poet Murat Veli. Welcome.

MURAT: Thank you, Jana. It's a pleasure to be here.

JANA: Murat, in your poetry, you often write about your memories of Turkey. Were you born there?

MURAT: Yes, I was. But I came to the United States in 1980, when I was ten. My parents came here in 1975—five years before me. They found jobs and bought a house. Then I joined them.

JANA: Who did you live with between 1975 and 1980?

MURAT: With my grandparents. Our family farm is in Sivas, in central Turkey. I missed my parents, of course, but my life with my grandparents was wonderful. My grandmother told stories, and she knew hundreds of riddles. Very entertaining for a little boy.

JANA: So then, in 1980, you left Turkey and joined your parents in the U.S.

MURAT: That's right. We lived in Baltimore. You know, Jana, I hated the city at first. I had no freedom. I rode a school bus instead of my grandfather's horses. I had no friends. So . . . I read. I escaped into books.

JANA: When did you start to write poetry?

MURAT: Well, first, you know, I wrote stories in Turkish all the time, from when I was only six or seven. But I wrote my first poem when I was twelve. I wrote poetry in English.

JANA: Did you study poetry in school?

MURAT: No, I didn't. In college I majored in farming—agriculture. But I wrote every day.

JANA: You won an award for your poetry at a very young age. When was that?

MURAT: That was in 1992. A year after I graduated from college.

JANA: What do you do when you *aren't* writing poetry?

MURAT: I teach it! I became a teacher in 1994, and I've been teaching since then. When I'm not farming, that is.

JANA: We have to pause for a break. When we return, Murat Veli will read one of his poems.

UNIT 4 EXERCISE 5, PAGE 35. LISTENING.

BETSY: Do you ever think back, say, ten years ago? We were so different then.

ROSA: Ten years?

BETSY: Yeah, I don't know about you, but when I was a little kid my life was really different. You know what I mean? I always used to get up really early, and I never used an alarm clock. Today, without an alarm clock, forget it. I'd never wake up.

ROSA: You're telling me. I can hardly get up *with* the alarm clock.

BETSY: No kidding! And I remember, as soon as I woke up, I used to have a huge breakfast. I mean huge—cereal, eggs, toast, the works.

ROSA: Me, too. These days we're lucky if we have time for a quick cup of coffee and a brief look at the newspaper.

BETSY: Really! And when we were kids we had endless energy. I used to run from morning to night. Now I'm exhausted after fifteen minutes of aerobics.

ROSA: We'd better stop talking like this. Imagine in another ten years. . . . What will we say we used to do then?

EXERCISE 3, PAGE 42. A TRAFFIC ACCIDENT

REPORTER: What was the cause of the accident, officer?

OFFICER: Well, it looks like there were many causes. First of all, when the accident occurred, the driver was driving much too fast. The driver is a suspect in a burglary, and she was leaving town. While she was driving, she was speaking to someone on her car phone. When she saw the pedestrian, she immediately stepped on the brakes, but it was too late. The victim wasn't paying attention, either. First of all, he didn't wait for the traffic light to change. He was crossing against a red light when the car hit him. He didn't see the approaching car because he was talking to his friend. The friend wasn't paying attention, either. He was eating an ice cream cone while he was crossing the street. When he noticed the car, he tried to push his friend out of the way, but it was too late.

REPORTER: How is the victim doing?

OFFICER: Well, when the ambulance arrived, he was bleeding from a head wound, but the doctors stopped the bleeding and they think he'll be OK.

EXERCISE 6, PAGE 44. LISTENING.

OFFICER: Did you see the accident, miss?

WITNESS: Yes I did, officer.

OFFICER: Can you tell me what happened?

WITNESS: I'll try, but it all happened so quickly . . .

OFFICER: That's OK, just tell me what happened.

WITNESS: Well, I was walking down the street when I heard this car honking. The driver was driving much too fast. In fact, I'm sure he was speeding. The two men were just starting to cross the street. They were talking to each other and not paying attention to traffic. I guess they noticed something when the driver honked. They started to run, but, um, the car was moving too fast and was much too close to stop. That's how they got hit.

EXERCISE 4, PAGES 53–54. RADIO CALL-IN QUESTIONS.

CALLER 1: Hello, Professor Vroom. My question is this: Will the car of the future run on gasoline?

VROOM: No, it won't. It will probably use solar energy. Thanks for calling. Next?

CALLER 2: I had a flat tire yesterday. I was wondering, will we still get flat tires on these future cars?

VROOM: No, we won't. In fact, by the year 2010, flat tires will be a thing of the past. Tires will have a special seal so they'll repair themselves automatically.

CALLER 3: Sounds great. In what other ways will the car of the future be different?

VROOM: Well, instead of keys, cars will have smart cards. These will look a lot like credit cards. They'll open doors, and they'll adjust the seats, mirrors, and steering wheels. They'll even control the inside temperature.

CALLER 3: Will they help prevent car thefts?

VROOM: Yes, they will! OK, next caller?

CALLER 4: Hello. I'm curious. How much will these cars cost?

VROOM: I don't know exactly, but they certainly won't be cheap.

UNIT 6 EXERCISE 6, PAGE 55. CHOOSE THE FUTURE.

JASON: I just heard the weather report.

ARIEL: Oh? What's the forecast?

JASON: It's going to rain tomorrow.

ARIEL: Oh, no. I hate driving in the rain. And it's a long drive to the Car Show.

JASON: Wait! I have an idea. We'll take the train instead!

ARIEL: Good idea! Do you have a train schedule?

JASON: Yes. Here's one. There's a train that leaves at 7:00 A.M.

ARIEL: What about lunch? Oh, I know, I'll make some sandwiches for us to take along. I don't like train food.

JASON: Sounds good. You know, it's a long trip. What are we going to do all those hours?

ARIEL: Don't worry. We'll think of something.

JASON: You know, we have to get up really early.

ARIEL: That's true. I think I'll go home now.

JASON: OK. I'll see you tomorrow. Good night.

UNIT 6 EXERCISE 7, PAGE 56. LISTENING.

1. **A:** I'm glad it's Friday. Let's go home.
   B: What are you doing tonight?
   A: The usual. I'm just staying home and watching TV.

2. **A:** Hi, Pete. What are you watching?
   B: Oh, it's a program about cars of the future. It's pretty interesting. Want to watch with me?

3. **A:** There's a phone call for Professor Vroom.
   B: Oh. He's working on his speech for the Car Show next week. Can you take a message?

4. **A:** There's a lecture at the Y tonight.
   B: Really? What's it on?
   A: Some professor's talking about the use of robots in the home. Do you want to go?

5. **A:** I wish I could go to the lecture, but my parents are flying in from Florida.
   B: Oh. Are you going to meet them at the airport?
   A: No. They're going to take a taxi to my place.

6. **A:** Excuse me. What time does the train to New Haven leave?
   B: The train to New Haven? It leaves at 2:05. You'd better hurry, it's two o'clock.
   A: Oh. Thanks.

EXERCISE 4, PAGE 63. LISTENING.

MAN: Jobs Are Us. How can I help you?

WOMAN: Do you have any jobs for people with word-processing skills?

MAN: Yes. Have you had any experience?

WOMAN: No, not really. I just graduated from college. But I have taken some word-processing classes.

MAN: OK. Do you have a resume?

WOMAN: Yes, I do.

MAN: Fine, why don't you mail or fax us your resume. As soon as we receive it, we'll set up an interview at our office.

WOMAN: OK. What happens then?

MAN: Well, after we interview you, you'll take a word-processing test. Then as soon as we score your test results, we'll arrange for you to speak with one of our job counselors. Together we'll determine the best kind of position for you.

WOMAN: Will you send me on interviews at different companies?

MAN: Yes. But before we send you to any companies, you'll probably receive some more job training.

WOMAN: I see. Do you have any written information about your agency that you could send to me?

MAN: Yes. I'll send you one of our brochures as soon as I get off the phone.

WOMAN: Thank you. And I'll send you my resume.

EXERCISE 4, PAGE 70. LISTENING.

1. I saw . . . at the restaurant.
2. The . . . car hit the truck.
3. It happened at . . .
4. . . . mother called me.
5. I reported it to . . .
6. There were . . . shouts.
7. . . . saw the man.
8. I have to hang up now because . . .

EXERCISE 2, PAGES 89–90. THE OFFICE PARTY.

1. **A:** Listen, guys! The food and drinks are over here. Please come and help yourselves.
   B: Thanks. We will.
2. **A:** Isn't that the new head of the accounting department over there?
   B: I think so. Let's go over and introduce ourselves.
3. **A:** I'm really nervous about my date with Nicole after the party. I cut myself twice while shaving, and then I lost my car keys.
   B: Come on. This is a party. Just relax and be yourself. You'll do fine.
4. **A:** What are you giving your boss for the holidays this year?
   B: We always give each other the same holiday gifts. Every year I give him a book and he gives me a scarf.

5. **A:** What do you think of the new computer program?

   B: I'm not sure. In our department, we're still teaching ourselves how to use it.

6. **A:** Jessica looks upset. Didn't she get a promotion?

   B: No, and she keeps blaming herself. I'll lend her that article about self-talk.

7. **A:** The Aguayos are going to Japan on vacation this year.

   B: Are they going by themselves or with a tour group?

8. **A:** This was a great party.

   B: Yeah. We really enjoyed ourselves.

UNIT 9 EXERCISE 5, PAGE 92. LISTENING.

1. **A:** Mark's department did a great job this year.

   B: I know. They're really proud of each other.

2. **A:** What's wrong? You look upset.

   B: I just heard Ed and Jeff talking. You know Ed blames himself for everything.

3. **A:** I hear you're going to Japan on vacation this year. Are you going by yourself or with a tour?

   B: Oh, with a tour.

4. **A:** Hillary looks happy tonight. Did Meredith give her the promotion?

   B: No, not yet. Meredith keeps asking herself if she can do the job.

5. **A:** How do you like the new computer system?

   B: I'm not sure. In our department, we're still teaching ourselves how to use it.

6. **A:** So long, now. Thanks for coming. It was good to see you.

   B: Oh, it was a great party.

   A: I'm glad you enjoyed yourselves.

UNIT 10 EXERCISE 7, PAGE 102. LISTENING.

1. **FEMALE STUDENT:** What's Terry doing?

   MALE STUDENT: She's handing out some lab reports.

2. **MALE TEACHER:** Are you done with your report, Rea?

   FEMALE STUDENT: Almost. I just have to look up some information.

3. **FEMALE STUDENT:** Hey, guys. That music is disturbing us.

   MALE STUDENT: Sorry. We'll turn it off.

4. **FEMALE STUDENT:** Jason is discouraged.

   MALE STUDENT: I know. He says he can't keep up in class.

5. **FEMALE STUDENT:** Did you hear about Lila?

   MALE STUDENT: Yes. We were all surprised when she dropped in yesterday.

6. **MALE TEACHER:** OK, class. It's time to take off your lab coats.

   FEMALE STUDENT: Oh, could we have a few more minutes? We're almost done.

UNIT 11 EXERCISE 6, PAGE 121. LISTENING.

ANNE: Our office is very busy, Karl. We get a lot of phone calls.

KARL: Oh, that's no problem. I can handle the phones.

ANNE: Good. Can you speak any other languages? Many of our students are foreign.

KARL: Well, I used to be able to speak Spanish, but I'm out of practice now.

ANNE: That's OK. Maybe with a little practice, you'll be able to get along. Now, what about computer skills? Can you use the computer?

KARL: Yes. I can do word processing and spreadsheets.

ANNE: How fast can you type?

KARL: Fifty words per minute.

ANNE: That's good. Can you do any desktop publishing? We're thinking of designing a monthly newsletter.

KARL: Well, I can't right now. But I *am* taking a course in desktop publishing, so I imagine I'll be able to do it pretty soon.

ANNE: You also have to schedule appointments. Many of our students take private dance lessons.

KARL: I can do that.

ANNE: Let's see. What else? Oh, can you drive?

KARL: Sure.

ANNE: That's good. I might need you to do some errands from time to time.

KARL: No problem.

ANNE: Oh! As you can hear, one of our classes is beginning right now. Can you dance, Karl?

KARL: No, but I hope I'll be able to take some classes here if I get the job.

UNIT 12 — EXERCISE 5, PAGE 132. LISTENING.

1.   MAN: May I see your driver's license please?

    WOMAN: Certainly. Here it is.

2.   GIRL: Mom, can I leave the table now? I'm finished eating, and I want to watch TV.

    WOMAN: No, you can't. Not yet. I want you to wait until we're all finished.

3.   WOMAN: I feel awful. I've got a headache, and I'm sick to my stomach. Do you mind if I leave work now?

     MAN: Not at all. Go home and get some rest.

4. YOUNG MAN: Hi, Mrs. Carter. This is Jeff. May I speak to Linda?

    WOMAN: Hi, Jeff. I'm sorry, Linda's sleeping. Could I take a message?

5.   WOMAN: This is Globe Travel, Mr. Sanchez. Have you decided what day you want to leave for Chicago?

     MAN: No, I haven't. Could I tell you tomorrow? I need to talk to my wife first.

    WOMAN: I'm sorry, but I'm afraid I have to know today. This is the last day I can book your flight.

UNIT 13 — EXERCISE 5, PAGE 140. LISTENING.

DARA: Hey Mom, can you drive me to the library on Saturday morning? I have a report to do for school.

MARCIA: Sorry, I can't. I'm taking Mark to the dentist on Saturday morning.

DARA: Will you take me in the afternoon?

MARCIA: Sure. We can all go to the library in the afternoon.

SALLY: Hello, Marcia? This is Sally. I have to ask you a big favor. We're going to a party on Saturday night. Could you babysit for us?

MARCIA: I'd like to, but I can't. We're going to the movies Saturday night. Why don't you try Ann? She babysits for us sometimes.

MOM: Hi, Marcia. This is Mom. Listen, we're going away for the day on Sunday. Could you come and walk the dog on Sunday morning?

MARCIA: Sure. I'd be glad to. What time should I come?

MOM: Come at about 8:00. Thanks a lot.

PAT: Hi, Marcia, this is Pat. Are you going to the gym on Sunday afternoon?

MARCIA: Yes, I am.

PAT: Would you mind giving me a ride? My car broke down this week.

MARCIA: Not at all. I'd be glad to.

UNIT 14 EXERCISE 6, PAGE 148. LISTENING.

We only have a few minutes left in class, and we'd better not forget to talk about your final exam. I want to give you some advice about getting ready for an important exam.

You've studied hard, and you're all going to be terrific travel agents. But it's not enough just to study. You have to get ready in other ways, too. First of all, you should get a good night's sleep and get up early so you can eat breakfast. You really ought to have a good breakfast before an examination—it's very important. Also, you'd better leave plenty of time to get here. Don't be late and get caught in traffic. That will upset you during the exam.

Now here are a few tips for taking the exam. When you first get the test paper, take a deep breath and relax. You shouldn't start answering questions right away. Instead, you should read the exam through completely before you write anything. Then pick the easiest sections and do those first. You should try the more difficult sections after you finish the easy ones. Remember, the test is very long and we don't expect anyone to answer all the questions. You shouldn't try to finish it.

See you tomorrow at the exam. And good luck, everybody.

UNIT 15 EXERCISE 4, PAGE 156. LISTENING.

EMILY: Lantau looks beautiful. Why don't we stay overnight? I think there's a hostel on the island.

MEGAN: You're right. According to this map, the S.G. Davis hostel is right over here. And there are quite a few interesting things we could do right around the hostel.

EMILY: Hmmm. How about going to see the Tian Tan Buddah? They say it's the largest seated outdoor Buddha statue in the world.

MEGAN: That sounds good. And it's just a few minutes' walk from here. Oh, look at that. There's a riding school right near the hostel. Maybe we could go horseback riding later on.

EMILY: Oh—I don't like horseback riding. Sorry.

MEGAN: No problem. There's plenty of other things we could do.

EMILY: Let's have lunch at the Tea Gardens Restaurant.

MEGAN: I have another idea. Why don't we spend some time at the Po Lin Monastery? It's supposed to be very beautiful, and we could have lunch there. They serve vegetarian meals all day.

EMILY: That's a good idea! Any ideas for later on?

MEGAN: How about hiking the Lantau Trail?

EMILY: Why don't we do that tomorrow? If we stay at the hostel, we can get up in time to hike the trail and then watch the sunrise at Lantau Peak. It's supposed to be spectacular!

MEGAN: Great idea! Let's get started! We've got a lot to do!

UNIT 16 EXERCISE 6, PAGE 174. LISTENING.

INTERVIEWER: So, tell me, Antonio, how long have you been a sports announcer?

ANTONIO: For twenty years. My first job was with Channel 8 News. I covered tennis and baseball for them. I left in 1990 when the station was sold.

INTERVIEWER: I see. And how many jobs have you had since then?

ANTONIO: Since 1990? Just two. I was a tennis coach for two years, and then I announced sports on radio WQRT until last year. That's when I moved here to Los Angeles.

INTERVIEWER: So you've been here for a year. How do you like it?

ANTONIO: Very much.

INTERVIEWER: Have you worked at all since you moved here?

ANTONIO: No, not since last year. I decided to go back to school. I've been enrolled in the business program at UCLA since September, but I really miss sports announcing. That's why I'd like this job.

UNIT 17 EXERCISE 4, PAGE 181. LISTENING.

HELMUT: Hi, Gisela. It's me.

GISELA: Helmut! I didn't expect to hear from you so soon. Why aren't you having your interview?

HELMUT: I've already had it!

GISELA: Really? I thought they were taping from 10:00 to 12:00. How'd it go?

HELMUT: OK, I guess. They didn't give me much time to speak, though. The whole thing lasted less than two minutes!

GISELA: Two minutes! You're kidding. Well, I want to hear all about it when you get home. What are you going to do now?

HELMUT: Well, believe it or not, I haven't gotten my flu shot yet, so I'm on my way to see Dr. Bellini.

GISELA: I thought you got your shot two weeks ago! I hope you have time to do everything. Have you been to the lab yet?

HELMUT: Uh-huh. I dropped by there before the interview. But I need to read some new article about that banana vaccine research, and I haven't gotten to the library yet.

GISELA: Well, good luck with all your stuff. Oh, and Helmut—don't forget to pick up the film for Rita's birthday party.

HELMUT: I've already done it.

GISELA: Great. And what about the rent check? Have you mailed it yet?

HELMUT: Not yet. I forgot. But I'll do that right now.

GISELA: OK, sweetie. See you later.

HELMUT: Bye.

GISELA: Bye.

URSULA: This is a nice restaurant. Have you had their steak?

JIMMY: No, but I've had the eggplant parmigiana. In fact, I always have that.

URSULA: Then try some of my steak tonight.

JIMMY: Actually, I've stopped eating meat.

URSULA: Are you a Save the Animals person?

JIMMY: Oh, no. It's not that I love animals. I just hate plants. Have you ever really talked to a plant? They have absolutely nothing to say.

URSULA: Right. So, have you ever wanted to live outside of New York?

JIMMY: Outside of New York? Where's that? But seriously, I've never wanted to try any other place. I love it here.

URSULA: But have you ever *traveled* to a different city?

JIMMY: Why should I do that? No, traveling is definitely not for me. You like it here too, right?

URSULA: It's OK, but I've traveled to other places, too. It's a big world out there.

JIMMY: I like it right here. Say, have you made plans for tomorrow night? How about dinner? Same time, same place, same eggplant parmigiana . . .

RECEPTIONIST: Happy Travels. How may I direct your call?

LYNETTE: Jake, please.

TRAVEL AGENT: Hello, this is Jake.

LYNETTE: Hi, Jake, it's Lynnette.

TRAVEL AGENT: Hey, how are you doing?

LYNETTE: I'm working really hard and I need a break. I'm trying to plan a vacation.

TRAVEL AGENT: Sure. How many days can you take?

LYNETTE: Well, let's see. I've just started working on this new show, but I really could use a rest. I guess I'll take six days.

TRAVEL AGENT: OK, that helps. Have you ever been on an organized tour?

LYNETTE: Never. Traveling with a group is not my idea of a vacation. I don't mind a package deal, but no tours.

TRAVEL AGENT: Have you ever been to Europe?

LYNETTE: Yes, several times. I really want to do something I've never done before.

TRAVEL AGENT: OK, I've got the perfect vacation. It's a wonderful vacation to beautiful—

LYNETTE: Hello? Hello?

JOE: Hi, honey! How are you?

MARIA: I'm OK—a little tired, I guess. I only slept a few hours last night. I'm writing this big report for tomorrow's meeting, and I haven't stopped worrying about it all week.

JOE: You need to rest. Listen—maybe I'll come see you this weekend. We've only seen each other twice this month.

MARIA: OK. But I really have to work. Remember the last time you came here? I didn't do any work at all.

JOE: OK. Now, why don't you go make yourself a cup of coffee and just relax?

MARIA: Coffee! You must be kidding! I've already had five cups today. And yesterday I drank at least six. No more coffee for me.

JOE: Well then, get some rest, and I'll see you tomorrow.

MARIA: OK. Good night!

 UNIT 19 EXERCISE 6, PAGE 199. LISTENING.

INTERVIEWER: As you know, we've been interviewing married faculty members. How long have the two of you been married?

MAN: For ten years.

WOMAN: But we lived in different cities for most of that time.

MAN: That's right. It was very hard, I should say impossible, to get a job in the same city.

WOMAN: In fact, this is the first time we've been at the same university since we were graduate students back in Boston.

INTERVIEWER: How long did you live in Boston?

MAN AND WOMAN: Six years.

INTERVIEWER: And how long have you been in Austin?

WOMAN: How long has it been? A year now?

MAN: That's right. We've been here for almost a year. July will be exactly a year.

WOMAN: Yes. We *finally* managed to find jobs in the same city *and* at the same university. It's been great!

MAN: And now that we don't have to pay rent for two apartments, we've been able to buy a house.

WOMAN: We've only had it for a month, and we love it.

MAN: It sure beats driving six hours every weekend to see each other!

UNIT 20 EXERCISE 2, PAGES 204–205. AN INTERVIEW.

INTERVIEWER: How long have you been living on the streets, Mr. Tarver?

MR. TARVER: For almost two years now.

INTERVIEWER: Where do you sleep?

MR. TARVER: It's been pretty warm, so I've been sleeping in the park. But winter will be here soon, and it'll be too cold to sleep outside. I've been worrying about that.

INTERVIEWER: What have you been doing about food?

MR. TARVER: I haven't been eating much lately. Sometimes someone gives me money, and I buy a sandwich and something to drink.

INTERVIEWER: How have you been spending your time?

MR. TARVER: I do a lot of thinking. Recently, I've been thinking a lot about my past and how I ended up without a home.

INTERVIEWER: Do you see any way out of your present situation?

MR. TARVER: I want to work, so I've been looking for a job. I've been reading the want ads every day in the paper, and I've been asking everyone I know for a job.

INTERVIEWER: Any luck?

MR. TARVER: So far, no.

MARTHA: Hi, Dave.

DAVE: Oh, hello, Martha. I've been reviewing your test results. Your computer skills are very good.

MARTHA: Oh, I've been working with computers since I graduated from high school. I've even been tutoring one of the clients here in word processing.

DAVE: That's great. Have you finished your resume?

MARTHA: Yes. And I've been making a list of places to send it.

DAVE: Good. I'll show you how to use the fax machine this morning. Now, let's talk about some practical things. How have you been getting here from the shelter?

MARTHA: I've been walking. The shelter isn't far away.

DAVE: OK. The program can give you bus tickets when you go on interviews. Do you have business clothes?

MARTHA: I've been looking in used clothing stores. I think I found a suit I can afford. But I'm worried about day care. How can I afford that?

DAVE: Um . . . who's been taking care of your children for the last two weeks?

MARTHA: A friend at the shelter. But she's been looking for work, too. What happens when she finds a job?

DAVE: I've been trying to set up a day care program here. Maybe it will be ready when you find a job.

1. **A:** Isn't it awful?
   B: What's so awful?
   A: Haven't you seen it? They've cut down that tree.
2. **A:** You must be so nervous about your safari trip.
   B: Well, we've planned the first few weeks, and we've packed all our stuff.
3. **A:** Isn't the new highway wonderful?
   B: What's so wonderful about it?
   A: Haven't you seen how nicely they've widened the road?
4. **A:** What is Professor Owen doing these days?
   B: She's been writing a book about elephants.
5. **A:** Will she ever stop?
   B: I don't know. She's been eating leaves all morning.

MAGGIE: What's the matter with Alice?

LUIS: Who knows? She's always annoyed about something.

MAGGIE: I know, but this time I'm really puzzled.

LUIS: Really? Why is this time so puzzling?

MAGGIE: Oh, I thought she was happy. She met an interesting man last week.

LUIS: That's nice. Was she interested in him?

MAGGIE: I thought she was. She said they saw a fascinating movie together. So I thought . . .

LUIS: Maybe she was fascinated by the movie, but it sounds to me like she might be disappointed with the guy.

MAGGIE: Maybe you're right. It's hard to tell with Alice. Her moods are always very surprising.

UNIT 22 EXERCISE 6, PAGE 233. LISTENING.

MAN: I found four apartments in today's paper that I think we should take a look at.

WOMAN: Good! Tell me about them.

MAN: Well, they're all two bedrooms in Smithfield, and they all cost between four fifty and five hundred a month.

WOMAN: Sounds good so far.

MAN: Let's see. The first one is described as a large, two bedroom in a new building. It's also near public transportation. It doesn't say anything else about it.

WOMAN: OK.

MAN: Now, the second one has more information. It sounds like it's sunny. It says it's just been painted and in excellent condition. It's also near stores and schools.

WOMAN: That sounds better. What about the other two?

MAN: OK. The third one is described as "cute and cozy."

WOMAN: Uh-oh. You know what that usually means!

MAN: Yeah, it's probably very small.

WOMAN: What else does it say?

MAN: It says it's in a quiet area.

WOMAN: Hmmm. That could mean there are no stores or anything around.

MAN: Maybe. Now, where's that fourth ad I circled? Oh, here it is. OK. This one says the apartment's in a completely renovated building with a modern kitchen and bathroom.

WOMAN: What's wrong with that?

MAN: Nothing. And it's available right away.

UNIT 23 EXERCISE 7, PAGE 243. LISTENING.

WOMAN: How about pizza for dinner?

MAN: Sounds good. Any special brand?

WOMAN: Well here's the frozen food section. Let's see what they have.

MAN: OK . . . there's Di Roma's and there's Angela's. Ever hear of those?

WOMAN: No. How do they compare in price?

MAN: Let's see. Angela's is $5.38, and Di Roma's is $4.41.

WOMAN: Di Roma's is cheaper, but the pizza isn't as big as Angela's.

MAN: Right. Angela's is bigger. You get five and a quarter slices from a Di Roma's pizza, but you get six slices from an Angela's.

WOMAN: Hmmm.

MAN: What are you looking at?

WOMAN: The nutrition information. Listen to this. Angela's uses low-fat cheese, so there are fewer grams of fat.

MAN: Sounds like Angela's is the healthier choice. What else does the label say? What ingredients do they list for the sauce?

WOMAN: Well, in addition to tomatoes and water, Angela's sauce just has basil and black pepper. Di Roma's has basil, oregano, garlic, onions, salt, and pepper.

MAN: Di Roma's sounds a lot tastier.

WOMAN: It's hard to choose. Let's see if there's an expiration date.

MAN: Di Roma's says sell by February 15 of this year.

WOMAN: That's in two weeks! The Angela's says sell by April 15 of next year.

MAN: Then, let's get the Angela's. It's fresher, and we can always add our own spices.

UNIT 24   EXERCISE 6, PAGE 253. LISTENING.

TIMOTHY: Hello! I would like to buy a very special gift for my wife.

SALES CLERK: You've come to the right place. What kind of gift are you looking for?

TIMOTHY: Well, I think . . .

SALES CLERK: Great . . . let me show you what we have. Over here, in the jewelry department, we have a gorgeous bracelet. It looks like real gold, but it's not. It's actually the least expensive gift we have in the store.

TIMOTHY: Actually, I was thinking of something . . .

SALES CLERK: Now, if beauty is not what you're after, but you still want to make it impressive . . . how about this winter coat? She'll feel warm and loved every time she wears it. This is definitely the most practical gift we have.

TIMOTHY: Hmmmmm. She has a winter coat. I want this gift to be very special.

SALES CLERK: OK. Here are two big sellers. You could buy her one of these lovely picture frames and put in any picture you like. Use a funny picture of the two of you, and this could be the silliest gift you've ever seen. You don't seem too excited about that. OK, and then there is the very special gift for that very special person.

TIMOTHY: Yes . . .

SALES CLERK: This basket of soap and bubble bath. Have you ever smelled anything so sweet? This is definitely the sweetest gift. . . . You're not looking for sweet?

TIMOTHY: Well, as I said, I'm looking for something really special. I mean soap and picture frames . . .

SALES CLERK: I've got it! Here is the most romantic gift of all. What's your wife's name?

TIMOTHY: Amalia. . . . But that's just a card you're holding.

SALES CLERK: No, no, no. With this card and less than fifty dollars, you can name a star Amalia, after your wife. Imagine—a real star in the sky that you have named for your wife.

TIMOTHY: You're kidding.

SALES CLERK: I'm not kidding. Just read the brochure. Now, am I right? Is this the most romantic gift you've ever heard of?

UNIT 25   EXERCISE 5, PAGE 260. LISTENING.

And what a race that was, ladies and gentlemen. Up until the last minute, those horses sure had us guessing. Nobody fell asleep during this race, I can tell you that.

Of course, you know that Get Packin' was the winner. He did come in first, but for a long time it looked like Inspired Winner was going to win. He was running as fast as Wild Whirl, and then suddenly he started to run slower and slower. The next thing we knew he was last in line, and he stayed last the rest of the race. Yes, Inspired Winner came in last, while Wild Whirl finished a close second to Get Packin'.

Now Señor Speedy and Exuberant King started running as slowly as two turtles in a sandbox. Then, after the second turn, Señor Speedy took off like lightning. That's all Exuberant King needed to see, and he was off, too. It was amazing. They were moving as fast as any horse can move, but it was too late to catch up. As fast as they were running, they still couldn't catch up with Get Packin' or Wild Whirl. They ran side by side most of the way, but at the end Exuberant King ran a little slower, and Señor Speedy came in third place.

UNIT 26 EXERCISE 4, PAGE 276. LISTENING.

PATIENT: So, doctor, what do you think?

DOCTOR: Well, first of all, you must stop smoking. You should also quit drinking coffee.

PATIENT: What about my weight?

DOCTOR: Avoid losing any more weight. Stay at 160 pounds. That's the perfect weight for you. As for your diet, you eat enough protein, but I suggest eating more complex carbohydrates.

PATIENT: And what about exercise?

DOCTOR: Well, exercise is very important, but avoid running every day. It is too stressful.

PATIENT: But I want to do some form of exercise every day.

DOCTOR: Have you considered riding a bike? Cycling is something you can do every day without harm.

PATIENT: OK. Any other advice?

DOCTOR: Yes. Keep working eight hours a day. Being active mentally and physically is the best thing for you.

UNIT 27 EXERCISE 5, PAGE 283. LISTENING.

Good evening, everyone, and thanks for coming tonight. My name is Latoya Williams, and I want to be your next Student Council president.

I believe that I am the best person for this position because of my experience in working for student government. For two years I have been a class representative to the Student Council. As a representative, I have been successful in bringing many new members into the Council. Elect me president, and I can do much more for you.

First of all, I am opposed to raising student activity fees. We pay the highest student activity fees of any college in this area, and the college plans on raising these fees again this year. I will insist on discussing this issue with the administration.

Second, when I am president you can look forward to eating better. Right now you have to choose between eating school cafeteria food or buying fast foods on campus. We need some more choices— how about some ethnic foods and health foods on campus?

The third and most important issue is campus safety. Many of us want to use the computer labs and libraries at night. However, we are nervous about walking back to our dorms at ten or eleven o'clock. I will ask the school president for more campus security guards on campus at night.

I am experienced, and I will be aggressive about talking to the school administration about student issues. I believe that these three issue—lower fees, better food, and most importantly, greater safety—are going to make a big difference. Vote for me next week and get the campus you deserve.

UNIT 28 EXERCISE 4, PAGE 290. LISTENING.

1. **WOMAN:** I've been married once before. I have a teenage daughter from my first marriage. She and my new husband always used to argue. I really wanted them to discuss their problems, but that was impossible at first.

2. MAN: I guess I'm a slow learner, but I finally learned not to argue with my stepdaughter.

3. WOMAN: Blended families always have a lot to learn. I expected to have problems with my daughter.

4. MAN: But it was much, much worse than we thought. For a while, my stepdaughter refused to talk to me at all. To be honest, sometimes I just wanted her to leave the house for a few hours.

5. WOMAN: I know what you mean. But we always tried to understand her feelings. After all, she didn't choose to live with us. I made that choice for her.

6. MAN: I almost gave up. Then one day, she asked me to go on a family vacation—the three of us went to California.

7. WOMAN: I was amazed. I didn't expect to have a good time, but it was wonderful.

8. MAN: We're still having problems, but we can talk about them now. In fact, sometimes, I'd like her to stop talking for a few minutes.

WOMAN: Oh, come on . . .

UNIT 29 EXERCISE 5, PAGE 296. LISTENING.

Hello, you have reached Lacy's Department Store.

If you are calling from a touchtone telephone, please press 0 now.

To speak to a customer service representative, please press 1 now.

To report a lost or stolen credit card, please press 2 now.

To place an order through our teleservice, please press 3 now.

To ask about billing accounts or merchandise delivery, please press 4 now.

To get information about our locations and hours, please press 5 now.

To listen to this recording again, please press 6 now, and thank you for calling Lacy's.

UNIT 30 EXERCISE 5, PAGE 304. LISTENING.

We're excited to report that our new recreation center is open to the public. The outside areas are all completely accessible by wheelchair, and soon the indoor pool and other indoor areas will be, too.

You'll notice that there are now ramps for all the steps going into the new building. These ramps are gradual enough to use without help. Each door also has an automatic door opener, and it's placed low enough so that you can reach it from a wheelchair.

The old water fountains were too high for everyone to use. We've put in new, lower ones—we know you get thirsty out there on the basketball courts.

Unfortunately, we haven't been able to change the outdoor telephones yet. They are still too high to reach from a wheelchair. However, indoor public telephones are already wheelchair accessible.

Oh—and some important news for you skateboarding dudes! These new entrances are too busy for you to skate around. Check out our new skateboarding park instead. You'll find plenty of challenge there.

UNIT 31 EXERCISE 7, PAGE 313. LISTENING.

INTERVIEWER: So, what types of things do you like to do when you are first starting to date someone?

MARTA: Oh. Well, I enjoy going for long walks. That gives you a chance to get to know the other person.

INTERVIEWER: And what about going dancing?

MARTA: Yes, I love to dance.

INTERVIEWER: Do you ever go bowling?

MARTA: Well, I stopped bowling last year when I sprained my wrist.

INTERVIEWER: I see. I suppose you enjoy movies. Everyone I've interviewed does.

MARTA: Yes, but I refuse to go to a movie on the first few dates. There's not enough time to talk.

INTERVIEWER: Well, what activities *do* you find good for getting to know someone?

MARTA: Well, just last week I was walking home with this guy from class. And we decided to stop and have a pizza. We talked for hours, and I really got to find out a lot about him.

INTERVIEWER: Would you ever invite him to your house for a home-cooked dinner?

MARTA: I've avoided doing things like that, but I don't mind preparing a picnic in the park.

INTERVIEWER: Well, thank you for answering all my questions.

MARTA: You're welcome.

UNIT 32 EXERCISE 6, PAGE 336. LISTENING.

WAITER: Have you decided what you'd like?

ARLENE: What are your specials tonight?

WAITER: We have a fish dinner and a steak dinner.

ARLENE: I think I'll have the fish dinner. What does that come with?

WAITER: Well, you have a choice of soup or a salad.

ARLENE: Hmmm. I think I'd prefer soup to a salad. What kind of soup do you have today?

WAITER: We have onion and tomato. The tomato soup is very good.

ARLENE: I think I'd rather have onion soup.

WAITER: OK, onion soup. And would you prefer rice or potato with your fish?

ARLENE: Could I have a vegetable instead?

WAITER: Sure. We have fresh broccoli today.

ARLENE: I'd rather not have broccoli. I guess I'll have the rice after all.

WAITER: And to drink?

ARLENE: A small soda. I prefer diet soda, if you have it.

WAITER: Yes, we do. And you have a choice of apple pie or ice cream for dessert.

ARLENE: Do you have chocolate ice cream?

WAITER: No, vanilla.

ARLENE: Then I'd prefer the pie.

UNIT 33 EXERCISE 7, PAGE 349. LISTENING.

1. **A:** Should I go left or right at the corner?
   B: You have to turn right. You can't make a left turn here.
2. **A:** Why are you stopping here?
   B: Look at the sign. There are men working.
   A: You don't have to stop. You just have to slow down.

3. **A:** Look. A parking spot. Let's just run in and pick up some groceries.

   B: You can't park here.

   A: Not even for a few minutes?

   B: Nope.

4. **A:** That car is going awfully slow.

   B: Why don't you pass?

   A: I have to wait. I can't pass here. It's not allowed.

5. **A:** Slow down a little. It's starting to rain.

   B: I can't. Look at the speed limit.

   A: But you don't have to drive 55 miles an hour.

6. **A:** You have to stop here.

   B: Why? There's no traffic.

   A: You've got to come to a complete stop when you see this sign.

UNIT 34 EXERCISE 4, PAGE 358. LISTENING.

1. **MAN:** Where's Netta? It's 2:00 already.

   WOMAN: Relax. She isn't supposed to be here until 2:30.

   MAN: Oh, OK. I guess I am a little nervous.

2. **WOMAN:** What's the photographer doing up there? He isn't supposed to take pictures during the ceremony.

   MAN: It's OK. He's just checking the light.

3. **MAN:** Let's go sit down. The ceremony's going to start soon.

   WOMAN: Where do we sit?

   MAN: We're with the bride's family, so we're supposed to sit on the right.

4. **WOMAN:** Here come the bridesmaids now. Ooh, don't they look beautiful!

   MAN: Where's Sophie?

   WOMAN: She'll come in later. She's the maid of honor, so she's supposed to walk behind the bride.

5. **MAN:** I've never been to an American wedding. What are we supposed to say to the bride and groom?

   WOMAN: Tell the bride she looks beautiful. Say "congratulations" to the groom.

   MAN: OK.

6. **MAN:** Why did the usher give me all this rice?

   WOMAN: You're supposed to throw it at the bride and groom when they come out of the church.

   MAN: Really?

UNIT 35 EXERCISE 6, PAGE 365. LISTENING.

And now for the weekend forecast.

A lot of you are still shoveling snow from Wednesday's storm, but take heart. Warm, dry air is moving in from the south. We might see sunny skies and temperatures in the low fifties by Friday.

Plan to get out on Saturday—it's going to be a beautiful day. It will be bright and sunny, and temperatures may reach sixty by Saturday afternoon. There will be some wind, though, with gusts reaching twenty miles per hour, so bring a jacket.

Unfortunately, this beautiful weather won't stay with us for the whole weekend. A new storm front is right behind this good weather. Cold, windy weather could be here again by Sunday afternoon, and there might even be some flurries Sunday evening.

Don't put away the snow shovel yet. Winter is still with us.

 UNIT 36 EXERCISE 8, PAGE 376. LISTENING.

HOLMES:	Dr. Watson, this is Captain Rogers from the Police Department.
CAPTAIN:	How do you do, Dr. Watson? Well, we're all here now. It must be 10:00. Let's go down to the basement.
HOLMES:	You lead, captain. We'll follow you.
CAPTAIN:	The storeroom is in here. Please close the door.
HOLMES:	Let's get comfortable. We may have a long wait.
WATSON:	I'm going to sit on one of these boxes. Uh . . . what's in all these boxes, captain?
CAPTAIN:	Gold. Two months ago, the bank borrowed a large amount of gold from France. There may be 2,000 gold coins in that box, Dr. Watson.
HOLMES::	John Clay must know about this gold. That's why he took the job at Wilson's.
WATSON:	And he invented the Red-Headed League to keep Wilson away from the shop. While Wilson was working at the League, John Clay was digging a tunnel to the bank.
HOLMES:	But Clay just ended the Red-Headed League. So his tunnel has to be finished.
CAPTAIN:	You're right, Mr. Holmes! This floor is hollow. The tunnel has got to be right here, under this floor!
HOLMES:	Did you bring your gun, Watson? John Clay could be dangerous.
WATSON:	Yes, I did. But what is he waiting for? It's after 10:00.
HOLMES:	He may want Wilson to be asleep before he comes.
CAPTAIN:	Shhh! I heard a noise in the tunnel!
HOLMES:	It might be him! Get ready!
CLAY:	Police?!
HOLMES:	How do you do? You must be Mr. John Clay!
CAPTAIN:	You're under arrest, Mr. Clay.

UNIT 37 EXERCISE 2, PAGE 394. MAKING PLANS.

JASON:	There's still a lot of work to do this evening. We have to plan the food for the trip.
MEGAN:	I've been reading this book about camping. There's some good advice about food in it.
JASON:	What does it say?
MEGAN:	We should bring a lot of beans and rice.
JASON:	Potatoes are good on camping trips, too.
MEGAN:	Fresh vegetables are too heavy to carry. Maybe we can get some when we pass through a town.
JASON:	Is the equipment ready? We should go over the checklist.
MEGAN:	I did that. We need some batteries for the radio.
JASON:	Why do we need a radio? I thought we were running away from civilization.
MEGAN:	But the news never stops. I still want to know what's happening.
JASON:	That's OK with me. By the way, do we have enough warm clothing? It gets chilly in the mountains.

MEGAN: That's true. And the cold really bothers me at night.

JASON: But we have warm sleeping bags.

MEGAN: And I have you!

EXERCISE 5, PAGE 397. LISTENING.

JASON: That book you found has a good recipe for cookie bars.

MEGAN: Let's make some and bring them along. What are the ingredients?

JASON: It says two cups of butter.

MEGAN: Hmmm. We don't have that much butter left. We'd better get some more.

JASON: How about brown sugar? We need three cups of that.

MEGAN: We still have a lot of brown sugar. What's next?

JASON: Oatmeal.

MEGAN: We only have a little oatmeal. What else? Is there any flour in this recipe?

JASON: Four cups.

MEGAN: Then there isn't enough flour either.

JASON: We'll also need a cup of cornflakes and some eggs.

MEGAN: OK. We have a lot of cornflakes. How many eggs do we need?

JASON: Eight.

MEGAN: Eight? What are we making, an omelet?

JASON: I'm just reading the recipe. It says eight eggs.

MEGAN: We don't have that many. We only have four.

JASON: The last things are raisins and chocolate chips. I know we have a lot of those.

MEGAN: We ate the chocolate chips last night, remember?

JASON: Oh, yeah.

MEGAN: But you're right. We still have a lot of raisins.

JASON: Why don't you make the list, and I'll go shopping.

EXERCISE 7, PAGE 406. LISTENING.

1. A: Let's go to an amusement park this weekend.
   B: That's a great idea. I haven't ridden a roller coaster in ages.

2. A: Is Mark a manager at Blare Gardens now?
   B: Yes, he is.

3. A: Have you played the video game yet?
   B: No, I haven't. I'm going to right now.

4. A: It's 6:00. Let's pick up the pizza.
   B: OK. Do you want me to go?

5. A: What's that?
   B: It's a new ride. Do you want to try it?

6. A: Look! A shark!
   B: That's not a shark, silly. It's the dolphin from the water show.

DIAGNOSTIC AND FINAL TESTS AND ANSWER KEY

These exams, which are linked to the eight parts of the Student's Book, test the material presented in the Grammar Charts, Grammar Notes, and Focused Practice exercises.

The results of each **Diagnostic Test** enable you to tailor your class to the needs of individual students. The format of both the Diagnostic and Final tests is the same, and all but the final two or three sections of each test are labeled by unit title. This labeling allows you to pinpoint each student's particular strengths and weaknesses. The final sections of each test are called Synthesis; these exercises cover the grammar points of the entire part. Included in the Synthesis section are questions in the format of the Structure and Written Expression sections of the TOEFL.

Students who do well on the part's Diagnostic Test should feel good about their high scores, but they should also realize that knowledge of a language requires communication in open-ended situations. If these students are weak in comprehension or communication skills, they should concentrate on the Listening and Comprehension Practice exercises in the book.

Students who do poorly on the Diagnostic Test will want to divide their time between the Focused Practice and Communication Practice exercises.

Students of diverse skills and abilities can be divided into groups that concentrate on the kinds of exercises they need the most. The teacher can work with the different groups and help each student to overcome his or her weaknesses.

The **Final Test** for each part gives students the chance to make certain that they understand the grammar points presented in the part. The tests are straightforward, and since the format of the Final Test is the same unit by unit as on the Diagnostic Test, the Final Test offers students who have studied the chance to succeed and gain a sense of accomplishment and confidence in their ability to learn and understand grammar.

NOTE: **The Tests, which are perforated so that they can be removed and copied, follow the Answer Key.**

DIAGNOSTIC AND FINAL TESTS
ANSWER KEY

Note: In this answer key, where the contracted form is given, the full form is also correct,
and where the full form is given, the contracted form is also correct.

PART I

Diagnostic Test

I. **(Unit 1: Present Progressive and Simple Present Tense)**
Total: 4 points—1/2 point per item

2. smells
3. share
4. is rising
5. are having
6. is passing
7. takes
8. is looking
9. eat

II. **(Unit 1: Present Progressive and Simple Present Tense)**
Total: 19 points—1 point per item

2. Do . . . need
3. do
4. want
5. don't drink
6. 'm dying
7. are . . . doing
8. are . . . calling
9. Do . . . have
10. don't
11. don't like
12. think
13. suppose
14. cause
15. are
16. Are
17. 'm not
18. 's crying
19. 's ringing
20. finish

III. **(Unit 2: Imperative)**
Total: 8 points—1 point per item

2. **a.** Get a good night's sleep.
   b. Don't stay up late.
3. **a.** Don't talk during the show.
   b. Stay in your seat during the show.
4. **a.** Stay in the car.
   b. Don't get out of the car.
5. **a.** Follow the pilot's instructions.
   b. Don't put your things in the aisle.

IV. **(Unit 3: Simple Past Tense)**
Total: 10 points—1/2 point per item

2. was born
3. named
4. started
5. didn't want

6. was
7. took
8. began
9. lasted
10. spent
11. went
12. broke out
13. felt
14. wasn't
15. returned
16. became
17. fought
18. published
19. wrote
20. died
21. won

V. **(Unit 3: Simple Past Tense)**
Total: 7 points—1/2 point per item

2. didn't
3. was
4. felt
5. Were
6. wasn't
7. were
8. went
9. had
10. was
11. gave
12. did . . . get
13. did
14. were
15. chose

VI. **(Unit 4: *Used to*)**
Total: 4 points—1 point per item

2. People didn't use to travel very much for pleasure.
3. People used to tell stories and play games in the evening.
4. Rita used to play softball.
5. Bob used to write articles for the school newspaper.

VII. **(Unit 5: Past Progressive and Simple Past Tense)**
Total: 12 points—1 1/2 points per item (1/2 point for each clause; 1/2 point for correct use / nonuse of comma between clauses)

2. . . . I fell down, I scraped my knee.
3. A storm started . . . we were waiting in the ticket line.

4. . . . we were waiting in the popcorn line, the movie started.
5. . . . we were looking for a seat, a man yelled, "Sit down!"
6. The movie screen suddenly went black . . . we were watching the movie.
7. . . . the lights came on, the manager explained, "The film broke."
8. . . . were going home, we rented a movie at a video store.
9. We watched the video on TV . . . we got home.

VIII. (Unit 6: Future)
Total: 4 points—1/2 point per item

2. I'll go
3. It's going to be
4. will you be
5. I'll make
6. I'm going to make
7. I'm going
8. I'll take
9. you'll understand

IX. (Unit 7: Future Time Clauses)
Total: 6 points—1/2 point per item

2. a. won't leave
   b. call
3. a. receives
   b. 'll send
4. a. 'll send
   b. is
5. a. 'll listen
   b. drive
6. a. know
   b. will be
7. a. weighs
   b. 'll take

X. (Unit 8: *Wh-* questions: Subject and Predicate)
Total: 6 points—1 point per item

2. Why did Ted come
3. Who(m) did you see
4. What was Arnie wearing
5. What happened
6. What did Sylvia spill
7. How did she feel

XI. (Units 1–8: Synthesis)
Total: 8 points—1 point per item

2. D   5. C   8. C
3. A   6. B   9. B
4. D   7. C

XII. (Units 1–8: Synthesis)
Total: 12 points—1 point per item

2. C   6. D   10. B
3. B   7. B   11. D
4. D   8. C   12. A
5. B   9. C   13. B

PART I

Final Test

I. (Unit 1: Present Progressive and Simple Present Tense)
Total: 4 points—1/2 point per item

2. sounds
3. passes
4. is taking
5. is sharing
6. rises
7. have
8. is going off
9. see

II. (Unit 1: Present Progressive and Simple Present Tense)
Total: 19 points—1 point per item

2. Is . . . raining
3. is
4. pours
5. Do . . . have
6. don't
7. 'm wearing
8. bothers
9. love
10. don't want
11. prefer
12. Do . . . hear
13. don't
14. don't hear
15. think
16. 's crying
17. Is . . . coming
18. is
19. 's getting
20. needs

III. (Unit 2: Imperative)
Total: 8 points—1 point per item

2. a. Walk on the sidewalk.
   b. Don't pick the flowers.
3. a. Don't feed the large animals
   b. Keep your hands away from the cages.
4. a. Don't go into the kitchen.
   b. Be polite to your waitperson.
5. a. Speak softly.
   b. Don't eat or drink.

IV. (Unit 3: Simple Past Tense)
Total: 10 points—1/2 point per item

2. died
3. took
4. spent
5. went
6. didn't stay
7. was
8. worked
9. became
10. wrote
11. didn't have
12. moved
13. were
14. returned
15. bought
16. published
17. won
18. was
19. read
20. said
21. didn't know

V. (Unit 3: Simple Past Tense)
Total: 7 points—1/2 point per item

2.	didn't	9.	did . . . go
3.	Did . . . call	10.	slept
4.	did	11.	were
5.	didn't answer	12.	did . . . want
6.	was	13.	wanted
7.	got	14.	wasn't
8.	went	15.	slept

VI. (Unit 4: *Used to*)
Total: 4 points—1 point per item

2. Bob used to write poetry.
3. He didn't use to tell people about his poems.
4. We didn't use to worry about time.
5. People didn't use to drive as much.

VII. (Unit 5: Past Progressive and Simple Past Tense)
Total: 12 points—1 1/2 points per item (1/2 point for each clause; 1/2 point for correct use / nonuse of comma between clauses)

2. . . . the earth moved, the lights went out.
3. The electricity went out . . . we were reviewing the simple past tense.
4. . . . we were sitting in the dark, my heart was beating very fast.
5. We went outside . . . the earth stopped moving.
6. . . . we were standing in the yard, the school principal came out.
7. Many parents arrived . . . the principal was speaking to the students.
8. I felt relieved . . . I saw my father.
9. . . . my father and I were driving home, we saw the damage from the earthquake.

VIII. (Unit 6: Future)
Total: 4 points—1/2 point per item

2.	We're going to go	6.	rises
3.	I'm going to be	7.	will win
4.	I'm going to make	8.	I'll go
5.	are studying	9.	I'm going

IX. (Unit 7: Future Time Clauses)
Total: 6 points—1/2 point per item

2.	a. won't come	5.	a. finish
	b. finishes		b. will be
3.	a. will feel	6.	a. 'll bring
	b. takes		b. hits
4.	a. see	7.	a. will retire
	b. 'll tell		b. turns

X. (Unit 8: *Wh-* Questions: Subject and Predicate)
Total: 6 points—1 point per item

2. What time / When did they go out?
3. Where did the lights go out?
4. Why did they go out?
5. What were Suzy and Bob doing when the lights went out?
6. Who lit some candles?
7. How long did they play chess by candlelight?

XI. (Units 1–8: Synthesis)
Total: 8 points—1 point per item

2.	A	5.	D	8.	C
3.	B	6.	B	9.	A
4.	C	7.	D		

XII. (Units 1–8: Synthesis)
Total: 12 points—1 point per item

2.	C	6.	D	10.	C
3.	D	7.	A	11.	D
4.	D	8.	C	12.	B
5.	B	9.	C	13.	B

PART II

Diagnostic Test

I. (Unit 9: Reflexive and Reciprocal Pronouns)
Total: 15 points—1 point per item

2.	yourself	10.	each other
3.	herself	11.	themselves
4.	each another	12.	yourselves
5.	yourselves	13.	ourselves
6.	myself	14.	yourself
7.	itself	15.	themselves
8.	each other		(each other)
9.	himself	16.	himself

II. (Unit 9: Reflexive and Reciprocal Pronouns)
Total: 25 points—1 point per item

2.	himself	10.	me
3.	you	11.	himself
4.	me	12.	yourself
5.	myself	13.	themselves
6.	you	14.	themselves
7.	itself	15.	herself
8.	yourself	16.	each other
9.	myself	17.	each other's

18. each other
19. me
20. you
21. myself
22. yourself

23. each other
24. our
25. ourselves
26. each other

III. (Unit 10: Phrasal Verbs)
Total: 30 points—2 points per item

2. got up
3. found out
4. talked over
5. wrote down
6. sign up
7. got back
8. lie down
9. woke up

10. eat out
11. dressed up
12. picked out
13. called up
14. went on
15. stayed up
16. get together

IV. (Unit 10: Phrasal Verbs)
Total: 10 points—1 point per item

2. turn it in
3. drop him off
4. turn it on
5. take them back
6. turn it down

7. Look them up
8. pay her back
9. call it off
10. point them out
11. pick you up

V. (Units 9–10: Synthesis)
Total: 10 points—1 point per item

2. B
3. A
4. D
5. A

6. D
7. B
8. C

9. C
10. B
11. D

VI. (Units 9–10: Synthesis)
Total: 10 points—1 point per item

2. D
3. C
4. D
5. B

6. C
7. A
8. B

9. B
10. C
11. D

PART II

Final Test

I. (Unit 9: Reflexive and Reciprocal Pronouns)
Total: 15 points—1 point per item

2. each other
3. themselves
4. herself
5. each other

6. yourself
7. myself
8. each other
9. ourselves

10. yourself
11. himself
12. yourselves
13. themselves

14. itself
15. each other
16. themselves

II. (Unit 9: Reflexive and Reciprocal Pronouns)
Total: 25 points—1 point per item

2. each other
3. himself
4. him
5. yourself
6. you
7. myself
8. ourselves
9. himself
10. themselves
11. himself
12. himself
13. itself
14. you

15. ourselves
16. myself
17. each other
18. me
19. you
20. yourself
21. myself
22. myself
23. themselves
24. each other
25. each other's
26. each other

III. (Unit 10: Phrasal Verbs)
Total: 30 points—2 points per item

2. put off
3. get together
4. get along
5. find out
6. left out
7. grew up
8. pointed out
9. came along

10. keep up
11. showed up
12. pick out
13. turned down
14. get back
15. clears up
16. comes out

IV. (Unit 10: Phrasal Verbs)
Total: 10 points—1 point per item

2. drop you off
3. laid them off
4. try them on
5. fill it out
6. shut them off

7. work them out
8. wake me up
9. Turn it down
10. threw them away
11. bring it up

V. (Units 9–10: Synthesis)
Total: 10 points—1 point per item

2. C
3. B
4. C
5. A

6. C
7. A
8. D

9. C
10. C
11. A

VI. (Units 9–10: Synthesis)
Total: 10 points—1 point per item

2. D
3. A
4. B
5. C

6. D
7. B
8. D

9. C
10. A
11. C

Part III

Diagnostic Test

I. **(Unit 11: Ability: *Can, Could, Be able to*)**
Total: 16 points—2 points per item

2. Could . . . hold
3. can't meet
4. can help
5. can understand
6. couldn't stick
7. to be able to exercise
8. can fit
9. 'll be able to stay

II. **(Unit 12: Permission: *May, Could, Can, Do you mind if . . . ?*)**
Total: 6 points—2 points per item

2. May I take an early lunch break today?
3. Do you mind if I sit next to you?
4. Can we change the radio station?

III. **(Unit 13: Requests: *Will, Would, Could, Can, Do you mind . . . ?*)**
Total: 8 points—2 points per item

2. Could you please trim the rose bushes?
3. Would you mind driving your grandfather to the clinic?
4. Will you take out the trash, please?
5. Would you please pick up the clothes at the cleaner's?

IV. **(Unit 14: Advice: *Should, Ought to, Had better*)**
Total: 8 points—1 point per item

2. Everyone ought to ~~taking~~ [take] a hurricane warning very seriously.
3. You'd ~~not better~~ [better not] leave your pets outside during a bad storm.
4. People ~~not should~~ [shouldn't] turn off their radios.
5. You shouldn't ~~being~~ [be] outside when the storm hits.
6. You ought [to] stay away from the windows.
7. ~~You~~ [You'd] better take care of yourself.
8. Everyone should ~~stays~~ [stay] inside until the hurricane is over.
9. Also, people ~~would~~ [had] better stay calm.

V. **(Unit 15: Suggestions: *Let's, Could, Why don't . . . ?, How about . . . ?*)**
Total: 8 points—1 point per item

2. Why don't
3. going
4. could
5. how about
6. Why not
7. take
8. let's not
9. How about

VI. **(Units 11–15: Synthesis)**
Total: 16 points—2 points per item

2. A
3. C
4. B
5. A
6. D
7. D
8. A
9. B

VII. **(Units 11–15: Synthesis)**
Total: 12 points—1 point per item

2. A
3. C
4. C
5. B
6. C
7. A
8. D
9. C
10. B
11. D
12. C
13. A

VIII. **(Units 11–15: Synthesis)**
Total: 12 points—1 point per item

2. C
3. C
4. A
5. C
6. A
7. B
8. C
9. A
10. B
11. B
12. C
13. A

IX. **(Units 11–15: Synthesis)**
Total: 14 points—1 point per item

2. B
3. B
4. C
5. A
6. B
7. C
8. B
9. C
10. A
11. B
12. C
13. C
14. D
15. B

Part III

Final Test

I. **(Unit 11: Ability: *Can, Could, Be able to*)**
Total: 16 points—2 points per item

2. 'll be able to cook
3. can make
4. 'll be able to have
5. could cook
6. can't cook
7. be able to invite
8. couldn't do
9. can cook

II. **(Unit 12: Permission: *May, Could, Can, Do you mind if . . . ?*)**
Total: 6 points—2 points per item

2. Do you mind if I pour myself a little more coffee?
3. May we borrow your camera?
4. Could I ask you some questions?

III. **(Unit 13: Requests: *Will, Would, Could, Can, Would you mind . . . ?*)**
Total: 8 points—2 points per item

2. Would you pick up the kids at school, please?
3. Could you take the VCR to the repair shop, please?
4. Can you please empty the dishwasher?
5. Would you mind mopping the kitchen floor?

IV. **(Unit 14: Advice: *Should, Ought to, Had better*)**
Total: 8 points—1 point per item

2. If there is a tornado warning in your area, you ~~don't should~~ *shouldn't* panic.
3. First, you should ~~to~~ get out of your car.
4. You'd better *not* ~~to~~ be outside when the tornado hits.
5. If you're outside, you ought to ~~lies~~ *lie* down on the ground.
6. If your house has a basement, you ~~would~~ *'d* better move to the basement.
7. People ought to ~~staying~~ *stay* away from windows or glass doors.
8. If possible, you'd better ~~to~~ get under a heavy piece of furniture.
9. Everyone should ~~stays~~ *stay* inside until the tornado passes.

V. **(Unit 15: Suggestions: *Let's, Could, Why don't . . . ?, Why not . . . ?, How about . . . ?*)**
Total: 8 points—1 point per item

2. could
3. make
4. How about
5. call
6. not
7. Why not
8. How about
9. Why don't

VI. **(Units 11–15: Synthesis)**
Total: 16 points—2 points per item

2. C
3. B
4. B
5. A
6. B
7. C
8. B
9. A

VII. **(Units 11–15: Synthesis)**
Total: 12 points—1 point per item

2. C
3. D
4. C
5. D
6. C
7. B
8. D
9. C
10. B
11. B
12. C
13. A

VIII. **(Units 11–15: Synthesis)**
Total: 12 points—1 point per item

2. C
3. A
4. B
5. B
6. B
7. A
8. C
9. B
10. A
11. A
12. A
13. C

IX. **(Units 11–15: Synthesis)**
Total: 14 points—1 point per item

2. C
3. B
4. A
5. A
6. B
7. C
8. C
9. B
10. C
11. D
12. A
13. D
14. C
15. C

PART IV

Diagnostic Test

I. **(Unit 16: Present Perfect: *Since* and *For*)**
Total: 6 points—1 point per item

2. for
3. since
4. for
5. since
6. for
7. since

II. **(Unit 16: Present Perfect: *Since* and *For*)**
Total: 12 points—1 point per item

2. A: How long have your parents been married?
   B: They've been married for
3. A: Have you and Greg known each other for very long?
   B: We've known each other since
4. A: How long has that tree been in the front yard?
   B: It's been in the front yard for
5. A: Has Bryan played soccer for a long time?
   B: He's played soccer since

6. A: How long has Angie worked as a hospital volunteer?
   B: She's worked as a hospital volunteer since

7. A: Has Elliot been on vacation all week?
   B: He's been on vacation for

III. (Unit 17: Present Perfect: *Already* and *Yet*)
Total: 15 points—1 point per item

2. a. Has . . . gone
   b. already
   c. he has
3. a. Have . . . had
   b. already
   c. I have
4. a. Have . . . gotten back
   b. yet
   c. they haven't
5. a. Has . . . taken
   b. yet
   c. she hasn't
6. a. Have . . . read
   b. already
   c. I haven't

IV. (Unit 18: Present Perfect: Indefinite Past)
Total: 12 points—1 point per item

2. A: Has Mom ever gone to that restaurant on Charles Street?
   B: Yes, she has.
3. A: Have we ever made a special breakfast for her?
   B: No, never.
4. A: Have we ever bought theater tickets for her?
   B: Yes, we have.
5. A: Has Mom ever taken a boat trip?
   B: No, never.
6. A: Have we ever forgotten about Mother's Day?
   B: No, never.
7. A: Has Mom ever complained about her present?
   B: No, never.

V. (Unit 19: Present Perfect and Simple Past Tense)
Total: 8 points—1/2 point per item

2. did you work
3. decided
4. have you played
5. has rung
6. 've had
7. wrote
8. has been
9. Have we met
10. met
11. 've been
12. Did you live
13. did you deposit
14. Did you watch
15. haven't seen
16. went
17. haven't read

VI. (Units 20: Present Perfect Progressive)
Total: 13 points—1 point per item

1. b. 's been spending
   c. 's been doing
2. a. has been answering
   b. 've been ringing
   c. 've been jumping up
3. a. has . . . been snowing
   b. 's been coming
4. a. 've been waiting
   b. has been complaining
   c. has been running
5. a. hasn't been coming
   b. 's been working
   c. 's been sleeping

VII. (Units 21: Present Perfect and Present Perfect Progressive)
Total: 8 points—1 point per item

2. 've been cleaning
3. has been working / has worked
4. 've finished
5. has been going off
6. has been talking
7. has given
8. has been teaching / has taught
9. has . . . lived

VIII. (Units 16–21: Synthesis)
Total: 14 points—1 point per item

2. A	7. D	12. A
3. B	8. A	13. D
4. D	9. B	14. B
5. B	10. D	15. A
6. C	11. C	

IX. (Units 16–21: Synthesis)
Total: 12 points—1 point per item

2. C	6. D	10. C
3. B	7. A	11. A
4. C	8. D	12. B
5. D	9. B	13. D

PART IV

Final Test

I. (Unit 16: Present Perfect: *Since* and *For*)
Total: 6 points—1 point per item

2. for
3. since
4. for

5. For
6. since
7. Since

II. (Unit 16: Present Perfect: *Since* and *For*)
Total: 12 points—1 point per item

2. A: How long has Tony gone to this school?
   B: He's gone to this school for
3. A: Have Ed and Lydia lived here for a long time?
   B: They've lived here since
4. A: How long has that stop sign been at the corner?
   B: It's been at the corner since
5. A: Has George worn an earring for a long time?
   B: He's worn an earring for
6. A: How long has Kate worked as a barber?
   B: She's worked as a barber since
7. A: Have the kids been asleep long?
   B: They've been asleep for

III. (Unit 17: Present Perfect: *Already* and *Yet*)
Total: 15 points—1 point per item

2. a. Has . . . given
   b. already
   c. she has
3. a. Has . . . retired
   b. yet
   c. he hasn't
4. a. Has . . . come
   b. already
   c. it has

5. a. Have . . . decided
   b. yet
   c. we haven't
6. a. Have . . . seen
   b. yet
   c. I haven't

IV. (Unit 18: Present Perfect: Indefinite Past)
Total: 12 points—1 point per item

2. A: Has Joey ever gone to the skating rink on Main Street?
   B: Yes, he has.
3. A: Have we ever taken him to his favorite restaurant?
   B: No, never.
4. A: Have we ever let him pick out a video game at the toy store?
   B: Yes, we have.
5. A: Has Joey ever been to the big amusement park in Centerville?
   B: No, never.
6. A: Have you ever made his favorite dinner?
   B: Yes, I have.
7. A: Have we ever invited all his friends here for a party?
   B: No, never.

V. (Unit 19: Present Perfect and Simple Past Tense)
Total: 8 points—1/2 point per item

2. haven't found
3. have gone out
4. did you live
5. has been
6. didn't hand it in
7. told
8. 've never seen
9. didn't understand

10. snowed
11. have you known
12. came
13. has been
14. were
15. hasn't rung
16. have you been
17. has given

VI. (Unit 20: Present Perfect Progressive)
Total: 13 points—1 point per item

1. b. have been giving
   c. 've been bathing
   d. 's been rolling
2. a. has . . . been doing
   b. haven't been doing
   c. 's been spending
   d. 's been feeling
3. a. have . . . been studying
   b. 've been going
   c. 've been studying
4. a. 've been sitting
   b. have been clearing up
   c. 've been hearing

VII. (Unit 21: Present Perfect and Present Perfect Progressive)
Total: 8 points—1 point per item

2. have been screaming
3. has turned off
4. have seen
5. has been studying
6. has . . . had
7. has been repairing / has repaired
8. hasn't changed
9. have been driving / have driven

VIII. **(Units 16–21: Synthesis)**
Total: 14 points—1 point per item

2. A	**7.** B	**12.** A
3. D	**8.** D	**13.** B
4. A	**9.** A	**14.** B
5. C	**10.** C	**15.** A
6. D	**11.** D	

IX. **(Units 16–21: Synthesis)**
Total: 12 points—1 point per item

2. B	**6.** A	**10.** B
3. B	**7.** B	**11.** A
4. B	**8.** B	**12.** B
5. B	**9.** C	**13.** A

PART V

Diagnostic Test

I. **(Unit 22: Adjectives and Adverbs)**
Total: 10 points—1/2 point per item

2. good	**12.** easy
3. well	**13.** nutritiously
4. hard	**14.** nice
5. interesting	**15.** freshly
6. clearly and thoroughly	**16.** bad
7. beautifully	**17.** extremely
8. completely	**18.** high
9. uncomfortable	**19.** late
10. lately	**20.** important
11. awful	**21.** interesting

II. **(Unit 22: Adjectives and Adverbs)**
Total: 8 points—1 point per item

2. exceptionally inspiring
3. extremely carefully
4. reasonably well
5. really high
6. beautifully poetic
7. unusually low
8. barely acceptable
9. childishly simple

III. **(Unit 22: Adjectives and Adverbs)**
Total: 5 points—1/2 point per item

2. a. amazed   **3. a.** terrified
   b. fascinating   **b.** frightened

4. a. shocking   **6. a.** surprised
   b. distressing   **b.** shocking
5. a. confused
   b. embarrassing

IV. **(Unit 23: Adjectives: Comparatives and Equatives)**
Total: 10 points—1 point per item

2. larger than
3. more nutritious than
4. sweeter than
5. a. bigger than
   b. more expensive
6. more intelligent than
7. a. faster than
   b. more economical
8. a. more popular
   b. better than

V. **(Unit 23: Adjectives: Comparatives and Equatives)**
Total: 10 points—2 points per item

2. . . . were as good as yesterday's (sales).
3. . . . isn't as heavy as the average tiger.
4. . . . isn't as talented as Tina's (dog).
5. . . . isn't as large as Russia's (population).
6. . . . were as popular as romance novels.

VI. **(Unit 24: Adjectives: Superlatives)**
Total: 10 points—1 point per item

1. b. the best
   c. The oldest
2. a. the most expensive
   b. the most popular
   c. the best
   d. the longest
3. a. the most recent
   b. the most boring
   c. the handsomest / the most handsome
   d. the worst

VII. **(Unit 25: Adverbs: Equatives, Comparatives, Superlatives)**
Total: 10 points—1 point per item

1. b. as hard as   **2. a.** the loudest
   c. more closely   **b.** more noisily than
   d. more regularly   **c.** as hard as
   e. more slowly   **d.** more softly
   f. as completely as   **e.** more quietly

VIII. (Units 22–25: Synthesis)
Total: 10 points—1 point per item

2. The apartment uptown is a little bigger
   ~~that~~ *than* the apartment downtown.
3. The downtown apartment is much
   ~~sunnyer~~ *sunnier* than the uptown one.
4. The uptown neighborhood seems more
   ~~interestingly~~ *interesting* than the downtown one.
5. The downtown apartment is on a ~~high~~ *higher*
   floor than the uptown one.
6. That's why it's ~~more quieter~~ *quieter/more quiet*.
7. That's important to me because the
   noiser it gets, *the* ~~,~~ less I sleep.
8. Another consideration is that the
   uptown apartment is very ~~closely~~ *close* to a
   subway stop.
9. That means I'll be able to get to work
   ~~more early~~ *earlier*.
10. The apartment I have now is the ~~cheaper~~ *cheapest*
    of the three.
11. However, it's also *the* ~~,~~ ugliest.

IX. (Units 22–25: Synthesis)
Total: 12 points—1 point per item

2. B	6. C	10. D
3. A	7. A	11. D
4. C	8. C	12. C
5. D	9. D	13. D

X. (Units 22–25: Synthesis)
Total: 15 points—1 point per item

2. B	7. A	12. C
3. A	8. C	13. A
4. B	9. D	14. C
5. C	10. D	15. C
6. C	11. B	16. B

PART V

Final Test

I. (Unit 22: Adjectives and Adverbs)
Total: 10 points—1/2 point per item

2. glad	4. well
3. good	5. nice

6. happy
7. affordably
8. extremely
9. expensive
10. carefully
11. fine
12. hard
13. surprisingly
14. lately
15. usually
16. quiet
17. special
18. wonderful
19. seriously
20. greatly
21. eager

II. (Unit 22: Adjectives and Adverbs)
Total: 8 points—1 point per item

2. extremely excited
3. greatly improved
4. absolutely perfect
5. really quickly/quick
6. totally boring
7. unreasonably strict
8. unusually late
9. terribly upset

III. (Unit 22: Adjectives and Adverbs)
Total: 5 points—1 1/2 point per item

2. a. annoyed
   b. pleased
3. a. embarrassing
   b. inspired
4. a. interested
   b. entertaining
5. a. alarming
   b. terrified
6. a. bored
   b. disappointing

IV. (Unit 23: Adjectives: Comparatives and Equatives)
Total: 10 points—1 point per item

1. b. nicer
2. a. bigger than
   b. larger
3. more dangerous than
4. a. farther
   b. livelier/more lively
5. a. more popular
   b. better
6. more economical than
7. more interesting than

V. (Unit 23: Adjectives: Comparatives and Equatives)
Total: 10 points—2 points per item

2. . . . isn't as old as the system/one in London.
3. . . . is as long as the Jiangyin Bridge.
4. . . . isn't as widely spoken as Hindi.
5. . . . was as successful as our team.
6. . . . wasn't as tall as Lincoln.

VI. (Unit 24: Adjectives: Superlatives)

Total: 10 points—1 point per item

1. **b.** the largest
2. **a.** The highest
   b. the largest
   c. the deepest
   d. longest
3. **a.** The most common
   b. the longest
4. **a.** The heaviest
   b. The fastest
   c. the sleepiest

VII. (Unit 25: Adverbs: Equatives, Comparatives, Superlatives)

Total: 10 points—1 point per item

1. **b.** the most dangerously
   c. faster than
   d. as slow as
   e. the worst
2. **a.** better than
   b. as well as
   c. longer
   d. less
   e. more seriously than
   f. the hardest

VIII. (Units 22–25: Synthesis)

Total: 10 points—1 point per item

2. Gary is a little ~~tall~~ *taller* than Dave.
3. Dave is ~~heavyer~~ *heavier* than Gary.
4. Dave is a much more ~~aggressively~~ *aggressive* boy than Gary.
5. Gary is quieter than Dave, but he expresses himself ~~more~~ better.
6. That's why Gary is a better student ~~that~~ *than* Dave.
7. The ~~big~~ *bigger* the boys get, the more different they become.
8. Dave is starting to become his parents' ~~worsest~~ *worst* problem.
9. Dave's teacher says he's not ^*as* well-behaved as the other students.
10. Also, he isn't working as ~~hardly~~ *hard* as he should.
11. Dave has promised he will work ~~hardest~~ *harder* from now on.

IX. (Units 22–25: Synthesis)

Total: 12 points—1 point per item

2. D   6. A   10. B
3. C   7. B   11. A
4. D   8. C   12. A
5. C   9. A   13. C

X. (Units 22–25: Synthesis)

Total: 15 points—1 point per item

2. B   7. A   12. B
3. A   8. B   13. D
4. C   9. C   14. D
5. D   10. D   15. C
6. B   11. B   16. A

PART VI

Diagnostic Test

I. (Unit 26: Gerunds: Subject and Object)

Total: 10 points—1 point per item

2. **a.** Not going
   b. losing
3. **a.** Bowling
   b. getting together
4. **a.** Staying
   b. running
5. **a.** going
   b. moving
6. **a.** trying
   b. hearing

II. (Unit 27: Gerunds after Prepositions)

Total: 15 points—1 point per item

2. with studying
3. in continuing
4. to graduating
5. (to) being
6. about finding
7. (about) supporting
8. on giving
9. to accepting
10. to feeling
11. to living
12. in making
13. of doing
14. about changing
15. about admitting
16. on entering

III. (Unit 28: Infinitives after Certain Verbs)

Total: 5 points—1 point per item

2. We usually remind them to come to the meetings.
3. That's why we asked to see the menu again.
4. I never expected to wait for an hour, though!

5. That's why she has decided to go to Miami next year, too.
6. In fact, we invited them to visit us at our beach house next weekend.

IV. (Unit 28: Infinitives after Certain Verbs)
Total: 6 points—1 point per item
3. . . . warned his daughter to be home by 10:00.
4. . . . would like her son / him to spend more time with his little sister.
5. . . . promised to call her mother as soon as she gets there.
6. . . . needs to use the car tonight.
7. . . . reminded her mother to sign her report card.
8. . . . advised his daughter / her to finish high school.

V. (Unit 29: Infinitives of Purpose)
Total: 6 points—1 point per item
2. We avoid eating in restaurants in order not to spend a lot of money.
3. Gerry rides a bicycle (in order) to stay in shape.
4. We're wearing heavy coats today in order not to feel cold.
5. I stopped by the post office (in order) to buy stamps.
6. Sylvia uses the Internet all the time (in order) to do research for her clients.
7. The Jacksons are staying home this weekend (in order) to paint the living room.

VI. (Unit 30: Infinitives with *Too* and *Enough*)
Total: 8 points—1 point per item
2. too late to stop
3. old enough to be
4. too noisy for me to concentrate
5. good enough for us to eat
6. too hot for me to eat
7. too heavy for us to carry
8. mature enough to be
9. too hard to give up

VII. (Unit 31: Gerunds and Infinitives)
Total: 10 points—1 point per item
2. trying out
3. competing
4. to change
5. being
6. to apply
7. receiving
8. studying
9. to help
10. to go
11. to give

VIII. (Unit 31: Gerunds and Infinitives)
Total: 4 points—1 point per item
2. to pick up
3. to exercise
4. to pay
5. meeting

IX. (Unit 31: Gerunds and Infinitives)
Total: 6 points—1 point per item
2. a. Swimming is great.
   b. It's great to swim.
3. a. Learning English isn't easy.
   b. It isn't easy to learn English.
4. a. Meeting new people is interesting.
   b. It's interesting to meet new people.

X. (Units 26–31: Synthesis)
Total: 6 points—1 point per item
2. Don't expect to ~~stopping~~ stop all at once.
3. Avoid ~~to be~~ being with other people who smoke.
4. Remember ~~drinking~~ to drink a lot of water.
5. It's important to ~~getting~~ get a lot of rest, too.
6. Don't be nervous about ~~tell~~ telling people you are quitting.
7. You will get used to ~~be~~ being a nonsmoker sooner than you think.

XI. (Units 26–31: Synthesis)
Total: 12 points—1 point per item
2. C
3. A
4. C
5. D
6. C
7. B
8. A
9. D
10. C
11. D
12. C
13. B

XII. (Units 26–31: Synthesis)
Total: 12 points—1 point per item
2. B
3. D
4. A
5. A
6. A
7. C
8. D
9. C
10. C
11. D
12. A
13. D

PART VI

Final Test

I. (Unit 26: Gerunds: Subject and Object)
Total: 10 points—1 point per item

2. a. arguing
   b. discussing
3. a. feeling
   b. Being
4. a. Not going
   b. allowing
5. a. translating
   b. signing up
6. a. cooking
   b. making

II. (Unit 27: Gerunds after Prepositions)
Total: 15 points—1 point per item

2. to allowing
3. to seeing
4. of failing
5. to doing
6. on sharing
7. of watching
8. in making
9. without raising
10. to acting
11. on hearing
12. in telling
13. to challenging
14. about describing
15. at speaking
16. in winning

III. (Unit 28: Infinitives after Certain Verbs)
Total: 5 points—1 point per item

2. I remind her all the time to wear her seat belt.
3. Yes. And the librarian would like me to return them immediately.
4. No. I asked to talk to the manager instead of to a salesperson.
5. Yes, and we've invited them to come for dinner tomorrow night.
6. That's why I've encouraged him not to go there again.

IV. (Unit 28: Infinitives after Certain Verbs)
Total: 6 points—1 point per item

2. . . . invited Steve / him to come for dinner on Saturday night.
3. . . . warned the woman / her to slow down.
   . . . promised not to drive that fast ever again.
4. . . . asked Burt / him to stop at the store on his way home.
   . . . agreed to stop at the store on his way home.
5. . . . reminded Patty / her to take her medicine at noon.

V. (Unit 29: Infinitives of Purpose)
Total: 6 points—1 point per item

2. We opened the windows (in order) to let in some fresh air.
3. The Garcias are going to the museum on Saturday (in order) to see the Picasso exhibit.
4. Politicians often appear on TV talk shows (in order) to talk about themselves.
5. I'm going to run into the supermarket (in order) to get a few things.
6. College students use the Internet all the time (in order) to look up information.
7. Allison walks to work (in order) to save money.

VI. (Unit 30: Infinitives with *Too* and *Enough*)
Total: 8 points—1 point per item

2. too delicate to fight
3. too afraid to accept
4. strongly enough for men to obey
5. fast enough to keep up
6. supportive enough for the government to let
7. mature enough to be
8. too emotional to go
9. too complicated for me to understand

VII. (Unit 31: Gerunds and Infinitives)
Total: 10 points—1 point per item

2. spending
3. earning
4. to go
5. to go
6. to take
7. attending
8. to transfer
9. living
10. getting
11. putting

VIII. (Unit 31: Gerunds and Infinitives)
Total: 4 points—1 point per item

2. to meet
3. sending
4. exercising
5. to send

IX. (Unit 31: Gerunds and Infinitives)
Total: 6 points—1 point per item

2. a. Talking during a movie is rude.
   b. It's rude to talk during a movie.
3. a. Listening to music is relaxing.
   b. It's relaxing to listen to music.
4. a. Taking tests is challenging.
   b. It's challenging to take tests.

X. **(Units 26–31: Synthesis)**
Total: 6 points—1 point per item

2. Don't forget to ~~buying~~ *buy* subway tokens.

3. I usually avoid ~~to stay~~ *staying* out late on weeknights.

4. Remember ~~asking~~ *to ask* your teacher about the homework assignment.

5. Don't be nervous about ~~speak~~ *speaking* English.

6. Are you used to ~~live~~ *living* here now?

7. This problem is too hard ~~for doing~~ *to do*.

XI. **(Units 26–31: Synthesis)**
Total: 12 points—1 point per item

2. A	6. A	10. A
3. C	7. C	11. D
4. D	8. B	12. D
5. C	9. C	13. B

XII. **(Units 26–31: Synthesis)**
Total: 12 points—1 point per item

2. C	6. D	10. B
3. B	7. A	11. C
4. C	8. A	12. C
5. D	9. C	13. D

PART VII

Diagnostic Test

I. **(Unit 32: Preferences: *Prefer, Would prefer, Would rather*)**
Total: 12 points—1 point per item

1. **b.** prefer
2. **a.** would . . . rather
   b. 'd rather
3. **a.** Would . . . prefer
   b. prefer
4. **a.** Would . . . prefer
   b. 'd rather
5. **a.** prefers
   b. prefer
6. **'d rather
7. **a.** Do . . . prefer
   b. would prefer

II. **(Unit 32: Preferences: *Prefer, Would prefer, Would rather*)**
Total: 8 points—2 points per item

2. an apartment to a house
3. live in the city than live in the suburbs
4. move to the East Side than live
5. taking public transportation to driving

III. **(Unit 33: Necessity: *Have (got) to, Don't have to, Must, Must not, Can't*)**
Total: 8 points—1 point per item

2. have to	6. don't have to
3. don't have to	7. can't
4. can't	8. don't have to
5. can't	9. have to

IV. **(Unit 33: Necessity: *Have (got) to, Don't have to, Must, Must not, Can't*)**
Total: 4 points—1 point per item

2. must	4. mustn't
3. mustn't	5. don't have to

V. **(Unit 34: Expectations: *Be supposed to*)**
Total: 6 points—1 point per item

2. 's supposed to be
3. are supposed to be
4. were supposed to hand in
5. 's supposed to rain
6. wasn't supposed to tell
7. were supposed to get

VI. **(Unit 35: Future Possibility: *May, Might, Could*)**
Total: 10 points—1 point per item

2. may	7. Are you going
3. will	8. 's starting
4. may	9. Maybe
5. might not	10. couldn't
6. might	11. may not

VII. **(Unit 36: Assumptions: *Must, Have (got) to, May, Might, Could, Can't*)**
Total: 10 points—2 points per item

2. B	4. B	6. C
3. A	5. A	

VIII. **(Units 32–36: Synthesis)**
Total: 10 points—1 point per item

2. You ~~don't~~ *aren't* supposed to arrive late for a wedding.

3. I'm tired, so I ~~wouldn't rather~~ *'d rather not* go out tonight.

4. We don't ~~got~~ *have* to rush, because we have plenty of time.

5. Thomas may not ~~to~~ graduate this year.

6. Would you ~~rather going~~ *rather go / prefer going* to a movie or to a ballgame?

7. I prefer chicken ~~than~~ *to* fish.

8. Sara doesn't ~~has~~ *have* to work tomorrow.

9. If you want to do well in this class, you must ~~studying~~ *study* very hard.

10. Bob ~~has~~ *had* to take his driving test several times, but he finally passed it.

11. Our teacher was supposed to ~~gives~~ *give* us a quiz yesterday, but he didn't.

IX. **(Units 32–36: Synthesis)**
Total: 6 points—1 point per item

2. B	**4.** A	**6.** C
3. C	**5.** B	**7.** C

X. **(Units 32–36: Synthesis)**
Total: 12 points—1 point per item

2. D	**6.** D	**10.** C
3. B	**7.** A	**11.** C
4. C	**8.** B	**12.** D
5. A	**9.** B	**13.** C

XI. **(Units 32–36: Synthesis)**
Total: 14 points—1 point per item

2. C	**7.** A	**12.** A
3. C	**8.** C	**13.** B
4. B	**9.** B	**14.** C
5. C	**10.** D	**15.** D
6. B	**11.** A	

PART VII

Final Test

I. **(Unit 32: Preferences:** *Prefer, Would prefer, Would rather)*
Total: 12 points—1 point per item

1. **b.** prefer
2. **a.** Would . . . rather
   b. 'd prefer
3. **a.** Do . . . prefer
   b. prefer
   c. prefer
4. **a.** Would . . . prefer
   b. prefer
   c. 'd rather
5. **a.** Would . . . rather
   b. 'd prefer
   c. 'd prefer

II. **(Unit 32: Preferences:** *Prefer, Would prefer, Would rather)*
Total: 8 points—1 point per item

2. small cars to large cars
3. drive an automatic than a stick shift
4. buying a Japanese car to buying a European car
5. have a safe car than drive a pretty car

III. **(Unit 33: Necessity:** *Have (got) to, Don't have to, Must, Must not, Can't)*
Total: 8 points—1 point per item

2. has to	**6.** can't
3. doesn't have to	**7.** has to
4. can't	**8.** doesn't have to
5. has to	**9.** has to

IV. **(Unit 33: Necessity:** *Have (got) to, Don't have to, Must, Must not, Can't)*
Total: 4 points—1 point per item

2. must	**4.** must
3. mustn't	**5.** doesn't have to

V. **(Unit 34: Expectations:** *Be supposed to)*
Total: 6 points—1 point per item

2. 's supposed to be
3. are supposed to be able to
4. are supposed to wear
5. was supposed to pick up
6. is supposed to fall
7. were supposed to study

VI. **(Unit 35: Future Possibility:** *May, Might, Could)*
Total: 10 points—1 point per item

2. could	**7.** couldn't
3. Are we going to	**8.** might not
4. couldn't	**9.** may
5. Maybe	**10.** might
6. may not	**11.** might not

VII. **(Unit 36: Assumptions:** *Must, Have (got) to, May, Might, Could, Can't)*
Total: 10 points—2 points per item

2. A	**4.** B	**6.** A
3. C	**5.** C	

VIII. **(Units 32–36: Synthesis)**
Total: 10 points—1 point per item

2. I really ~~must to~~ *must / have (got) to* finish this letter this morning.

3. Oksana knows how to drive, but ~~she~~ *she'd* rather not.

4. What time does he ~~has~~ (have) to go to work today?

5. Do you prefer ~~eat~~ (to eat / eating) a big lunch or a big dinner?

6. The weather ~~is~~ (was) supposed to be beautiful, but it rained all weekend.

7. I don't think Mr. Sato is here today, but he ~~maybe~~ (may be).

8. Mike ~~mayn't~~ (may not) come if he can't get off work early.

9. Do you ~~got~~ (have) to do a lot of homework tonight?

10. ~~May~~ (Could) the children be hiding under the bed?

11. Our neighbors prefer using public transportation ~~than~~ (to) driving.

IX. (Units 32–36: Synthesis)
Total: 6 points—1 point per item

2. C	**4.** C	**6.** A
3. A	**5.** A	**7.** B

X. (Units 32–36: Synthesis)
Total: 12 points—1 point per item

2. D	**6.** C	**10.** A
3. C	**7.** B	**11.** C
4. B	**8.** D	**12.** C
5. C	**9.** B	**13.** B

XI. (Units 32–36: Synthesis)
Total: 14 points—1 point per item

2. D	**7.** C	**12.** D
3. C	**8.** A	**13.** D
4. B	**9.** B	**14.** A
5. A	**10.** C	**15.** C
6. A	**11.** C	

PART VIII

Diagnostic Test

I. (Unit 37: Nouns and Quantifiers)
Total: 9 points—1 point per item / 1/2 point (for each proper noun in 5A)

1. B: Really? My mom and dad were in Asia last month, too.

2. A: When is Ramadan this year?

B: I think it starts in October.

3. A: I like Alicia Bernstein.

B: I do too. She's a really good English teacher.

4. A: Are you busy Saturday?

B: I'll be out of town. I'm going to St. Louis for the weekend.

5. A: When did Europeans first come to America?

B: Most historians think it was a long time before Columbus.

II. (Unit 37: Nouns and Quantifiers)
Total: 19 points—1 point per item

2. a. electricity		**6. a.** any
b. it		**b.** a little
3. a. a few		**c.** a lot of
b. There's		**7. a.** several
c. time		**b.** a little
4. a. windows		**8. a.** much
b. They've		**b.** How much
c. a little		**c.** some
5. a. There's		
b. chocolate		
c. some		

III. (Unit 38: Articles: Indefinite and Definite)
Total: 18 points—1 point per item

2. The	**8.** a	**14.** the
3. a	**9.** The	**15.** some
4. the	**10.** the	**16.** a
5. some	**11.** the	**17.** the
6. the	**12.** the	**18.** the
7. the	**13.** The	**19.** the

IV. (Unit 38: Articles: Indefinite and Definite)
Total: 11 points—1 point per item

1. b. a	**3. a.** a	**5. a.** an
2. a. a	**b.** the	**b.** a
b. a	**4. a.** the	**6. a.** the
	b. the	**b.** the

V. (Unit 38: Articles: Indefinite and Definite)
Total: 8 points—1 point per item

2. the	**5.** The	**8.** the
3. Ø	**6.** The	**9.** The
4. Ø, Milk	**7.** Ø	

VI. (Unit 38: Articles: Indefinite and Definite)
Total: 5 points—1 point per item

2. a. Ø   3. a. Ø   4.   Ø
   b. Ø   b. Some

VII. (Units 37–38: Synthesis)
Total: 10 points—1 point per correction

We're going to the beach soon, but I have a little ~~few~~ time to write this note.

Our ~~H~~hotel room is beautiful.

It's ~~a~~ the nicest place we've ever stayed in.

~~A~~ The pool is lovely, too.

We swam in it yesterday, and the water ~~were~~ was just the right temperature.

After that, we had lunch here in the hotel, and

we met ~~the~~ a man from Centerville.

He's ~~the~~ a pilot, and he travels all over the world.

I know we're going to meet ~~a great deal of~~ a lot of / many interesting people here.

VIII. (Units 37–38: Synthesis)
Total: 10 points—1 point per item

2. C   6. B   9. C
3. B   7. C   10. C
4. A   8. B   11. A
5. A

IX. (Units 37–38: Synthesis)
Total: 10 points—1 point per item

2. C   6. A   9. B
3. C   7. B   10. B
4. D   8. A   11. A
5. B

PART VIII

Final Test

I. (Unit 37: Nouns and Quantifiers)
Total: 9 points—1 point per item

1. B: Really? I've heard that ~~c~~California is a beautiful state.

2. A: My birthday is on ~~F~~friday this year.

B: Why don't we have dinner at the new ~~I~~italian restaurant?

3. A: Which course does ~~p~~professor ~~H~~hugo teach?

B: I think she teaches ~~R~~russian.

4. A: What are you doing for ~~C~~christmas?

B: I'm going to the ~~P~~philippines to visit my family.

5. A: Where did ~~E~~eskimos come from originally?

B: They probably came from ~~A~~asia.

II. (Unit 37: Nouns and Quantifiers)
Total: 19 points—1 point per item

2. a. luggage   6. a. How much
   b. How much   b. a lot of
3. a. water   c. a
   b. is   7. a. enough
   c. It's   b. few
4. a. soil   c. many
   b. corn   8. a. much
   c. beans   b. a little
5. a. There are   c. much
   b. advice
   c. it

III. (Unit 38: Articles: Indefinite and Definite)
Total: 18 points—1 point per item

2. a   8. the   14. the
3. the   9. the   15. The
4. a   10. the   16. the
5. a   11. the   17. the
6. some   12. some   18. an
7. an   13. a   19. the

IV. (Unit 38: Articles: Indefinite and Definite)
Total: 11 points—1 point per item

2. a. an   4. a. a
   b. a   b. the
   c. a   5. an
   d. the   6. a. The
3. a. a   b. the
   b. the

V. (Unit 38: Articles: Indefinite and Definite)
Total: 8 points—1 point per item

2. the   5. The   8. The
3. The   6. The   9. Ø
4. Ø, Water   7. Ø, Video

VI. (Unit 38: Articles: Indefinite and Definite)

Total: 5 points—1 point per item

2. a. Ø   3. a. Ø   4.   Ø
   b. some   b. Ø

VII. (Units 37–38: Synthesis)

Total: 10 points—1 point per correction

Woodrow University is a good school, but our instructors give a great deal of ~~homeworks~~ homework.

I'm taking ~~r~~Russian, ~~m~~Math, and English this semester.

I also have a part-time job, in the evenings and on ~~s~~Saturday; so I have ~~few~~ little time to study.

I'm living in ~~a~~ the same apartment as last year, but I have two new roommates: Ruth and Sumalee.

They're ~~the~~ nursing students.

Our apartment is crowded, but we have ~~an~~ a good arrangement.

Ruth studies in ~~a~~ the kitchen, I study in my bedroom, and Sumalee studies in the living room.

I don't get ~~many~~ much mail these days, so please write soon.

VIII. (Units 37–38: Synthesis)

Total: 10 points—1 point per item

2. B	6. B	10. B
3. A	7. C	11. C
4. C	8. B	
5. A	9. A	

IX. (Units 37–38: Synthesis)

Total: 10 points—1 point per item

2. D	6. A	9. C
3. B	7. A	10. D
4. C	8. A	11. D
5. C		

TESTS

PART I PRESENT, PAST, AND FUTURE: REVIEW AND EXPANSION

DIAGNOSTIC TEST

I. PRESENT PROGRESSIVE AND SIMPLE PRESENT TENSE

Complete each sentence with the present progressive or simple present form of the verb in parentheses.

1. The telephone _____is ringing_____ . Could you answer it, please?
   (rings / is ringing)

2. Oh, we're having stew. Mmm, it _____ wonderful.
   (smells / is smelling)

3. Many identical twins are very close. They _____ the
   (share / are sharing)
   same thoughts and interests.

4. The temperature _____ quickly today. It's already hotter
   (rises / is rising)
   than it was at this time yesterday.

5. Can you call us back later? We _____ dinner.
   (have / are having)

6. Look at the eclipse! The moon _____ in front of the sun, and now it's dark outside.
   (passes / is passing)

7. Sylvia _____ a shower every morning after her exercise class.
   (takes / is taking)

8. The cat _____ at the fish. Don't let her eat it!
   (looks / is looking)

9. In Spain, most people _____ dinner after 8:00 P.M.
   (eat / are eating)

II. PRESENT PROGRESSIVE AND SIMPLE PRESENT TENSE

Complete the conversations with short answers and the present progressive or simple present tense of the verbs in parentheses. Use contractions when possible.

1. **A:** Why _____are_____ we _____stopping_____ here? _____ we
   1. (stop)

   _____ gas?
   2. (need)

   B: Yes, we _____ . And I _____ a cold soda to drink. I usually
   3.   **4. (want)**

   _____ sodas, but right now I _____ of thirst!
   5. (not drink)   **6. (die)**

2. **A:** Hello?

   B: Hi, Terry. It's Pam. How _____ you _____ ?
   7. (do)

   A: I'm fine, thanks. Where _____ you _____ from, Pam?
   8. (call)

B: From my car. _____ you _____ a car phone?
9. (have)

A: No, I _____ . I _____ car phones. I _____ they're
10.   11. (not like)   12. (think)
dangerous.

B: I _____ you're right. They _____ a lot of accidents every
13. (suppose)   14. (cause)
year. What _____ those noises? _____ you OK?
15. (be)   16. (be)

A: No. I _____ . The baby _____ , and someone _____
17. (not be)   18. (cry)   19. (ring)
the doorbell. I never _____ my phone conversations! Good-bye, Pam.
20. (finish)

III. IMPERATIVE

Write an affirmative and a negative imperative for each of the situations. Use the sentences in the box. Use each sentence only once.

> Talk during the show.
> Follow the pilot's instructions.
> ~~Pay attention~~.
> Stay in the car.
> Get a good night's sleep.
> ~~Take a nap~~.
> Put your things in the aisle.
> Stay up late.
> Stay in your seat during the show.
> Get out of the car.

1. In English class: **a.** Pay attention.
   b. Don't take a nap.

2. On the night before an exam: **a.** _____
   b. _____

3. In a theater **a.** _____
   b. _____

4. In a traffic jam: **a.** _____
   b. _____

5. On an airplane: **a.** _____
   b. _____

IV. SIMPLE PAST TENSE

Complete the biography of the Chilean poet Pablo Neruda. Use the simple past tense form of the verbs in parentheses. Use contractions when possible.

Pablo Neruda, one of the world's most popular poets, ____lived____ from 1904 to 1973. He
1. (live)

_____ in Chile, and his parents _____ him Neftali Ricardo Reyes. In 1920,
2. (be born)   3. (name)

he _____ using the name Pablo Neruda because he _____ his father to
    4. (start)   **5. (not want)**

know that he _____ a poet.
               6. (be)

    Early in life, Neruda _____ an interest in politics. His government service
                               7. (take)

_____ in 1927 and _____ most of his life. He _____ six years
 8. (begin)   **9. (last)**   **10. (spend)**

as the Chilean consul in several Asian countries and then _____ to Spain, France, and
                                          11. (go)

Mexico. The Spanish Civil War _____ during Neruda's term in Spain; he
                        12. (break out)

_____ the tragedy of the war, and he _____ the same man after that.
 13. (feel)   **14. (not be)**

When he _____ to Chile in 1945, he _____ a senator; as a senator, he
        15. (return)   **16. (become)**

_____ for human rights in his country.
 17. (fight)

    At the age of twenty, Neruda _____ his most popular book—*Twenty Love Poems*
                                18. (publish)

and a Song of Despair. For the next forty-nine years, Neruda _____ . In 1971, two years
                                                    19. (write)

before he _____ , Pablo Neruda _____ the Nobel Prize for literature.
        20. (die)   **21. (win)**

V. SIMPLE PAST TENSE

Complete the conversation with short answers or the simple past form of the verbs in the box. Use contractions when possible. Use some verbs more than once.

be   choose   come   feel   get   give   go   have

A: <u> Did </u> you <u> come </u> to class Friday?
                              1.

B: No, I _____ . I _____ sick all last week.
               2.   **3.**

     I _____ terrible. _____ you here?
       4.   **5.**

A: No, I _____ here either.
               6.

B: Where _____ you?
                7.

A: I _____ to Centerville. I _____ a job interview at the Tropicana
            8.   **9.**
    Company.

B: How _____ the interview?
                10.

A: Hard! And after the interview, they _____ me a test.
                                     11.

B: So, _____ you _____ the job?
                           12.

A: Yes, I _____ . There _____ lots of other applicants for my job,
              13.   **14.**

    but Tropicana _____ me. I start tomorrow.
                    15.

VI. _USED TO_

Write the underlined information in a different way, using a form of used to.

1. In the nineteenth century, <u>most women didn't go to school.</u>

   Most women didn't use to go to school.

2. Before trains and cars, <u>people didn't travel very much for pleasure</u>.

   _____

3. Before television, <u>people told stories and played games in the evening</u>.

   _____

4. <u>Rita played softball</u> last year and the year before, but she doesn't play anymore.

   _____

5. <u>Bob wrote articles for the school newspaper</u> when he was a freshman, but he doesn't have time this year.

   _____

VII.   PAST PROGRESSIVE AND SIMPLE PAST TENSE

Combine these pairs of sentences. Use the simple past tense or the past progressive form of the verbs. Use commas when necessary.

1. We walked to the movie theater.
   I tripped on the sidewalk.

   While _we were walking to the movie theater, I tripped on the sidewalk._

2. I fell down.
   I scraped my knee.

   When _____

3. A storm started.
   We waited in the ticket line.

   _____ while _____

4. We waited in the popcorn line.
   The movie started.

   While _____

5. We looked for a seat.
   A man yelled, "Sit down!"

   While _____

6. The movie screen suddenly went black.
   We watched the movie.

   _____ while _____

7. The lights came on.
   The manager explained, "The film broke."

   When _____

8. We went home.
We rented a movie at a video store.

While _____

9. We got home.
We watched the video on TV.

_____ when _____

VIII.   FUTURE

Circle the most appropriate form to complete each sentence.

1. **A:** I'm dizzy. I think (I'm going to faint)/ I'll faint.

   B: Come sit down. You'll feel better in a minute.

2. **A:** There's a jazz concert in the park tonight.

   B: Great! I think I'll go / I'm going. I'd like to hear some good music.

3. **A:** Look at that blue sky!

   B: Yes. It's going to be / It will be a beautiful day.

4. **A:** I'm flying to Cairo next week.

   B: Really? When will you be / are you back?

5. **A:** I'm starving. I think I'm making / I'll make a sandwich.

   B: Can you make me one, too?

6. **A:** Do you need anything from the store?

   B: I'd like a loaf of fresh bread. I'm going to make / I make some sandwiches for lunch.

7. **A:** Do you have any plans for this summer?

   B: Yes, I do. I'm going / I'll go to France.

8. **A:** You look tired.

   B: I *am* tired. Maybe I'm taking / I'll take a nap.

9. **A:** I didn't understand the grammar we did today.

   B: Don't worry. Soon you'll understand / you're understanding it.

IX.   FUTURE TIME CLAUSES

Complete the sentences with the correct form of the verbs in parentheses. Use will *where necessary.*
Use contractions when possible.

1. I _____'ll fix_____ that leaky faucet when I _____get_____ home tonight.
   a. (fix)   **b.** (get)

2. Ron _____ here until you _____ .
   a. (not leave)   **b.** (call)

3. When Hassan _____ the contract, he _____ you a copy.
   a. (receive)   **b.** (send)

4. We _____ a repairperson as soon as someone _____ available.
   a. (send)   **b.** (be)

5. I _____ to your tape while I _____ to work tomorrow.
   a. (listen)   b. (drive)

6. Before you _____ it, the holidays _____ here.
   a. (know)   b. (be)

7. The nurse is going to weigh you. After she _____ you, she _____ your
   a. (weigh)   b. (take)
blood pressure.

X.   *WH-* QUESTIONS: SUBJECT AND PREDICATE

Read the answers. Then complete the wh- *questions about the underlined words.*

1. Q: _____Who invited you_____ to a party last weekend?

   A: <u>Hua</u> invited us to a party last weekend.

2. Q: _____ late?

   A: Ted came late <u>because he had to study</u>.

3. Q: _____ there?

   A: I saw <u>Arnie and Sylvia</u> there.

4. Q: _____ ?

   A: Arnie was wearing <u>a white tuxedo</u>.

5. Q: _____ to his tuxedo?

   A: <u>Something awful</u> happened to his tuxedo.

6. Q: _____ on it?

   A: Sylvia spilled <u>tomato juice</u> on it.

7. Q: _____ ?

   A: She felt <u>terrible</u>.

XI.   SYNTHESIS

Circle the letter of the correct answer to complete each sentence.

1. What's the name of that song that's playing? It _____ familiar.   **A B Ⓒ D**
   (A) is sounding   (C) sounds
   (B) will sound   (D) sounded

2. Jason, please _____ give your little sister any soda.   **A B C D**
   (A) doesn't   (C) no
   (B) not   (D) don't

3. I love old movies. That's why I _____ rent videos on the weekends.   **A B C D**
   (A) often   (C) rarely
   (B) seldom   (D) never

4. When we were younger, we _____ play in the playground after school.   **A B C D**
   (A) using   (C) use to
   (B) were used to   (D) used to

5. What time _____ for San Francisco?　　A B C D
   (A) our plane leaves　　　　(C) do we leave
   (B) we leave　　　　　　　　(D) our plane leaving

6. The old factory on the corner was on fire when we _____ by this afternoon.　　A B C D
   (A) are driving　　　　　　(C) drive
   (B) drove　　　　　　　　　(D) driving

7. Whose baseball cap _____?　　A B C D
   (A) that's　　　　　　　　　(C) is that
   (B) that is　　　　　　　　　(D) that

8. Maggie wants to get a job as soon as she _____ next June.　　A B C D
   (A) is graduating　　　　　(C) graduates
   (B) will graduate　　　　　(D) is going to graduate

9. Where _____ to elementary school?　　A B C D

   (A) you go　　　　　　　　(C) you went
   (B) did you go　　　　　　(D) you're going

XII.　SYNTHESIS

Each sentence has four underlined words or phrases. The four underlined parts of the sentence are marked A, B, C, and D. Circle the letter of the ONE underlined part that is NOT CORRECT.

1. I <u>used to</u> <u>going</u> hiking <u>every weekend</u>, but I <u>don't</u> anymore.　　A Ⓑ C D
   　　A　　　　B　　　　　　　C　　　　　　　D

2. <u>When</u> the man <u>came</u> into the store, <u>did</u> he <u>wearing</u> a blue jacket?　　A B C D
   　A　　　　　　B　　　　　　　　C　　　D

3. It <u>rarely</u> <u>is snowing</u> here, but <u>last year</u> it <u>did</u>.　　A B C D
   　　　A　　　B　　　　　　　　C　　　　D

4. <u>There's</u> <u>going to be</u> a play in the park tonight, and I <u>think</u> I <u>go</u>.　　A B C D
   　　A　　　　B　　　　　　　　　　　　　　　C　　　D

5. The lake <u>is</u> very deep on this side, so <u>no</u> <u>swim</u> here: <u>It's</u> dangerous.　　A B C D
   　　　　　A　　　　　　　　　　　B　　C　　　D

6. I <u>used to</u> <u>hate</u> tomatoes, but <u>now</u> <u>I'm loving</u> them.　　A B C D
   　　A　　　B　　　　　　　　　C　　D

7. Kevin <u>usually</u> <u>work</u> in the morning, but <u>this month</u> he's <u>working</u> in the afternoon.　　A B C D
   　　　　　A　　　B　　　　　　　　　　C　　　　　D

8. <u>Were</u> you <u>having</u> dinner when I <u>was calling</u> <u>last night</u>?　　A B C D
   　　A　　　　B　　　　　　　　C　　　D

9. <u>Don't forget</u> to come see me <u>as soon as</u> <u>you'll arrive</u> in Boston <u>next week</u>.　　A B C D
   　　A　　　　　　　　　　　B　　　　C　　　　　　　D

10. <u>Read</u> the directions and <u>looking at</u> the first example <u>before</u> you <u>start</u> the test.　　A B C D
   　A　　　　　　　　　　B　　　　　　　　　C　　　D

11. <u>While</u> we <u>were driving</u> to work <u>this morning</u>, we <u>were seeing</u> a bad accident.　　A B C D
   　A　　　　B　　　　　　C　　　　　　D

12. <u>Whom</u> <u>is going to</u> correct our tests <u>when</u> we <u>finish</u>?　　A B C D
   　A　　　B　　　　　　　　　C　　　D

13. <u>Did</u> you <u>used to</u> live on Central Avenue <u>when</u> you <u>were</u> a child?　　A B C D
   　A　　　B　　　　　　　　C　　　D

PART I PRESENT, PAST, AND FUTURE: REVIEW AND EXPANSION

I. PRESENT PROGRESSIVE AND SIMPLE PRESENT TENSE

Complete each sentence with the present progressive or simple present form of the verb in parentheses.

1. Today is a beautiful day, and many people ___are enjoying___ the weather.
    (enjoy / are enjoying)

2. That song _____ strange. Is there something wrong with the CD player?
    (sounds / is sounding)

3. During a solar eclipse, the moon _____ in front of the sun.
    (passes / is passing)

4. Steve _____ a shower. Can he call you back later?
    (takes / is taking)

5. Dora _____ her apartment with Carol this semester because Carol doesn't have any-
    (shares / is sharing)
    where else to live.

6. In the summer, the temperature _____ quickly in the morning.
    (rises / is rising)

7. We _____ a lot of students in our class this year.
    (have / are having)

8. The car alarm _____. Please go down and find out if the car is all right.
    (go off / is going off)

9. I _____ Ken over there. Let's go say hello.
    (see / am seeing)

II. PRESENT PROGRESSIVE AND SIMPLE PRESENT TENSE

Complete the conversations with short answers and the present progressive or simple present tense of the verbs in parentheses. Use contractions when possible.

1. **A:** Oh, no! The street ___looks___ wet. _____ it _____?
           1. (look)   2. (rain)

    B: Yes, it _____. It _____ every day at this time during rainy season.
                        3.   4. (pour)

    A: _____ you _____ an umbrella?
                              5. (have)

    B: No, I _____, but I _____ my raincoat. Anyway, a little rain
                    6.   7. (wear)

            never _____ me. I _____ to walk in the rain!
                     8. (bother)   9. (love)

    A: Not me! I _____ to get my new dress wet, and I _____ not to get sick.
                       10. (not want)   11. (prefer)

2. **A:** Listen! _____ you _____ something?
                                    12. (hear)

    B: No, I _____. I _____ anything. Oh, wait! I _____
                    13.   14. (not hear)   15. (think)

            someone _____. _____ that sound _____ from
                     16. (cry)   17. (come)

            the apartment upstairs?

    A: Yes, it _____. And it _____ louder. Maybe someone
                     18.   19. (get)

            _____ our help. Let's go find out.
             20. (need)

Diagnostic and Final Tests **153**

III. IMPERATIVE

Write an affirmative and a negative imperative for each of the situations. Use the sentences in the box. Use each sentence only once.

> Speak softly.
> Walk on the sidewalk.
> Go into the kitchen.
> Feed the large animals.
> Pick the flowers.
> Be polite to the waiter.
> ~~Write with a pen.~~
> Eat or drink.
> Keep your hands away from the cages.
> ~~Use a pencil.~~

1. In math class: **a.** _Don't write with a pen._
   b. _Use a pencil._

2. In the park: **a.** _____
   b. _____

3. At the zoo: **a.** _____
   b. _____

4. In a restaurant: **a.** _____
   b. _____

5. In a library: **a.** _____
   b. _____

IV. SIMPLE PAST TENSE

Complete this biography of an American poet, Robert Frost. Use the simple past tense of the verbs in parentheses. Use contractions when possible.

Robert Frost, one of the most popular American poets, _____was born_____ in California
                                                                1. (be born)

in 1874. After his father _____ , his mother _____ her
                              2. (die)   **3. (take)**

family to New England, where Frost _____ most of his life. He
                                          4. (spend)

_____ to Harvard University, but he _____ there
5. (go)   **6. (not stay)**

very long because he _____ sick all the time.
                            7. (be)

    He _____ as a farmer for seven years, and then he
                   8. (work)

_____ a teacher. He _____ poetry, but he
9. (become)   **10. (write)**

_____ much success. In 1912, he and his family _____
11. (not have)   **12. (move)**

to England. Soon several of his poems _____ in print.
                                         13. (be)

In 1915, Frost _____ 14. (return) to the United States and _____ 15. (buy) a farm in New Hampshire. He _____ 16. (publish) many poems and later

_____ 17. (win) four Pulitzer prizes. Frost _____ 18. (be) a wonderful speaker, and he often _____ 19. (read) his poems in public. He

once _____ 20. (say) that poetry "makes you remember what you

_____ 21. (not know) you knew."

V. SIMPLE PAST TENSE

Complete the conversation with short answers or the simple past form of the verbs in the box. Use contractions when possible. Use some verbs more than once.

answer	be	call	get	go	sleep	want

A: _____Did_____ you _____go_____ out last night?
1.

B: No, I _____ . Why? _____ you _____ me?
2.   3.

A: Yes, I _____ . You _____ .
4.   5. (negative)

B: I'm sorry. I _____ really tired when I _____ home from work,
6.   7.

so I _____ to bed early.
8.

A: What time _____ you _____ to sleep?
9.

B: I _____ for twelve hours—from 7:00 P.M. to 7:00 A.M.
10.

A: Wow! You really _____ tired!
11.

B: So why _____ you _____ to speak to me?
12.

A: I _____ to invite you to a movie. It _____ interesting, though.
13.   14. (negative)

I _____ from 8:00 to 10:00 P.M.—in my seat at the movie, instead of in bed!
15.

VI. *USED TO*

Write the underlined information in a different way, using a form of used to.

1. <u>Emily had a good imagination</u> when she was a child, but she doesn't make up stories anymore.

   Emily used to have a good imagination.

2. <u>Bob wrote poetry</u> when he was in high school, but he's not interested in poetry anymore.

   _____

3. <u>He didn't tell people about his poems</u> before, but now he doesn't mind.

   _____

4. In the past, <u>we never worried about time</u>, but now we always feel rushed.

_____

5. <u>People didn't drive as much</u> in the past. They walked more.

_____

VII. PAST PROGRESSIVE AND SIMPLE PAST TENSE

Combine these pairs of sentences. Use the simple past tense or the past progressive form of the verbs. Use commas when necessary.

1. I sat in English class.
The earthquake struck.

_____I was sitting in English class_____ when ___the earthquake struck.___

2. The earth moved.
The lights went out.

When _____

3. The electricity went out.
We reviewed the simple past tense.

_____ while _____

4. We sat in the dark.
My heart beat very fast.

While _____

5. We went outside.
The earth stopped moving.

_____ when _____

6. We stood in the yard.
The school principal came out.

While _____

7. Many parents arrived.
The principal spoke to the students.

_____ while _____

8. I felt relieved.
I saw my father.

_____ when _____

9. My father and I drove home.
We saw the damage from the earthquake.

While _____

VIII. FUTURE

Circle the most appropriate form to complete each sentence.

1. A: What (are we going to do) / will we do today? It's too cold to go outside.

 B: Let's play cards.

2. **A:** Do you have any plans for this weekend?

   B: Yes, we do. <u>We're going to go / We go</u> camping.

3. **A:** I feel strange. I think <u>I'm going to be / I'll be</u> sick.

   B: I'll pull over and stop the car.

4. **A:** What do we need for dinner?

   B: We need some chopped meat. <u>I'm going to make / I make</u> spaghetti sauce tonight.

5. **A:** Martina and I <u>are studying / study</u> for the test every day next week.

   B: That's a great idea.

6. **A:** What time does the sun rise tomorrow morning?

   B: Tomorrow the sun <u>rises / is rising</u> at 5:10.

7. **A:** Do you have any predictions about next year's election?

   B: I think Brown is <u>winning / will win</u>.

8. **A:** There's a time-management seminar next week.

   B: Really? I think <u>I'm going to go / I'll go</u>. I missed the last one.

9. **A:** Do you have any plans for the fall?

   B: Yes. Didn't I tell you? <u>I'm going / I'll go</u> to Mexico for a semester.

IX. FUTURE TIME CLAUSES

Complete the sentences with the correct form of the verbs in parentheses. Use will *where necessary. Use contractions when possible.*

1. When dinner _____is_____ ready, I _____'ll call_____ you.
   a. (be)   b. (call)

2. Bill _____ until he _____ his math assignment.
   a. (not come)   b. (finish)

3. Chris _____ better after he _____ a nap.
   a. (feel)   b. (take)

4. When we _____ the neighbors tonight, we _____ them the news.
   a. (see)   b. (tell)

5. By the time you _____ this course, your grammar _____ excellent!
   a. (finish)   b. (be)

6. We _____ the patio furniture inside before the storm _____ .
   a. (bring)   b. (hit)

7. My grandfather _____ next year—as soon as he _____ 62.
   a. (retire)   b. (turn)

X. *WH-* QUESTIONS: SUBJECT AND PREDICATE

Read the answers. Then write wh- *questions about the underlined words.*

1. **Q:** ___What happened last night?_____

   A: <u>The lights went out</u> last night.

2. **Q:** _____

   A: They went out <u>at about nine o'clock</u>.

3. Q: _____

A: The lights went out <u>all over Miami</u>.

4. Q: _____

A: They went out <u>because there was a big storm</u>.

5. Q: _____

A: Suzy and Bob <u>were playing chess</u> when the lights went out.

6. Q: _____

A: <u>Suzy</u> lit some candles.

7. Q: _____

A: They played chess <u>for hours</u> by candlelight.

XI. SYNTHESIS

Circle the letter of the correct answer to complete each sentence.

1. The World Cup _____ every four years. Where will the next one be?   A (B) C D
    (A) is taking place   (C) was taking place
    (B) takes place   (D) took place

2. When you were a child, _____ eat a lot of candy?   A B C D
    (A) did you use to   (C) were you used to
    (B) you used to   (D) were you using

3. Kate told me about your cruise to Alaska. When _____?   A B C D
    (A) you leave   (C) leave you
    (B) do you leave   (D) you do leave

4. When you see Alex, please don't _____ him I'm here.   A B C D
    (A) to tell   (C) tell
    (B) telling   (D) tells

5. When that famous gymnast was younger, she used to _____ for six   A B C D
    hours a day.
    (A) practicing   (C) be practicing
    (B) practiced   (D) practice

6. My sister and her family live very far from us. That's why we _____ see   A B C D
    them during the week.
    (A) usually   (C) often
    (B) rarely   (D) always

7. Please wait here. The doctor will see you as soon as he _____ with his   A B C D
    other patient.
    (A) will finish   (C) is finishing
    (B) is going to finish   (D) finishes

8. What _____ when you got to the stadium?   A B C D
   (A) the players were doing   (C) were the players doing
   (B) the players will do   (D) do the players do

9. It _____ me two hours to do my homework last night.   A B C D

   (A) took   (C) used to take
   (B) was taking   (D) is going to take

XII. SYNTHESIS

Each sentence has four underlined words or phrases. The four underlined parts of the sentence are marked A, B, C, and D. Circle the letter of the ONE part that is NOT CORRECT.

1. <u>What</u> <u>were</u> you doing <u>when</u> the lights <u>were going out</u>?   A B C **(D)**
     A   B   C   D

2. Laura <u>is</u> <u>studying</u> hard because <u>she's wanting</u> to <u>be</u> a doctor.   A B C D
          A   B   C   D

3. <u>How</u> old <u>will you be</u> <u>when</u> you<u>'ll finish</u> this course?   A B C D
     A   B   C   D

4. <u>Don't</u> <u>drink</u> that milk: I <u>think</u> <u>it's smelling</u> bad.   A B C D
     A   B   C   D

5. The Costa family <u>used to</u> <u>ate</u> dinner at Paul's Steakhouse <u>every</u> Friday <u>night</u>.   A B C D
                 A   B   C   D

6. Lee <u>invited</u> me to the movies <u>tonight</u>, and I <u>think</u> I <u>go</u>.   A B C D
        A   B   C D

7. Sue <u>reads</u> an interesting article <u>yesterday</u> <u>while</u> she <u>was riding</u> to school.   A B C D
        A   B   C   D

8. It <u>didn't</u> <u>rain</u> today, and it probably <u>don't</u> <u>rain</u> tomorrow either.   A B C D
        A   B   C   D

9. <u>After</u> you <u>turn</u> left at the light, <u>going</u> straight <u>for</u> about a mile.   A B C D
     A   B   C   D

10. What time <u>is</u> your party <u>tomorrow night</u>, and <u>whom</u> <u>is going to</u> be there?   A B C D
             A   B   C   D

11. I <u>went</u> to five interviews <u>today</u>, but I still <u>don't</u> <u>having</u> a job.   A B C D
       A   B   C   D

12. <u>What</u> <u>you're doing</u> <u>after</u> you <u>finish</u> this test?   A B C D
      A   B   C   D

13. <u>How long</u> <u>was</u> you and <u>your friends</u> at the beach <u>on</u> Sunday afternoon?   A B C D
        A   B   C   D

PART II PRONOUNS AND PHRASAL VERBS

I. REFLEXIVE AND RECIPROCAL PRONOUNS

Complete each sentence, using the correct reflexive or reciprocal pronoun in the box. Use some pronouns more than once.

each other	herself	himself	itself	myself	ourselves	themselves	yourself	yourselves

1. When Mr. Chase was young, he taught _____*himself*_____ Japanese.

2. Your life isn't so hard. Stop feeling sorry for _____.

3. Did Sally enjoy _____ on the cruise she took last month?

4. By the end of the year, you and your classmates will know _____ very well—and I hope you'll be friends.

5. If you and Koji want to meet Professor Chang, go over and introduce _____ to him.

6. If you don't want to go to the movies tonight, I'll go by _____.

7. Did you see the new TV drama last night? The show _____ isn't great, but the lead actress is very talented.

8. It's easy to see that the bride and groom love _____ very much.

9. Mike often imagines _____ quitting his job, buying a boat, and sailing around the world.

10. Did you and Kristina help _____ with your math homework? You have all the same answers!

11. I'm glad that all our guests are helping _____ to the food.

12. Children, please behave _____ while I'm gone.

13. We couldn't afford to pay someone to paint the house, so we painted it _____.

14. If you're hungry, Marie, make _____ a sandwich.

15. Their parents used to work all day, so Oliver and Jack took care of _____ after school.

16. Juan is going to start his own business because he wants to work for _____.

II. REFLEXIVE AND RECIPROCAL PRONOUNS

Choose the correct pronouns to complete this TV interview between a talk-show host and her guest.

HOST: Welcome to all our viewers. Sit back and make _____*yourselves*_____ comfortable. Tonight we
　　　　　　　　　　　　　　　　　　　　　　　　　　　　1. (you / yourselves)

have a fascinating guest: the writer of the most popular show on television. Yes, that's right.

Tonight's guest is Chris Connors _____. Good evening, Chris. We're excited to
　　　　　　　　　　　　　　　　　　　2. (him / himself)

have _____ with us.
　　　　3. (you / yourself)

GUEST: Thanks for inviting _____ , Joanne. I always enjoy _____ on your
               4. (me / myself)   **5.** (me / myself)

show.

HOST: I don't really need to introduce _____ to our audience. Everyone already knows
                  6. (you / yourself)

you. Are you enjoying your sudden success?

GUEST: Yes, Joanne, I am. I'm enjoying my success with the series and I'm enjoying the series

_____ .
7. (it / itself)

HOST: The whole country enjoys your series. You should be proud of _____ .
                8. (you / yourself)

GUEST: Well, yes, I am. I've always believed in _____ . Many people told
                  9. (me / myself)

_____ that my scripts weren't good. Mr. George Pappas turned down my first
10. (me / myself)

script for this series. He's probably pretty angry at _____ for that now.
                  11. (him / himself)

HOST: Well, congratulations! And how did you get the idea for the series? Did you come up with it

by _____ ?
12. (yourself / yourselves)

GUEST: Yes, I did. But the story of the main character, Alicia, is really the story of my cousin Sarah.

After high school, Sarah and her best friend taught _____ how to run a business.
                  13. (herself / themselves)

Within two years, they opened their first shop. And they did it by _____ , with no
                  14. (them / themselves)

help from anyone. Today they have stores in five different cities and lead very exciting lives.

HOST: Well, Alicia is very good at taking care of _____ and all her friends. Is your
                  15. (her / herself)

cousin as good?

GUEST: Absolutely! Sarah's great! Unfortunately, we don't see _____ often because we're
                  16. (each other / ourselves)

both so busy. But we're very interested in _____ work. And we call
                  17. (each other / each other's)

_____ all the time.
18. (each other / ourselves)

HOST: Very interesting. Tell _____ , Chris. Has anyone written a book about
                  19. (me / myself)

_____ yet?
20. (you / yourself)

GUEST: No, I don't think so. But if someone's going to tell my story, I'd prefer to do it _____ .
                  21. (me / myself)

HOST: And where do you see _____ in five years?
                  22. (you / yourself)

GUEST: In five years, my wife and I will have a large house in the country. She and I will be taking

care of our children and of _____ . . . you know, just enjoying
                  23. (each other / one another's)

_____ life together. It should be easy, because we never fight: We sometimes
24. (our / ourselves)

blame _____ for problems, but we never blame _____ .
        25. (each other / ourselves)   **26.** (each other / ourselves)

III. PHRASAL VERBS

Complete the letter from someone visiting the city of New Orleans. Choose the phrasal verb in the box that is closest in meaning to the words in parentheses. Use the correct form of the phrasal verb.

call up	dress up	eat out	find out	get back	get together	get up	go on
lie down	talk over	wake up	write down	~~play around~~	pick out	sign up	stay up

Dear Lou,

New Orleans is a wonderful city—especially for anyone who likes to __play around__ and have a
1. (have fun)

good time. We _____ really early our first day here. First, we talked to a woman who
2. (rise from bed)

works for the hotel, and we _____ about all the interesting things to do. Then, while we
3. (learn information)

were having breakfast, we _____ our plans for the day. After I _____ all our
4. (discuss)   5. (write on a piece of paper)

ideas, we decided to _____ for a tour.
6. (register)

We went on the tour and _____ to the hotel at around five. Since we were really
7. (return)

tired, we decided to _____ for a while and take a nap. When we _____ , we
8. (recline)   9. (awaken after sleeping)

were hungry. We wanted to _____ at a fancy restaurant, so we _____ .
10. (have a meal in a restaurant)   11. (wore special clothes)

Then we _____ a place that sounded good and _____ the restaurant for a
12. (select)   13. (phone)

reservation.

After dinner (it was delicious!), our party _____ for a few more hours. We heard
14. (continue)

some great jazz in a small club, and then we went dancing. You know me, I usually go to bed early—

but we _____ almost all night.
15. (remain awake)

Let's _____ next week when I get back. See you then!
16. (meet)

Love,

Melissa

IV. PHRASAL VERBS

Complete each conversation with a phrasal verb and a pronoun.

1. **A:** What should we take out of the freezer for dinner?
   B: There's some chicken. I'll _____ take it out _____ right now.

2. **A:** Are you going to turn in your paper this week?
   B: Yes. I have to _____ tomorrow morning.

3. **A:** Can we drop off Ernie on our way downtown?
   B: How can we _____ ? He lives in the opposite direction!

4. **A:** It's getting warm in here. Do you mind if I turn on the fan?

   B: Not at all. Go ahead and _____ .

5. **A:** I need to take back these library books.

   B: I'm going to the library. I'll _____ for you.

6. **A:** Would you please turn down the TV?

   B: But if I _____ , I won't be able to hear my show.

7. **A:** Where's my dictionary? I need to look up a few words.

   B: You lost your dictionary, remember? _____ on the Internet.

8. **A:** Did you ever pay back your aunt?

   B: No, not yet. I promise I'll _____ when I get paid on Friday.

9. **A:** Why did they call off the concert?

   B: They had to _____ because the singer got sick.

10. **A:** Be sure to point out your friends. I'm eager to see what they look like.

    B: OK. I'll _____ as soon as I find them.

11. **A:** Mom, can you pick up Sam and me after school today?

    B: Sure I can _____ . I might be a little late, though.

V. SYNTHESIS

Circle the letter of the sentence that best describes each situation.

1. Mary and her sisters always help one another.   **A   B   C (D)**
   (A) Mary and her sisters always do things without help from other people.
   (B) Mary always helps one of her sisters.
   (C) Mary helps her sisters by herself.
   (D) Mary helps her sisters, and her sisters help her.

2. Joe and Helen talk to themselves all the time.   **A   B   C   D**
   (A) He talks to her, and she talks to him.
   (B) He talks to himself, and she talks to herself.
   (C) They talk to other people.
   (D) He talks to himself, she talks to herself, and they talk to each other.

3. Please throw this book out.   **A   B   C   D**
   (A) Put it in the garbage.
   (B) Throw it outside.
   (C) Sell it.
   (D) Put it on the shelf.

4. When do you have to turn in your report?   A   B   C   D
    (A) When do you have to write it?
    (B) When do you have to change it?
    (C) When do you have to return it to someone?
    (D) When do you have to give it to someone?

5. Javier gets along with his coworkers.   A   B   C   D
    (A) He has a good relationship with them.
    (B) He doesn't like them.
    (C) He tells them what to do.
    (D) He knows them very well.

6. Salah isn't himself today.   A   B   C   D
    (A) He's with a friend.
    (B) He isn't here.
    (C) He needs some help.
    (D) He isn't acting the way he usually acts.

7. The mayonnaise is running out.   A   B   C   D
    (A) We're going to the store for mayonnaise.
    (B) We don't have much mayonnaise left.
    (C) The mayonnaise is going bad.
    (D) We have no mayonnaise.

8. When you gave me your phone number, you left out the area code.   A   B   C   D
    (A) You wrote the wrong area code.
    (B) I couldn't read your area code.
    (C) You didn't give me your area code.
    (D) I forgot your area code.

9. Don't hurt yourselves.   A   B   C   D
    (A) The person is saying this to one other person.
    (B) The person is saying this to two other people.
    (C) The person is saying this to two or more people.
    (D) The person is saying this to three or more people.

10. Abby lives by herself.   A   B   C   D
    (A) She earns all the money she needs to pay her expenses.
    (B) She lives alone.
    (C) She lives in the usual way.
    (D) She lives in a house she built.

11. I'd like to eat out today.   A   B   C   D
    (A) I want to have a picnic.
    (B) I want to eat at a friend's house.
    (C) I want to cook outside.
    (D) I want to go to a restaurant.

Circle the letter of the correct answer to complete each sentence.

1. What do you like to do when you're _____ yourself?   A B C Ⓓ
    (A) with   (C) for
    (B) at   (D) by

2. I'm gaining weight, so I'm going to _____ fattening foods.   A B C D
    (A) give off   (C) give out
    (B) give in   (D) give up

3. No, we can't lend you our notes because we need them _____.   A B C D
    (A) yourself   (C) ourselves
    (B) themselves   (D) one another

4. You're moving tomorrow? We can _____ if you want.   A B C D
    (A) you help out   (C) help yourself out
    (B) help yourselves out   (D) help you out

5. Carol, can't I talk _____ into staying for dinner? There's plenty of food.   A B C D
    (A) me   (C) yourself
    (B) you   (D) herself

6. Is your story true, or did you _____?   A B C D
    (A) make yourself   (C) make it up
    (B) make it   (D) make up

7. Why is Vanessa _____? I thought she loved school.   A B C D
    (A) dropping out   (C) dropping by
    (B) dropping in   (D) dropping off

8. When you finish playing, please put _____ your toys.   A B C D
    (A) them away   (C) yourselves away
    (B) away   (D) away yourselves

9. It's not always easy for friends to stay in touch with _____ when one   A B C D
    of them moves to another city.
    (A) themselves   (C) ourselves
    (B) each other   (D) yourselves

10. Your shirt is missing two buttons. _____ and I'll sew them back on for you.   A B C D
    (A) Take off   (C) Take it off
    (B) Take it yourself   (D) Take it

11. The meeting was going to be this morning, but the boss _____ until   A B C D
    this afternoon.
    (A) turned it off   (C) shut it off
    (B) let it off   (D) put it off

PART II PRONOUNS AND PHRASAL VERBS

FINAL TEST

I.   REFLEXIVE AND RECIPROCAL PRONOUNS

Complete each sentence, using the correct reflexive or reciprocal pronoun in the box. Use some pronouns more than once.

each other	herself	himself	itself	myself	ourselves	themselves	yourself	yourselves

1. I'm sorry, but I can't lend you my car tonight. I need it _____myself_____.

2. Todd and I see _____ a few times each year.

3. It's a beautiful day, and a lot of people are enjoying _____ outdoors.

4. Whenever Jill walks by a store window, she looks at _____ in the glass.

5. I'm not sure why you and Ricardo dislike _____ so much. You're very much alike.

6. Good morning, Mrs. Carson. Help _____ to some coffee and donuts while you wait.

7. When I was a child, I used to imagine _____ becoming a famous inventor.

8. Following a tragedy, it's important for friends and relatives to comfort _____.

9. Come on, Mei. Let's go introduce _____ to the new student.

10. Do you ever talk to _____ when you're alone?

11. I hope Steve didn't hurt _____ when he fell off his bike.

12. Kids, if you eat all that cake, you're going to make _____ sick.

13. Many kids today spend a lot of time by _____ because their parents are away at work.

14. The music _____ wasn't bad; it was just too loud!

15. I think we'll get this job done faster if we all help _____.

16. Our neighbors pride _____ on their beautiful garden.

II. REFLEXIVE AND RECIPROCAL PRONOUNS

Choose the correct pronouns to complete this interview between a reporter and several spectators at an international tennis tournament.

REPORTER: Hi! Are you enjoying _____yourself_____ today?
                                    1. (you / yourself)

SPECTATOR 1: Oh, yeah. This is great. It's always exciting when these two guys play against

_____ .
2. (each other / themselves)

REPORTER: Did you know that Andrew taught _____ to play tennis when he was only
                                                3. (him / himself)

four years old?

SPECTATOR 1: Wow! His parents are probably very proud of _____ .

4. (him / himself)

REPORTER: I'm sure they are. Do you _____ play any tennis?

5. (you / yourself)

SPECTATOR 1: Me? No, but I love to watch it.

REPORTER: Hello. Can I talk to _____ for a minute?

6. (you / yourself)

SPECTATOR 2: Of course.

REPORTER: Some people think Andrew and Sergei will be the best players in the world someday.

SPECTATOR 2: I _____ think that they're already the best players. We always have to

7. (me / myself)

remind _____ that Andrew is only seventeen years old.

8. (us / ourselves)

REPORTER: Well, Sergei _____ is only eighteen!

9. (he / himself)

SPECTATOR 2: That's true. Both players push _____ really hard. I saw Andrew practicing

10. (himself / themselves)

this morning.

REPORTER: Who was he practicing with?

SPECTATOR 2: He was by _____ . He was practicing his serve.

11. (him / himself)

REPORTER: Well, he prides _____ on his serve.

12. (him / himself)

SPECTATOR 2: His serve _____ isn't that great, but his opponents have trouble returning it.

13. (itself / himself)

REPORTER: And who is this lovely person sitting next to _____ ?

14. (you / yourself)

SPECTATOR 2: This is Lily, my wife. We're big tennis fans, and we _____ play a lot of tennis.

15. (each other / ourselves)

REPORTER: Hello. Let me introduce _____ . I'm Cindy Carlson from SBM Sports.

16. (me / myself)

SPECTATOR 3: We already know _____ . Don't you remember _____ ? We

17. (each other / ourselves) 18. (me / myself)

met at last year's Italian Open.

REPORTER: Stephanie! I'm sorry. I didn't recognize _____ for a moment. What are you

19. (you / yourself)

doing with _____ these days?

20. (you / yourself)

SPECTATOR 3: Well, I hurt _____ last year, so I can't play tennis anymore. But I'm not

21. (me / myself)

sitting around feeling sorry for _____ . I'm coaching two young sisters.

22. (me / myself)

These two girls believe in _____ , and they believe in _____ ,

23. (herself / themselves) 24. (each other / each other's)

too. They watch _____ tennis matches, and then they give

25. (each other / each other's)

_____ advice. They're the future of women's tennis. I'm sure of it!

26. (each other / themselves)

III. PHRASAL VERBS

Complete the letter from someone visiting the island of Puerto Rico. Choose the phrasal verb in the box that is closest in meaning to the words in parentheses. Use the correct form of the phrasal verb.

clear up	come along	come out	find out	get along	get back	get together	grow up
keep up	leave out	pick out	point out	put off	show up	~~take off~~	turn down

Dear Ellen,

Here we are in beautiful Puerto Rico. Our plane _____took off_____ from New York Monday
                                   1. (depart)

morning, and 3 1/2 hours later, we were in a new world! I'm glad we didn't _____
                                                           2. (postpone)

this trip until next year. I wanted to meet Pedro's family, and this was a wonderful chance to

_____ . They all _____ really well, and they talk a lot. Each time I talk to
  3. (meet)   **4. (relate)**

someone I _____ all kinds of interesting things about my husband. It's funny to hear
          5. (learn information)

some of the details that Pedro _____ when he told me about his life!
                      6. (omit)

    Yesterday we drove to the small town where Pedro _____ , and he
                                       7. (become an adult)

_____ all the places he used to go when he was a child. His sister _____ ,
  8. (indicate)   **9. (accompany)**

too. She has a lot of energy and walks really fast; sometimes I can't even _____ .
                                           10. (go as fast as)

    While we were at the outdoor market, Pedro's oldest brother _____ . He helped us
                                       11. (appear)

_____ some fresh fruit, but he _____ our lunch invitation because he
  12. (select)   **13. (reject)**

had to _____ to work.
       14. (return)

    The weather here is a little strange. Every afternoon, the sky suddenly gets very dark, it rains

really hard for a minute or two, and then it _____ and the sun _____
                                 15. (become clear)   **16. (appear)**

again.

    Well, I have to say goodbye now. See you soon.

Love,

Kay

IV. PHRASAL VERBS

Complete each conversation with a phrasal verb and a pronoun.

1. **A:** Do you want me to put these clothes away?

   B: No, thanks. We'll _____put them away_____ ourselves.

2. **A:** Could you drop Tony and me off at the mall on your way to work?

   B: I can _____ if you're ready to leave the house at 9:00 sharp.

3. A: My company laid off some workers today.

   B: Do you know why the company _____ ?

4. A: Did you try on all those clothes at the store?

   B: No, I didn't. I'll _____ when I get home.

5. A: Here is the form you have to fill out.

   B: Is it all right if I _____ tomorrow?

6. A: Be sure to shut off all the lights before you go to bed.

   B: OK. I'll _____ .

7. A: I don't know if the Coopers will ever work out their problems.

   B: I think they can _____ if they sit down and talk to each other calmly.

8. A: You have to wake up very early tomorrow.

   B: I know. You always get up early. Could you please _____ when you get up?

9. A: Do you want me to turn down my radio?

   B: Yes, please. _____ just a little.

10. A: Why in the world did you throw away your favorite shoes?

   B: I _____ because they were old and I was tired of them.

11. A: Why do you always bring up the past?

   B: I _____ because I think we can learn from it.

V. SYNTHESIS

Circle the letter of the sentence that best describes each situation.

1. Matthew turned up at around midnight.   Ⓐ   **B**   **C**   **D**
   - (A) He appeared at about 12:00.
   - (B) He woke up at about 12:00.
   - (C) He went home at about 12:00.
   - (D) He worked until around 12:00.

2. Who talked you into taking this class?   **A**   **B**   **C**   **D**
   - (A) Who told you about it?
   - (B) Who discussed it with you?
   - (C) Who persuaded you to take it?
   - (D) Who registered you for it?

3. Emily doesn't like to go shopping by herself.   **A**   **B**   **C**   **D**
   - (A) She doesn't like to spend money on herself.
   - (B) She doesn't like to shop alone.
   - (C) She doesn't like to buy things.
   - (D) She doesn't like shopping.

4. Let's work out today. A B C D
   (A) Let's take our work outside.
   (B) Let's be careful.
   (C) Let's exercise.
   (D) Let's have fun.

5. Mona and Irene hurt themselves in the soccer game. A B C D
   (A) Mona hurt herself, and Irene hurt herself.
   (B) Mona and Irene hurt each other.
   (C) Mona and Irene hurt other soccer players.
   (D) Other soccer players hurt Irene and Mona.

6. Please do your homework over. A B C D
   (A) Hand it in.
   (B) Look it over.
   (C) Do it again.
   (D) Turn it over.

7. After Wanda and Terry spoke to their friends, they made themselves dinner. A B C D
   (A) Wanda and Terry made dinner for Wanda and Terry.
   (B) Wanda made Terry dinner, and Terry made Wanda dinner.
   (C) Wanda and Terry made dinner for their friends.
   (D) Wanda and Terry made dinner for Wanda and Terry and their friends.

8. If they offer me the job, I'm going to turn it down. A B C D
   (A) I'm going to think about the job offer.
   (B) I'm going to accept the job offer.
   (C) I'm going to find out more about the job offer.
   (D) I'm going to reject the job offer.

9. My brother and I ourselves taught French. A B C D
   (A) He taught himself, and I taught myself.
   (B) We taught each other.
   (C) We taught French.
   (D) Someone taught us French together.

10. This math problem is really hard. I give up! A B C D
    (A) I'm turning it in.
    (B) I'm giving it back.
    (C) I'm quitting.
    (D) I'm starting again.

11. Someone shut off the lights. A B C D
    (A) The lights went out.
    (B) Someone turned the lights down.
    (C) The lights are brighter now.
    (D) The lights went on.

VI. SYNTHESIS

Circle the letter of the correct answer to complete each sentence.

1. Connie and Wally asked _____ for dinner tonight. Do you want to go?   A Ⓑ C D
   (A) over us
   (B) us over
   (C) over
   (D) ourselves

2. Young athletes often _____ a normal life to pursue excellence in their sport.   A B C D
   (A) give out
   (B) give in
   (C) give back
   (D) give up

3. I heard that you and Tom are finally talking to each other again. How did that _____ ?   A B C D
   (A) come about
   (B) come along
   (C) come in
   (D) come off

4. How can you kids expect other people to respect you if you don't respect _____ ?   A B C D
   (A) themselves
   (B) yourselves
   (C) ourselves
   (D) yourself

5. I know you're nervous, but just _____ yourself and everything will be fine.   A B C D
   (A) believe
   (B) by
   (C) be
   (D) be by

6. Oh, no! Did you cut _____ ?   A B C D
   (A) myself
   (B) you
   (C) me
   (D) yourself

7. Did Yolanda and her new friend get _____ phone numbers?   A B C D
   (A) themselves
   (B) each other's
   (C) one another
   (D) herself

8. If you think an answer is wrong, _____.
   (A) cross it
   (B) cross
   (C) cross out
   (D) cross it out

A B C D

9. Mrs. Costa took her new vacuum cleaner back to the store because it _____ the second time she used it.
   (A) broke up
   (B) broke in
   (C) broke down
   (D) broke out

A B C D

10. Last year Fernando didn't know anything about photography. But that course _____ an expert.
   (A) turned him into
   (B) turned him in
   (C) turned him on
   (D) turned him up

A B C D

11. We weren't in the mood to go to a movie. But Teresa talked _____ into it.
   (A) herself
   (B) ourselves
   (C) us
   (D) her

A B C D

PART III MODALS AND RELATED VERBS AND EXPRESSIONS

I. ABILITY: *CAN, COULD, BE ABLE TO*

Complete the advertisement. Use the appropriate form of can, could, *or* be able to *with each verb. Use* can *or* could *when possible.*

Think about your last exercise program: _____Could_____ you _____find_____ time for the
                                                                           1. (find)

program in your busy schedule? _____ the program _____ your interest
                                                                                    2. (hold)

for longer than a few weeks? If you answer "no," you're not alone. There are many programs, but

most programs _____ people's fitness needs.
                        3. (not / meet)

   Kathy Swift's Exercise Program is different. It has helped many people get in shape, and it

_____ you, too! We spoke to someone who tried it and loves it. Here's what she said:
      4. (help)

"I _____ why so many people love the Kathy Swift program. I tried other programs,
      5. (understand)

but I _____ with them for more than a week or two. I want _____ at
         6. (not / stick)   **7. (exercise)**

any time. With Kathy Swift, I _____ exercise into my regular routine. I know I
                                            8. (fit)

_____ fit for the rest of my life."
      9. (stay)

II. PERMISSION: *MAY, COULD, CAN, DO YOU MIND IF...?*

Write questions asking for permission, using the words in parentheses.
1. I'd like to use your car tomorrow.
   (Could) ___Could I use your car tomorrow?___
2. I need to take an early lunch break today.
   (May) _____
3. I'd like to sit next to you.
   (Do you mind if) _____
4. We want to change the radio station.
   (Can) _____

III. REQUESTS: *WILL, WOULD, COULD, CAN, WOULD YOU MIND...?*

Change each imperative to a polite request. Use the words in parentheses.
1. Vacuum the living room, please.
   (Can) ___Can you vacuum the living room, please?___

2. Please trim the rose bushes.

   (Could) _____

3. Drive your grandfather to the clinic.

   (Would you mind) _____

4. Take out the trash, please.

   (Will) _____

5. Please pick up the clothes at the cleaner's.

   (Would) _____

IV.   ADVICE: *SHOULD, OUGHT TO, HAD BETTER*

Find and correct the mistake in each sentence.

1. How should people ⋈ prepare for a hurricane?

2. Everyone ought to taking a hurricane warning very seriously.

3. You'd not better leave your pets outside during a bad storm.

4. People not should turn off their radios.

5. You shouldn't being outside when the storm hits.

6. You ought stay away from the windows.

7. You better take care of yourself.

8. Everyone should stays inside until the hurricane is over.

9. Also, people would better stay calm.

V.   SUGGESTIONS: *LET'S, COULD, WHY DON'T . . . ?, WHY NOT . . . ?, HOW ABOUT . . . ?*

Circle the correct words to complete the conversation.

A: Let's (do) / to do something fun on Saturday.
         1.

B: OK. Why don't / Why not we go to the zoo? I hear it's fantastic.
         2.

A: I know, but I really want to go shopping.

B: Then how about go / going to Old Town? There are a lot of nice stores there.
                        3.

A: OK. Maybe we would / could go to the zoo on Sunday.
                     4.

B: That's fine with me. And remember that I want to go to the harbor one of these days.

A: Well, how about / why don't Saturday night? Why not / Why don't go there for dinner? We could
         5.   **6.**

   take / taking the trolley from Old Town.
   7.

B: That sounds great, but let's / let's not go to an expensive restaurant. I don't like to spend a lot of
                        8.

   money on food.

A: I don't either. How about / Why not deciding on a restaurant when we get to the harbor?
         9.

VI. SYNTHESIS

Read the first sentence in each set. Then circle the letter of the information that completes the second sentence.

1. "May I borrow your pen?"   A B C Ⓓ
   The speaker is _____ .
   (A) making a suggestion   (C) asking about ability
   (B) asking for advice   (D) asking for permission

2. "Why don't we give the dog a bath?"   A B C D
   The speaker is _____ .
   (A) making a suggestion   (C) asking for permission
   (B) giving advice   (D) asking about ability

3. "Why weren't you able to come to class yesterday?"   A B C D
   The speaker is _____ .
   (A) asking for permission   (C) asking about ability
   (B) making a request   (D) giving advice

4. "Would you mind coming back later?"   A B C D
   The speaker is _____ .
   (A) asking for advice   (C) giving advice
   (B) making a request   (D) making a suggestion

5. "What time should we leave for the airport?"   A B C D
   The speaker is _____ .
   (A) asking for advice   (C) asking for permission
   (B) making a request   (D) making a suggestion

6. Let's have a party this weekend!"   A B C D
   The speaker is _____ .
   (A) making a request   (C) giving advice
   (B) giving permission   (D) making a suggestion

7. "Why don't we leave now? Otherwise, we'll hit rush-hour traffic."   A B C D
   The speaker is _____ .
   (A) giving permission   (C) asking for permission
   (B) making a request   (D) making a suggestion

8. "Can I call you by your first name?"   A B C D
   The speaker is _____ .
   (A) asking for permission   (C) making a request
   (B) asking for advice   (D) asking about ability

9. "You ought to buy yourself something nice."   A B C D
   The speaker is _____ .
   (A) making a request   (C) giving permission
   (B) giving advice   (D) talking about ability

Circle the letter of the correct answer to complete each sentence.

1. Mei has a fever. We _____ call the doctor right away.　　A　B　Ⓒ　D
    (A) would   (C) had better
    (B) are able to   (D) could

2. I'd love to see the Picasso exhibit. Would you _____ with me?　　A　B　C　D
    (A) go   (C) to go
    (B) if you go   (D) going

3. When Tito was younger, he used to _____ swim 50 meters underwater.　　A　B　C　D
    (A) could   (C) be able to
    (B) can   (D) would

4. I _____ play tennis when I was a kid, but I was a good volleyball player.　　A　B　C　D
    (A) can't   (C) couldn't
    (B) am not able to   (D) shouldn't

5. If you don't like your new shirt, why not _____ it for another one?　　A　B　C　D
    (A) to exchange   (C) exchanging
    (B) exchange   (D) you exchange

6. _____ I turn up the radio?　　A　B　C　D
    (A) Why not   (C) Do you mind if
    (B) Would you mind   (D) How about

7. Your English is so good that you _____ speak fluently by next year.　　A　B　C　D
    (A) will be able to   (C) were able to
    (B) can   (D) could

8. The team did best in 1998, when it _____ take second place.　　A　B　C　D
    (A) can   (C) is able to
    (B) could   (D) was able to

9. It's too bad that you're having trouble with math. Why don't we _____ together?　　A　B　C　D
    (A) to study   (C) study
    (B) studying   (D) don't study

10. Would you mind _____ me your dictionary? I'd like to look something up.　　A　B　C　D
    (A) lend   (C) lent
    (B) lending   (D) to lend

11. It's snowing hard. Maybe we _____ to take the train instead of driving to work.　　A　B　C　D
    (A) aren't able   (C) 'd better
    (B) can't   (D) ought

12. _____ you please open the window? It's hot in here. **A B C D**
    (A) Would you mind   (C) Can
    (B) Should   (D) Why don't

13. You _____ walk home. It's almost five miles. Let me drive you. **A B C D**
    (A) can't   (C) aren't
    (B) don't   (D) wouldn't

VIII. SYNTHESIS

Circle the letter of the appropriate response to each question.

1. Could you lend me some money? **A Ⓑ C**
    (A) Yes, I could.
    (B) I'm sorry. I can't. I'm broke.
    (C) No, not at all.

2. I'm going to paint my bedroom walls black. What do you think? **A B C**
    (A) Maybe you couldn't.
    (B) Maybe you wouldn't.
    (C) Maybe you shouldn't.

3. Would you mind passing the salt? **A B C**
    (A) Go right ahead.
    (B) No, I wouldn't.
    (C) Not at all.

4. Why don't we see a movie this afternoon? **A B C**
    (A) That's a great idea.
    (B) No, we don't.
    (C) Because I'm busy today.

5. Could I use the phone? **A B C**
    (A) Yes, you could.
    (B) No, you couldn't.
    (C) Yes, you can.

6. Lisa has a bad cold. Do you think she should stay home? **A B C**
    (A) Yes, she ought to stay in bed.
    (B) No, she'd better rest.
    (C) Why doesn't she stay home?

7. Do you mind if I change the radio station? **A B C**
    (A) Yes, go right ahead.
    (B) Yes, actually, I do. It's my favorite station.
    (C) No, you don't.

8. Were you able to contact Mr. Lewis?   A   B   C
   (A) No, I didn't.
   (B) Yes, I can.
   (C) Yes, we were.

9. Tony and Gene are failing biology. What should they do?   A   B   C
   (A) They ought to talk to their teacher.
   (B) They'll study harder.
   (C) They may hire a tutor.

10. Can you make a call for me?   A   B   C
    (A) Yes, I'm able to.
    (B) Certainly.
    (C) Yes, I may.

11. How about a movie tomorrow night?   A   B   C
    (A) No, please don't.
    (B) Sure.
    (C) Yes, we can.

12. May I go to the restroom?   A   B   C
    (A) Not at all.
    (B) Why not?
    (C) Yes, you can.

13. Where can we get some good sushi?   A   B   C
    (A) You ought to try Yoshino's.
    (B) You would eat at Saga Restaurant.
    (C) We may go to the Kyoto Cafe.

IX.   SYNTHESIS

*Each sentence has four underlined words or phrases. The four underlined parts of the sentence
are marked A, B, C, and D. Circle the letter of the ONE underlined part that is NOT CORRECT.*

1. <u>Would</u> <u>please you</u> <u>wake me up</u> early tomorrow morning<u>?</u>   A (B) C D
      A   B   C   D
2. Frank <u>can't</u> <u>comes</u> to class tomorrow because he <u>isn't</u> <u>feeling</u> well.   A B C D
         A   B   C D
3. <u>Why</u> <u>we don't</u> <u>find out</u> how much the airfare is to Paris<u>?</u>   A B C D
    A   B   C   D
4. <u>Do you</u> <u>mind</u> if I <u>parking</u> in your driveway<u>?</u>   A B C D
     A   B   C   D
5. <u>You better</u> <u>call</u> your parents, <u>or</u> <u>they'll be</u> worried about you.   A B C D
       A   B   C D
6. <u>Should</u> I <u>to lock</u> the door <u>when</u> I <u>leave</u> tonight?   A B C D
      A   B   C   D
7. <u>Would</u> you <u>mind</u> <u>check</u> the air in my front tire<u>?</u>   A B C D
      A   B   C   D

8. If you like comedies, <u>how about</u> <u>we're</u> <u>renting</u> the new Billy Crystal movie<u>?</u>   **A B C D**
                              A   B   C   D

9. The sun <u>is</u> very strong today, so <u>you'd</u> <u>not better</u> <u>stay</u> outside for too long.   **A B C D**
             A   B   C   D

10. Terry <u>can't</u> <u>play</u> in the game yesterday <u>because</u> she <u>hurt herself</u> last week.   **A B C D**
           A   B   C   D

11. If you <u>come</u> home past your curfew tonight, you <u>mayn't</u> <u>go out</u> at all <u>next</u> weekend.   **A B C D**
            A   B   C   D

12. Paolo <u>wants</u> to <u>take</u> the TOEFL next year, so he <u>oughts to</u> <u>start</u> studying soon.   **A B C D**
          A   B   C   D

13. I usually <u>can't</u> <u>finish</u> my homework in less than three hours, but last night I   **A B C D**
                A   B

<u>could</u> <u>finish</u> it in an hour.
 C   D

14. We <u>need</u> bread, so <u>why</u> <u>don't we go</u> to the store to get some<u>.</u>   **A B C D**
           A   B   C   D

15. <u>May</u> <u>please I</u> <u>speak to</u> you for a minute<u>?</u>   **A B C D**
      A   B   C   D

PART III MODALS AND RELATED VERBS AND EXPRESSIONS

FINAL TEST

I. ABILITY: *CAN, COULD, BE ABLE TO*

Complete the advertisement. Use the appropriate form of can, could, *or* be able to *with each verb. Use* can *or* could *when possible.*

<u>Can</u> you <u>cook</u>? If you join Ken's Cooking Club, in just a few weeks you
___1. (cook)___

_____. Here is what some of our satisfied students said:
___2. (cook)___

"I've had only two classes, but already I _____ a delicious meal. By the holidays
___3. (make)___

next month, I think I _____ a dinner party and invite all my friends."
___4. (have)___

"When I was younger, I _____ pretty well. But in college, I lived in a dorm—and
___5. (cook)___

you know you _____ in a dorm! After college, I wanted to _____ my
___6. (not cook)___ ___7. (invite)___

friends and family for a meal, but I _____ anything in the kitchen. My cousin told me
___8. (not do)___

about Ken's, and now I _____ better than anyone I know!"
___9. (cook)___

II. PERMISSION: *MAY, COULD, CAN, DO YOU MIND IF...?*

Write questions asking for permission, using the words in parentheses.
1. I want to go to the mall.
   (Can) <u>Can I go to the mall?</u>
2. I'd like to pour myself a little more coffee.
   (Do you mind if) _____
3. We need to borrow your camera.
   (May) _____
4. I'd like to ask you some questions.
   (Could) _____

III. REQUESTS: *WILL, WOULD, COULD, CAN, WOULD YOU MIND...?*

Change each imperative to a polite request. Use the words in parentheses.
1. Please mow the lawn this afternoon.
   (Will) <u>Will you please mow the lawn this afternoon?</u>
2. Pick up the kids at school, please.
   (Would) _____

3. Take the VCR to the repair shop, please.

(Could) _____

4. Please empty the dishwasher.

(Can) _____

5. Mop the kitchen floor.

(Would you mind) _____

IV. ADVICE: *SHOULD, OUGHT TO, HAD BETTER*

Find and correct the mistake in each sentence.

1. Everyone ~~had~~ better take the following advice very seriously.

2. If there is a tornado warning in your area, you don't should panic.

3. First, you should to get out of your car.

4. You'd better no be outside when the tornado hits.

5. If you're outside, you ought to lies down on the ground.

6. If your house has a basement, you would better move to the basement.

7. People ought to staying away from windows or glass doors.

8. If possible, you'd better to get under a heavy piece of furniture.

9. Everyone should stays inside until the tornado passes.

V. SUGGESTIONS: *LET'S, COULD, WHY DON'T . . . ?, WHY NOT . . . ?, HOW ABOUT . . . ?*

Circle the correct words to complete the conversation.

A: Meg's birthday is on Saturday. How about <u>throw /(throwing)</u> her a party?

　　　　　　　　　　　　　　　　　　　　　1.

B: What a great idea! We <u>could / would</u> have it at my apartment.

　　　　　　　　　　　　　　　2.

A: OK. Let's <u>make / to make</u> a list of people to invite. Lily, Tom, Velia, . . .

　　　　　　　3.

B: <u>How about / Why doesn't</u> Carlos?

　　　　　4.

A: Of course. You know, I have an idea. Why don't we <u>call / calling</u> Meg and ask her who she wants

　　　　　　　　　　　　　　　　　　　　　　　　　5.

us to ask to the party?

B: No. Let's <u>don't / not</u> tell Meg about the party. <u>Why not / Why don't</u> make it a surprise?

　　　　　6.　　　　　　　　　　　　　　**7.**

A: That's a good idea, too. <u>How about / Why not</u> getting Meg's boyfriend to help?

　　　　　　　　　　　8.

B: Definitely! <u>Why don't / Why not</u> we call him right now?

　　　　　　9.

VI. SYNTHESIS

Read the first sentence in each set. Then circle the letter of the information that completes the second sentence.

1. "Let's buy the teacher some flowers."   A B C (D)
   The speaker is _____.
   (A) giving permission   (C) giving advice
   (B) making a request   (D) making a suggestion

2. "How long should I boil these potatoes?"   A B C D
   The speaker is _____.
   (A) asking for permission   (C) asking for advice
   (B) making a suggestion   (D) making a request

3. "May I see your notes?"   A B C D
   The speaker is _____.
   (A) asking for advice   (C) asking about ability
   (B) asking for permission   (D) making a suggestion

4. "Jim, you and Pete ought to practice more often."   A B C D
   The speaker is _____.
   (A) making a request   (C) talking about ability
   (B) giving advice   (D) giving permission

5. "Why don't we eat out tonight? I'm too tired to cook."   A B C D
   The speaker is _____.
   (A) making a suggestion   (C) giving permission
   (B) asking for permission   (D) making a request

6. "How much are you able to pay for a new car?"   A B C D
   The speaker is _____.
   (A) making a request   (C) giving advice
   (B) asking about ability   (D) asking for permission

7. "Would you mind putting your books away?"   A B C D
   The speaker is _____.
   (A) making a suggestion   (C) making a request
   (B) asking for advice   (D) giving advice

8. "Do you mind if I turn on the radio?"   A B C D
   The speaker is _____.
   (A) asking for advice   (C) making a request
   (B) asking for permission   (D) making a suggestion

9. "Could you speak English when you were a child?"   A B C D
   The speaker is _____.
   (A) asking about ability   (C) making a request
   (B) asking for permission   (D) asking for advice

VII. SYNTHESIS

Circle the letter of the correct answer to complete each sentence.

1. _____ I open this window? It's hot in here.   (Ⓐ) B C D
   - (A) May
   - (B) Would
   - (C) Do
   - (D) Am

2. This restaurant looks very expensive. Maybe we _____ to go somewhere else.   A B C D
   - (A) could
   - (B) 'd better
   - (C) ought
   - (D) should

3. _____ I use your phone?   A B C D
   - (A) Why not
   - (B) How about
   - (C) Would you mind
   - (D) Do you mind if

4. We _____ spend much time with you yesterday because we were very busy.   A B C D
   - (A) are not able to
   - (B) can't
   - (C) couldn't
   - (D) shouldn't

5. I'm sorry we can't meet today. _____ meeting tomorrow instead?   A B C D
   - (A) Let's
   - (B) Why not
   - (C) Why don't we
   - (D) How about

6. Sarah hurt her leg badly. I think we _____ take her to the emergency room right away   A B C D
   - (A) would
   - (B) could
   - (C) 'd better
   - (D) can

7. The kids want to go swimming. Would you please _____ them to the beach this afternoon?   A B C D
   - (A) to take
   - (B) take
   - (C) taking
   - (D) will take

8. Did you know that Mr. Lewis used to _____ run 100 meters in less than ten seconds?   A B C D
   - (A) could
   - (B) would
   - (C) can
   - (D) be able to

9. I have an idea for this weekend. _____ go fishing.   A B C D
   - (A) How about
   - (B) Why not
   - (C) We could
   - (D) Why don't we

10. _____ you please turn down the music? It's giving me a headache.   A B C D
    - (A) Should
    - (B) Can
    - (C) Why don't
    - (D) Would you mind

11. My grandchildren are growing so fast, when I see them next year, I _____ recognize them.   **A B C D**

    (A) can't   (C) 'm not able to

    (B) won't be able to   (D) couldn't

12. _____ chicken for dinner?   **A B C D**

    (A) Let's have   (C) How about

    (B) Why don't   (D) Could we

13. Would you mind _____ me home? My car is in the shop.   **A B C D**

    (A) driving   (C) drove

    (B) drive   (D) to drive

VIII. SYNTHESIS

Circle the letter of the appropriate response to each question.

1. Would you lend me your pen?   **A Ⓑ C**

    (A) Yes, I would.

    (B) I'm sorry. I can't. I'm using it.

    (C) No, not at all.

2. How about going dancing Friday night?   **A B C**

    (A) Yes, go right ahead.

    (B) No, don't.

    (C) Good idea.

3. Do you know a good coffee shop around here?   **A B C**

    (A) You should go to Alex's Cafe.

    (B) You may eat at Mel's Diner.

    (C) You would try Joe's.

4. Why don't we wash the car this afternoon?   **A B C**

    (A) Because it isn't dirty.

    (B) OK.

    (C) No, we don't.

5. Could you please take a picture of us?   **A B C**

    (A) No, not at all.

    (B) I'd be glad to.

    (C) I'm sorry, but you can't.

6. Was Ms. Green able to get in touch with Jay's mother?   **A B C**

    (A) No, she didn't.

    (B) Yes, she was.

    (C) Yes, she does.

7. I have a terrible stomachache. What should I do?   A   B   C
   (A) You ought to see a doctor.
   (B) You may go to the hospital.
   (C) You'll go lie down.

8. Could I practice English with you?   A   B   C
   (A) Yes, you could.
   (B) No, you weren't able to.
   (C) Yes, you can.

9. Do you mind if I try your new video game?   A   B   C
   (A) No, you may not.
   (B) No, not at all.
   (C) Yes, go right ahead.

10. Will you please explain this to me?   A   B   C
    (A) Sure I will.
    (B) No, you won't.
    (C) Yes, I could.

11. May I take the day off on Friday, Mr. Abbott?   A   B   C
    (A) No, you'd better not. We have a lot to do.
    (B) Yes, of course you could.
    (C) No, not at all. Enjoy yourself.

12. Will you and your girlfriend be at the dance?   A   B   C
    (A) No, we can't go.
    (B) Yes, we were able to go.
    (C) We'd be glad to go.

13. Would you mind stopping at the store on your way home?   A   B   C
    (A) No, I don't. What should I buy?
    (B) Yes, I would. Why not?
    (C) No. What do we need?

IX. SYNTHESIS

Each sentence has four underlined words or phrases. The four underlined parts of the sentence are marked A, B, C, and D. Circle the letter of the ONE *underlined part that is* NOT CORRECT.

1. I can't lending you any money because I don't have any myself.   A (B) C D
      A   B   C   D

2. Would you mind write down your address on this piece of paper?   A   B   C   D
      A   B   C   D

3. Why no we try to save some money this month?   A   B   C   D
      A   B C   D

4. Jessie couldn't come to work tomorrow because she has a doctor's appointment   A   B   C   D
           A   B   C
   in the morning.
      D

5. <u>We better</u> <u>study</u> for our exams this week, <u>or</u> we'll <u>do</u> very badly.   A B C D
   A   B   C D

6. You and I both like Thai food, so <u>how about</u> <u>we're</u> <u>having</u> dinner at the   A B C D
                                    A   B   C

    Siam Restaurant tonight<u>?</u>
                      D

7. If you kids <u>don't behave</u> <u>yourselves</u>, you <u>mayn't</u> have <u>any</u> dessert tonight.   A B C D
          A   B   C   D

8. <u>Could</u> you <u>translate</u> <u>please</u> this letter into English<u>?</u>   A B C D
  A   B   C   D

9. <u>Should</u> people <u>to turn off</u> their computers <u>when</u> a thunderstorm <u>starts</u>?   A B C D
  A   B   C   D

10. Mrs. Wagner <u>won't</u> <u>be able to</u> <u>leaves</u> the hospital today because she <u>has</u> a fever.   A B C D
             A   B   C   D

11. Tommy should <u>wear</u> something nice to school tomorrow, so <u>why don't</u> we <u>go</u> to   A B C D
               A   B   C

    the store and buy him a new shirt<u>.</u>
                              D

12. <u>Could</u> you <u>mind</u> <u>if</u> my band practices in our garage after school on Friday<u>?</u>   A B C D
  A   B C   D

13. You <u>may use</u> my computer <u>to write</u> your report, but you <u>ought to buy</u> your   A B C D
      A   B   C

    own computer, if you <u>could afford</u> it.
                         D

14. If Tomiko <u>wants</u> to <u>do well</u> in this class, she <u>oughts to</u> <u>study</u> a lot harder.   A B C D
        A   B   C   D

15. This neighborhood <u>is</u> dangerous at night, so <u>we'd</u> <u>not better</u> <u>go out</u> after dark.   A B C D
              A   B   C   D

PART IV PRESENT PERFECT

I. PRESENT PERFECT: *SINCE* AND *FOR*

Complete the story with since *or* for.

Maureen and Randy have lived in New Hampshire _____since_____ 1998. Maureen works at
the University of New Hampshire. She's worked there _____ three years. Randy is a
construction worker. He's worked in the construction business _____ he graduated
from high school. It's spring break at the university, so Maureen hasn't had to work
_____ a week now. She'd like to spend more time with Randy, but he hasn't taken
a vacation _____ their honeymoon. Maureen and Randy have argued about this
_____ the past few months: Maureen has dreamt of traveling _____ she
was very young, but Randy isn't interested in seeing new places.

II. PRESENT PERFECT: *SINCE* AND *FOR*

Use the words in parentheses to write questions. Then complete the answers, using since *or* for.

1. (You and your family / live here / for long?)

   A: _Have you and your family lived here for long?_

   B: _We've lived here since_ _____ 1998.

2. (How long / your parents / be married?)

   A: _____

   B: _____ almost thirty years.

3. (you and Greg / know each other / for very long?)

   A: _____

   B: _____ we were in college.

4. (How long / that tree / be in the front yard?)

   A: _____

   B: _____ at least ten years.

5. (Bryan / play soccer / for a long time?)

   A: _____

   B: _____ junior high.

6. (How long / Angie / work as a hospital volunteer?)

A: _____

B: _____ she retired three years ago.

7. (Elliot / be on vacation / all week?)

A: _____

B: _____ almost two weeks now.

III.   PRESENT PERFECT: *ALREADY* AND *YET*

Complete the conversations. Use the present perfect form of the verbs in parentheses, already *or* yet, *and short answers.*

1. A: _____Have_____ you and your husband _____eaten_____ at Alfredo's
       a. (eat)
       _____yet_____?
       b.

   B: No, _____we haven't_____. I hear it's very good.
           c.

2. A: _____ Larry _____ to bed _____? It's only 9:30!
                          a. (go)   **b.**

   B: Yes, _____. He was very tired.
             c.

3. A: _____ you _____ dinner _____? I thought you
                          a. (have)   **b.**
       were going to wait for me.

   B: Yes, _____. I'm really sorry. I was too hungry to wait.
             c.

4. A: _____ the Ryders _____ from their vacation _____?
                          a. (get back)   **b.**

   B: No, _____. They won't be back until Sunday.
            c.

5. A: _____ Marianne _____ her final exams _____?
                          a. (take)   **b.**

   B: No, _____. Exams start next week.
            c.

6. A: _____ you _____ that whole book _____? We don't
                          a. (read)   **b.**
       have to read it until next month.

   B: No, _____. I still have about 100 pages to read.
            c.

IV.   PRESENT PERFECT: INDEFINITE PAST

A brother and sister are making plans for Mother's Day. They want to do something different this year, so they're trying to remember what they did in past years. Use the words in parentheses to write questions and answers. Use ever *with the questions and, when appropriate, use* never *in short answers.*

1. (we / have / a picnic in the park?)

A: _____Have we ever had a picnic in the park?_____

B: No, _____never._____

2. (Mom / go / to that restaurant on Charles Street?)

    A: _____

    B: Yes, _____

3. (we / make / a special breakfast for her?)

    A: _____

    B: No, _____

4. (we / buy / theater tickets for her?)

    A: _____

    B: Yes, _____

5. (Mom / take / a boat trip?)

    A: _____

    B: No, _____

6. (we / forget /about Mother's Day?)

    A: _____

    B: No, _____

7. (Mom / complain / about her present?)

    A: _____

    B: No, _____

V. PRESENT PERFECT AND SIMPLE PAST TENSE

Circle the correct words to complete the sentences.

1. Ted and Sally (have lived)/ lived in Los Angeles since 1995.

2. I heard that you just left your job at the *Gazette*. How long have you worked / did you work there?

3. In 1995, Mr. and Mrs. Costa have decided / decided to move to a larger apartment.

4. How long have you played / did you play the piano? You're really good.

5. The phone has rung / rang more than twenty times this morning, and it's not even noon.

6. We 've had / had a lot of rain lately. I wish the sun would come out.

7. Carol has written / wrote to her cousin several times last month.

8. Shara has been / was a sportscaster for many years, but she's thinking of changing professions.

9. Have we met / Did we meet ? You look familiar.

10. We 've met / met last year at a soccer match.

11. I 've been / was awfully busy lately.

12. We heard you just moved here from Canada. Have you lived / Did you live there for very long?

13. How much money have you deposited / did you deposit in your account last week?

14. <u>Have you watched / Did you watch</u> the news last night?

15. Kenny just got back from Disney World, but I <u>haven't seen / didn't see</u> him yet. We're going to get together tomorrow.

16. Louis <u>has been / went</u> to the dentist three times last month, and his tooth doesn't hurt anymore.

17. I hope today's newspaper is still around. I <u>haven't read / didn't read</u> it yet.

VI. PRESENT PERFECT PROGRESSIVE

Complete the conversations. Use the present perfect progressive form of the verbs in parentheses.

1. A: ___Has___ Jason ___been handing in___ his homework lately?
a. (hand in)

He _____ more time on it at home.
b. (spend)

B: Yes, he has. And the work he _____ is excellent.
c. (do)

2. A: Who _____ the phones today?
a. (answer)

B: I have. And they _____ all day. I _____ every
b. (ring)   c. (jump up)

few minutes to answer them.

3. A: How long _____ it _____?
a. (snow)

B: For about an hour. And it _____ down really hard.
b. (come)

4. A: I _____ for over an hour. Will the doctor see me soon?
a. (wait)

B: We're sorry. Everyone _____ today because the doctor
b. (complain)

_____ behind schedule all day.
c. (run)

5. A: Sandra _____ to class lately. I wonder what's wrong.
a. (not come)

B: She _____ the night shift this month, so she
b. (work)

_____ during the day. That's why we haven't seen her.
c. (sleep)

VII. PRESENT PERFECT AND PRESENT PERFECT PROGRESSIVE

Complete the sentences. Use the present perfect or the present perfect progressive form of the verbs in the box. In some cases, either form is possible.

~~argue~~ clean finish give go off live talk teach work

1. Ted ___has argued___ with his neighbors several times about the noise they make. Now he's going to call the landlord.

2. I _____ the house all day, and it's still a mess.

3. Carol _____ with computers since she was a teenager. She never wants to do anything else.

4. I _____ this book. Do you want to borrow it?

5. A car alarm _____ for the last hour. I hope someone turns it off soon.

6. Diana _____ on the phone with her cousin in Argentina for over an hour. Doesn't she know how expensive long-distance calls are?

7. Our English teacher _____ us three quizzes so far this term.

8. Professor Collins _____ at this university for over 30 years, but he plans to retire next year.

9. Roberto _____ always _____ in the city, and he doesn't want to move to the suburbs.

VIII. SYNTHESIS

Circle the letter of the correct answer to complete each sentence.

1. Have you ever _____ to a movie studio?   **A B Ⓒ D**
   (A) go   (C) gone
   (B) went   (D) going

2. Mrs. Sato has been _____ a lot of progress with her English.   **A B C D**
   (A) making   (C) make
   (B) makes   (D) made

3. She _____ that paper for three days, and she's not done yet.   **A B C D**
   (A) 's written   (C) wrote
   (B) 's been writing   (D) writes

4. _____ you lived here long, Ali?   **A B C D**
   (A) Has   (C) Were
   (B) Did   (D) Have

5. I've _____ wanted to go to Paris, but I'm afraid of flying.   **A B C D**
   (A) never   (C) just
   (B) always   (D) lately

6. We're sorry that we _____ your game last night.   **A B C D**
   (A) 've missed   (C) missed
   (B) 've been missing   (D) were missing

7. Laura's flight hasn't gotten in _____. It's late because of the bad weather.   **A B C D**
   (A) since   (C) never
   (B) already   (D) yet

8. My family loves this house. We _____ here since I was born.   **A B C D**
   (A) have lived   (C) were living
   (B) lived   (D) live

9. _____ Tomas ever thought about going back to school?   A B C D

(A) Have

(B) Has

(C) Did

(D) Was

10. Akira has been a carpenter for _____.   A B C D

(A) 1998

(B) he was twenty-one years old

(C) he finished school

(D) many years

11. Where _____ before you moved here?   A B C D

(A) have you lived

(B) have you been living

(C) did you live

(D) you lived

12. The company accountant _____ my office because they're painting his.   A B C D

(A) has been sharing

(B) share

(C) shared

(D) has shared

13. Look! The flowers have bloomed _____, and spring hasn't even arrived.   A B C D

(A) yet

(B) lately

(C) since

(D) already

14. How _____ your birthday last year?   A B C D

(A) have you celebrated

(B) did you celebrate

(C) have you been celebrating

(D) do you celebrate

15. Mrs. Reynolds has been our teacher since _____.   A B C D

(A) January

(B) two months

(C) always

(D) a few weeks

IX. SYNTHESIS

Each sentence has four underlined words or phrases. The four underlined parts of the sentence are marked A, B, C, and D. Circle the letter of the ONE underlined part that is NOT CORRECT.

1. <u>Has</u> you and <u>your</u> family <u>lived</u> in this apartment <u>for</u> a long time?   Ⓐ B C D
     A   B   C   D

2. The kitchen <u>is</u> a mess because <u>I've</u> been <u>cooked</u> <u>since</u> noon.   A B C D
            A   B   C   D

3. We <u>haven't</u> <u>been knowing</u> Pat <u>for</u> <u>very</u> long.   A B C D
      A   B   C D

4. Ms. Scott's assistant <u>has left</u> <u>already</u> because <u>he's</u> <u>had</u> a doctor's   A B C D
                      A   B   C D

appointment at 4:00.

5. Carlos looks and feels great because <u>he's</u> <u>been</u> <u>exercising</u> every day <u>for</u> the   A B C D
                              A   B   C   D

day after New Year's.

6. I <u>haven't given</u> Dan the message because he <u>hasn't</u> <u>come</u> in <u>already</u>.   A B C D
    A   B   C   D

7. Mark's teacher <u>told</u> him to study more <u>for</u> almost a year, <u>but</u> he doesn't take   A B C D
              A   B   C

her very <u>seriously</u>.
           D

8. <u>Before</u> I <u>bought</u> my car, I <u>always</u> <u>have taken</u> the bus to work. A B C D
      A   B   C   D

9. Silvia <u>has been</u> out of school <u>since</u> about a week <u>because</u> she <u>has</u> the flu. A B C D
           A   B   C   D

10. I'<u>ve been going</u> to Japan on business <u>for years</u>, but I <u>haven't never</u> <u>gone</u> to China. A B C D
       A   B   C   D

11. Rafael <u>took</u> a nap <u>for</u> the last two hours, but I think we <u>ought to</u> wake <u>him up</u> now. A B C D
         A   B   C   D

12. <u>Have</u> you <u>gave</u> your parents the news that you'<u>re getting</u> married <u>next</u> year? A B C D
      A   B   C   D

13. That actor's movies <u>have</u> <u>always</u> <u>been</u> good, but his last one <u>has been</u> terrific. A B C D
                   A   B   C   D

PART IV PRESENT PERFECT

I. PRESENT PERFECT: *SINCE* AND *FOR*

Complete the story with since *or* for.

Grace and Julio have lived in New York City _____since_____ 1991. Grace has worked
                                              1.

at the Museum of Modern Art _____ almost ten years. She's a cashier. Julio is
                              2.

a waiter at an elegant French restaurant. He's worked there _____ he moved to
                                                              3.

New York twenty-five years ago. Grace has been bored with her job _____ a long
                                                                    4.

time now. _____ months, she's wanted to go back to school and study computer
          5.

science. She and Julio have talked about this _____ last July. Grace is sure they'll
                                               6.

find a way. _____ they got married almost twenty years ago, she and Julio have
            7.

always worked things out.

II. PRESENT PERFECT: *SINCE* AND *FOR*

Use the words in parentheses to write questions. Then complete the answers, using since *or* for.

1. (How long / you / be on a diet?)
   A: ___How long have you been on a diet?___
   B: ___I've been on a diet since___ last Monday.

2. (How long / Tony / go to this school?)
   A: _____
   B: _____ four years.

3. (Ed and Lydia / live here / for a long time?)
   A: _____
   B: _____ they were in high school.

4. (How long / that stop sign / be at the corner?)
   A: _____
   B: _____ we moved here.

5. (George / wear an earring / for a long time?)
   A: _____
   B: _____ about a year.

6. (How long / Kate / work as a barber?)

A: _____

B: _____ she got her license a few years ago.

7. (the kids / be asleep / long?)

A: _____

B: _____ almost an hour.

III. PRESENT PERFECT: *ALREADY* AND *YET*

Complete the conversations. Use the present perfect form of the verbs in parentheses, already *or* yet, *and short answers.*

1. A: ___Have___ you ___gone___ to the eye doctor ___yet___?
           a. (go)   b.

   B: Yes, ___I have___. I had an early appointment.
                     c.

2. A: _____ your teacher _____ you homework _____?
                                      a. (give)   b.

   It's the first day of class!

   B: Yes, _____. Ms. Chen wants us to write two paragraphs about ourselves.
                  c.

3. A: _____ your father _____ _____?
                                      a. (retire)   b.

   B: No, _____. He's only fifty-six years old.
                  c.

4. A: _____ the mail _____ _____? It's only noon.
                              a. (come)   b.

   B: Yes, _____, but there wasn't anything for you.
                  c.

5. A: _____ you and Jack _____ _____ what you want
                                      a. (decide)   b.

   to do for the holidays?

   B: No, _____. Is it okay if we let you know next week?
                 c.

6. A: _____ you _____ Lee's new apartment _____?
                          a. (see)   b.

   B: No, _____. But I've heard it's really nice.
                 c.

IV. PRESENT PERFECT: INDEFINITE PAST

A mother and father are making plans for their son's thirteenth birthday. They want to do something different this year, so they're trying to remember what they did in past years. Use the words in parentheses to write questions and answers. Use ever *with the questions and, when appropriate, use* never *in short answers.*

1. (we / have / a barbecue at the beach?)

   A: ___Have we ever had a barbecue at the beach?___

   B: No, ___never.___

2. (Joey / go / to the skating rink on Main Street?)

A: _____

B: Yes, _____

3. (we / take / him to his favorite restaurant?)

A: _____

B: No, _____

4. (we / let / him pick out a video game at the toy store?)

A: _____

B: Yes, _____

5. (Joey / be / to the big amusement park in Centerville?)

A: _____

B: No, _____

6. (you / make / his favorite dinner?)

A: _____

B: Yes, _____

7. (we / invite / all his friends here for a party?)

A: _____

B: No, _____

V.   PRESENT PERFECT AND SIMPLE PAST TENSE

Circle the correct words to complete the sentences.

1. Anne (lived) / has lived in Mexico City last year.

2. I need to make a deposit to my checking account today, but I haven't found / didn't find the time to go to the bank.

3. Vincent and Julie have gone out / went out on three dates so far this month. I think they like each other a lot.

4. Sharon told me you just moved here from Seattle. How long have you lived / did you live there?

5. The weather has been / was really awful lately. Do you think it will ever stop raining?

6. I got a bad grade on my composition because I haven't handed it in / didn't hand it in on time.

7. A few years ago, Gaby's parents have told / told her she was adopted.

8. I 've never seen / never saw a James Bond film, but I'm really looking forward to seeing the new one tonight.

9. We haven't understood / didn't understand the present perfect last year, but we understand it now.

10. Did you know that it has snowed / snowed last night?

11. Your girlfriend is very nice. How long have you known / did you know her?

12. The mail carrier <u>has come / came</u> about an hour ago.

13. Chris <u>has been / was</u> sick a lot lately. I don't think he takes very good care of himself.

14. There <u>have been / were</u> some really interesting programs on TV last night.

15. The phone <u>hasn't rung / didn't ring</u> for the last hour. Are you sure it's working?

16. I'm sorry you don't like your new job. How long <u>have you been / were you</u> there?

17. The teacher <u>has given / gave</u> us three quizzes this week, and the week's not over yet!

VI. PRESENT PERFECT PROGRESSIVE

Complete the conversations. Use the present perfect progressive form of the verbs in parentheses.

1. A: Why is your hair wet? _____ Have _____ you _____ been swimming _____?
  a. (swim)

  B: No, I haven't. Maryanne and I _____ the dog a bath. We
  b. (give)

  _____ him a lot lately, because he _____
  c. (bathe)   **d. (roll)**

  in the mud every chance he gets.

2. A: What _____ Eva _____ lately?
  a. (do)

  B: She and Jim _____ much these days. Jim
  b. (do not)

  _____ a lot of time at the doctor's office. He
  c. (spend)

  _____ sick, and the doctor can't figure out what's wrong.
  d. (feel)

3. A: How long _____ you _____ medicine here?
  a. (study)

  B: I _____ here for two terms. Last year I was at another university.
  b. (go)

  Altogether I _____ medicine for three years.
  c. (study)

4. A: This traffic jam is awful! We _____ here for fifteen minutes.
  a. (sit)

  B: Stop complaining. The radio said that the police _____ a very serious
  b. (clear up)

  accident. And we _____ an ambulance siren, so some people are
  c. (hear)

  probably hurt.

VII. PRESENT PERFECT AND PRESENT PERFECT PROGRESSIVE

Complete the sentences. Use the present perfect or the present perfect progressive form of the verbs in the box. In some cases, either form is possible.

change   drive   have   repair   scream   see   study   ~~teach~~   turn off

1. Professor Stein _____ has taught _____ this course three times.

2. The neighbors _____ at each other for the past hour. I wish they'd stop.

3. Lisa _____ her alarm clock, but she's still not up.

4. This is my favorite movie. I _____ it more than ten times!

5. Bill _____ in the library for hours. He should probably take a break.

6. How long _____ Dina _____ her driver's license?

7. Carlos _____ televisions since he graduated from high school, but he'd like to find a new career by the time he's thirty.

8. We've been eating at this restaurant for years, and it _____ a bit.

(negative)

9. We _____ around in circles all morning. Why don't we stop and ask for directions?

VIII.   SYNTHESIS

Circle the letter of the correct answer to complete each sentence.

1. Have you ever _____ to Italy?   A   B   Ⓒ   D
   (A) be   (C) been
   (B) were   (D) being

2. How long _____ Mr. Valdes worked here?   A   B   C   D
   (A) has   (C) did
   (B) has been   (D) was

3. Jack and Jill _____ a lot of time working in their yard last spring.   A   B   C   D
   (A) have spent   (C) were spending
   (B) have been spending   (D) spent

4. I haven't done the laundry _____. I'm going to try to do it tonight.   A   B   C   D
   (A) yet   (C) never
   (B) since   (D) already

5. Suzanne and I have been best friends since _____.   A   B   C   D
   (A) almost twenty years   (C) we were in college
   (B) two months   (D) always

6. Where _____ on your vacation last year?   A   B   C   D
   (A) have you gone   (C) did you use to go
   (B) have you been going   (D) did you go

7. Can you call back a little later? Tadashi and I _____ an interesting   A   B   C   D
   discussion and I'd like to finish it.
   (A) have   (C) had
   (B) have been having   (D) have had

8. Has anyone in your family _____ won the lottery?   A   B   C   D
   (A) always   (C) yet
   (B) never   (D) ever

9. I've been exercising for _____, and I'm exhausted.   A B C D
   (A) an hour   (C) noon
   (B) all morning   (D) I got home from work

10. Mara and I are good friends. We _____ each other since we were five years old. A B C D
   (A) know   (C) 've known
   (B) knew   (D) 've been knowing

11. My boss has just _____ me a promotion and a raise!   A B C D
   (A) been giving   (C) give
   (B) gave   (D) given

12. Where _____? I've been calling you for hours.   A B C D
   (A) have you been   (C) you've been
   (B) you were   (D) have you been being

13. Mario has been on a diet for two weeks, and he's _____ lost ten pounds.   A B C D
   (A) lately   (C) since
   (B) already   (D) yet

14. How _____ Pete lose that game?   A B C D
   (A) has   (C) has been
   (B) did   (D) have

15. Where _____ before you took this job?   A B C D
   (A) did you work   (C) have you worked
   (B) have you been working   (D) you were working

IX. SYNTHESIS

Each sentence has four underlined words or phrases. The four underlined parts of the sentence are marked A, B, C, and D. Circle the letter of the ONE underlined part that is NOT CORRECT.

1. <u>Have</u> your father <u>always</u> <u>been</u> a baker, or <u>is</u> baking his new hobby?   (A) B C D
   A   B   C   D

2. Before I <u>met</u> you, I <u>haven't known</u> anyone here <u>in</u> the city and I <u>was</u> very lonely.   A B C D
             A   B   C   D

3. The kids next door <u>have been</u> home <u>since</u> almost a week <u>now</u> because they   A B C D
                        A   B   C
   <u>have</u> bad colds.
   D

4. Rex <u>has been</u> <u>taken</u> flying lessons at the airport, and <u>he'll</u> probably have his   A B C D
        A   B   C
   license <u>by</u> next year.
           D

5. <u>How</u> long <u>you have</u> <u>been</u> <u>sitting</u> there in the dark?   A B C D
   A   B   C   D

6. Emily <u>has wanted</u> to go to college <u>last year</u>, <u>but</u> she <u>couldn't</u> afford the tuition.   A B C D
          A   B   C   D

7. Paula's parents <u>have</u> always <u>took</u> her with them <u>when</u> they <u>go</u> on vacation.   A B C D
                    A   B   C   D

8. I've been owning this car for a long time, and I haven't needed to repair it often.   **A B C D**
      A   B   C   D

9. I've always worn my hair long, but last week I've decided to get a haircut.   **A B C D**
      A   B   C   D

10. We haven't done our holiday shopping already because we're waiting until   **A B C D**
          A   B   C

we get our paychecks on Friday.
   D

11. Alyson didn't eat well since Adam has been on his business trip, because he   **A B C D**
              A   B   C

usually does all the cooking.
       D

12. I've ever been to Asia, but I traveled all around Europe last year.   **A B C D**
      A B   C   D

13. My mother has taught for many years before she retired, and recently she's been   **A B C D**
                A   B   C   D

busy as a volunteer at the hospital.

PART V ADJECTIVES AND ADVERBS: REVIEW AND EXPANSION

I. ADJECTIVES AND ADVERBS

Circle the correct words to complete the letter.

Dear Sally,

Thanks for your letter. I was (happy) / happily to hear from you!
                                1.

   I'm writing with good / well news. Everything is going good / well here at school. I've been
                      2.   3.

working hard / hardly , but my courses are interesting / interestingly . Most of my professors
            4.   5.

seem to know what they're talking about, and they explain everything

clear and thorough / clearly and thoroughly . My roommate and I are getting along
            6.

beautiful / beautifully , and living in a dormitory isn't as complete / completely
            7.   8.

uncomfortable / uncomfortably as I thought it would be. In fact, it's kind of fun. The only problem
            9.

I've been having late / lately is with the food here. The cafeteria food is awful / awfully , so it's not
                     10.   11.

easy / easily to eat nutritious / nutritiously . Sometimes I go to a nice / nicely store near here that
    12.   13.   14.

sells things like fruit and fresh / freshly made salads. The bad / badly thing is that they charge
                            15.   16.

extreme / extremely high / highly prices. I paid $1.00 for an apple yesterday.
    17.   18.

   Well, I'd better go now. It's getting late / lately , and I have an important / importantly paper
                                    19.   20.

due tomorrow. Write me more about your new friends. They seem interesting / interestingly .
                                                                        21.

Love,

F.

II. ADJECTIVES AND ADVERBS

Complete the story, combining the pairs of words in parentheses. Use the correct adjective or adverb forms.

Today was the last day of the semester and the end of a _____truly wonderful_____ experience
                                                          1. (true / wonderful)

for me: my poetry class. This was an _____ course, and the professor
                                        2. (exceptional / inspiring)

always prepared _____. I did _____ in the course
                  3. (extreme / careful)   4. (reasonable / good)

(I got a B), but Sid got a _____ grade (an A+) because his writing is
                            5. (real / high)

_____. Jill almost always gets A's in her English courses, but this time
  6. (beautiful / poetic)

Diagnostic and Final Tests **201**

she got a B–, an _____ grade for her. Poor Jim! His grade was
           7. (unusual / low)

_____; he got a D because the professor thought his poetry was
   8. (bare / acceptable)

_____ .
   9. (childish / simple)

III. ADJECTIVES AND ADVERBS

Circle the correct adjectives to complete the conversations.

1. **A:** This is such a bored /(boring) movie!
             a.

   B: I'm really (bored)/ boring , too. Let's leave.
          b.

2. **A:** I was amazed / amazing when I saw the Grand Canyon.
         a.

   B: Me, too. It's a fascinated / fascinating sight.
            b.

3. **A:** We were terrified / terrifying the first time we flew.
        a.

   B: Well, you don't seem frightened / frightening at all now.
            b.

4. **A:** The story about the family that disappeared is really shocked / shocking .
                  a.

   B: I agree. And it's truly distressed / distressing that the police don't have a single clue as to what
              b.

   happened to them.

5. **A:** You look confused / confusing .
        a.

   B: I am. I don't understand this exercise, and it's too embarrassed / embarrassing to ask the
                 b.

   teacher for help.

6. **A:** I was surprised / surprising at the judge's decision today in court.
        a.

   B: That judge is famous for his shocked / shocking decisions.
           b.

IV. ADJECTIVES: COMPARATIVES AND EQUATIVES

Complete the sentences with the correct comparative form of the adjectives in parentheses. Add than *where necessary.*

1. Ted has grown two inches since December. He's _____ taller than _____ I am, now.
                               (tall)

2. Is Jupiter _____ Earth?
           (large)

3. Spinach is _____ lettuce.
        (nutritious)

4. I put a lot of sugar in the cake, so it's probably _____ the pie.
                                 (sweet)

5. This apartment is much _____ your old one. Is it much
                     a. (big)

   _____ , too?
      b. (expensive)

6. Dolphins are mammals. They learn fast and can communicate with each other. They are

_____ fish.
　　　(intelligent)

7. The plane to Boston takes an hour, and the train takes seven hours. The plane is

_____ the train, but I think the train is _____.
　　a. (fast)　　　　　　　　　　　　　　　　　　　　　　　　　　b. (economical)

8. Which flavor of ice cream is _____ in your country: vanilla or chocolate?
　　　　　　　　　　　　　　　　a. (popular)

In the United States, most people think vanilla ice cream is _____
　　　　　　　　　　　　　　　　　　　　　　　　　　　　　b. (good)

chocolate.

V. ADJECTIVES: COMPARATIVES AND EQUATIVES

Read the first two sentences. Complete the third sentence with the correct form of be, as . . . as *or* not as . . . as *and the adjective in parentheses.*

1. Dario's grandfather is ninety-three.
　　Dario's grandmother is ninety-six.

　　(old) Dario's grandfather ___isn't as old as his grandmother.___

2. The store sold almost $1,000 in merchandise today.
　　Yesterday the store took in close to $1,000, too.

　　(good) Today's sales _____

3. An adult leopard weighs about 90 kg.
　　An adult tiger weighs about 200 kg.

　　(heavy) The average leopard _____

4. Tina's dog can fetch a ball and roll over.
　　Nancy's dog can't do any tricks.

　　(talented) Nancy's dog _____

5. Approximately 150 million people live in Russia.
　　Approximately 145 million people live in Pakistan.

　　(large) Pakistan's population _____

6. In the 1990s, publishing companies sold many romance novels.
　　Mysteries also sold very well.

　　(popular) In the 1990s, mysteries _____

VI. ADJECTIVES: SUPERLATIVES

Complete the paragraphs about American movies in the twentieth century. Use the superlative form of the adjectives in the box. Use one adjective more than once.

bad　boring　expensive　good　handsome　long　old　popular　recent　young

1. Tatum O'Neal was ___the youngest___ actor ever to win an Academy Award; she was
　　　　　　　　　　　　　　　a.

　　only ten years old when the Academy chose her as _____ actress of the
　　　　　　　　　　　　　　　　　　　　　　　　　　　　　　　b.

year for her role in the movie *Paper Moon*. _____ c. _____ actor to win an Oscar was Jessica Tandy, who was almost eighty-one when she won for *Driving Miss Daisy*.

2. The movie *Titanic* cost $200 million, making it _____ a. _____ film ever produced. Almost 2 billion people saw the movie, meaning that it was also _____ b. _____ film ever made. Many movie fans think it is _____ c. _____ movie they have ever seen. Personally, I didn't think it was very good, but it is certainly _____ d. _____ movie I've ever seen: It lasts more than three hours!

3. I just saw _____ a. _____ James Bond movie—the one that came out last week. I was very disappointed. There was no action, so it was _____ b. _____ movie of the Bond series so far; I almost fell asleep. The actor playing Bond is probably _____ c. _____ actor in Hollywood, but his good looks couldn't save the movie. Some Bond movies aren't as good as others. This one was definitely _____ d. _____!

VII. ADVERBS: EQUATIVES, COMPARATIVES, SUPERLATIVES

Complete the conversations with the equative, comparative, or superlative form of the adverbs in parentheses. Use as *or* than *where necessary.*

1. **A:** You look great!

   B: Thanks. Yes, I'm certainly doing ___better than___ a. (well) the last time you saw me. I haven't been working _____ b. (hard) I used to. Also, I've been watching my diet _____ c. (closely), and I've been exercising _____ d. (regularly). In general, I've been taking life _____ e. (slowly) than before and enjoying it _____ f. (completely) I can.

2. **A:** I don't know what to do about my neighbors. Their stereo plays _____ a. (loud) of any stereo I've ever heard. And yesterday they were fighting even _____ b. (noisily) usual. I was trying _____ c. (hard) I could to concentrate, but I couldn't hear myself think.

   B: You should talk to them. Ask them to play their music _____ d. (softly) and to talk _____ e. (quietly).

VIII. SYNTHESIS

Find and correct the mistake in each sentence.

1. I looked at two apartments, and the first one was almost as nice‸the second. ^{as}
2. The apartment uptown is a little bigger that the apartment downtown.
3. The downtown apartment is much sunnyer than the uptown one.
4. The uptown neighborhood seems more interestingly than the downtown one.
5. The downtown apartment is on a high floor than the uptown one.
6. That's why it's more quieter.
7. That's important to me because the noisier it gets, less I sleep.
8. Another consideration is that the uptown apartment is very closely to a subway stop.
9. That means I'll be able to get to work more early.
10. The apartment I have now is the cheaper of the three.
11. However, it's also ugliest.

IX. SYNTHESIS

Circle the letter of the correct answer to complete each sentence.

1. I really enjoyed the exhibit. Those were _____ photographs I've ever seen.   A B Ⓒ D

   (A) beautiful   (C) the most beautiful
   (B) most beautiful   (D) more beautiful

2. The United States _____ Canada. Canada is much larger.   A B C D

   (A) is larger than   (C) is as small as
   (B) isn't as large as   (D) is as large as

3. The weather has been bad all morning, and I think it's getting _____.   A B C D

   (A) worse   (C) worst
   (B) bad   (D) more bad

4. Drive _____! The roads are wet.   A B C D

   (A) safer   (C) safely
   (B) safe   (D) safest

5. Who works _____: a teacher, a doctor, or a lawyer?   A B C D

   (A) hardly   (C) more hard
   (B) harder   (D) the hardest

6. Why have you gotten to class _____ every day this week?   A B C D

   (A) lately   (C) late
   (B) later   (D) latest

7. Sahima is _____ salesperson in the store.   A B C D

   (A) the best   (C) the good

   (B) the better   (D) the well

8. That music is very _____. Could you turn it down a little?   A B C D

   (A) louder   (C) loud

   (B) loudly   (D) loudest

9. Sharon speaks four languages, but I speak only one. She learns languages   A B C D
_____ than I do.

   (A) as easily   (C) easiest

   (B) easier   (D) more easily

10. Last year we won the championship. But this year we're not playing _____   A B C D
and we haven't won a game yet.

   (A) good   (C) best

   (B) better   (D) well

11. Ali has the _____ habit of interrupting people while they're speaking.   A B C D

   (A) annoy   (C) annoys

   (B) annoyed   (D) annoying

12. The more you exercise, _____.   A B C D

   (A) you'll feel better   (C) the better you'll feel

   (B) you'll feel well   (D) you'll feel the best

13. Waleed got an A on the exam, but Alberto only got a B. The teacher doesn't know   A B C D
why Alberto hasn't been doing _____ Waleed this term.

   (A) worse than   (C) better

   (B) as good as   (D) as well as

X. SYNTHESIS

*Each sentence has four underlined words or phrases. The four underlined parts of the
sentence are marked A, B, C, and D. Circle the letter of the ONE underlined part that is
NOT CORRECT.*

1. I've just finished a really well book about wildlife in Alaska.   A B C (D)
   A   B   C   D

2. In the United States and Canada, Thanksgiving weekend is the busier and   A B C D
                                               A   B
most dangerous traveling time of the year.
   C   D

3. You'll improve tremendously your English if you practice much more regularly.   A B C D
            A   B   C   D

4. Are you really interesting in going to a better college?   A B C D
        A   B   C D

5. There <u>were</u> over 100 runners in the race, and Alice <u>won</u> because she ran
A   B

 <u>the faster</u> <u>of all of</u> them.   **A B C D**
  C   D

6. I think Isabel Allende's <u>most recent</u> novel is <u>beautiful</u> and <u>incredible</u> <u>touching</u>. **A B C D**
           A   B   C   D

7. Eduardo is <u>the older</u> in the family, but he <u>doesn't read</u> <u>as well as</u> his <u>younger</u> **A B C D**
       A   B   C   D

 sisters.

8. <u>The later</u> you <u>wait</u>, <u>worse</u> the traffic <u>will be</u>.   **A B C D**
   A   B   C   D

9. Ms. Carlin tried to teach the lesson, <u>but</u> her students <u>just</u> got <u>more and more</u> **A B C D**
                   A   B   C

 <u>noisily</u>.
 D

10. We're <u>the busiest</u> we<u>'ve ever been</u> <u>right</u> now, so we've <u>hard</u> had time to sleep. **A B C D**
     A   B   C   D

11. The house on the corner is <u>smaller</u> but <u>beautifuler</u> <u>than</u> <u>the one</u> across the street. **A B C D**
            A   B   C D

12. Your <u>new</u> car is <u>prettier than</u> your old one, but it's <u>least</u> <u>comfortable</u>. **A B C D**
    A   B   C   D

13. <u>The worse</u> epidemic <u>of</u> all time <u>was</u> the Black Plague, which killed <u>more than</u> **A B C D**
   A   B   C   D

 750 million people in the fourteenth century.

14. We were <u>really</u> <u>surprised</u> to see Lou at the mall last night because he <u>usual</u> **A B C D**
      A   B   C

 works <u>late</u> on Fridays.
    D

15. In some countries, <u>the wealthiest</u> citizens <u>often</u> give money to <u>charitably</u> **A B C D**
           A   B   C

 organizations that help <u>less fortunate</u> people.
          D

16. This filmmaker usually makes <u>wonderful</u> films, but this was <u>the less</u> <u>interesting</u> **A B C D**
            A   B   C

 documentary I<u>'ve ever seen</u>.
    D

PART V ADJECTIVES AND ADVERBS: REVIEW AND EXPANSION

 FINAL TEST

I. ADJECTIVES AND ADVERBS

Circle the correct words to complete the letter.

Dear Nick,

Your letter arrived (late)/ lately this morning, and I was glad / gladly to receive it. It's good / well to
      1.   **2.**   **3.**
know that things are going good / well for you at your new job. Your apartment sounds nice / nicely,
                            4.   **5.**
and I'm happy / happily that you've found a way to live affordable / affordably in the city. I know
           6.   **7.**
how extreme / extremely expensive / expensively everything can be if you don't shop
      8.   **9.**
careful / carefully.
    10.

      Everything is fine / finely here. I've been working hard / hardly and finding my job
                  11.   **12.**
surprising / surprisingly enjoyable. I've also been seeing a lot of Tara late / lately. We usual / usually
  13.   **14.**   **15.**
go out once or twice during the week—for quiet / quietly dinners. Most weekends, we spend a lot of
                                        16.
time together, too; even when we don't make special / specially plans, we always have fun. Tara is a
                                    17.
wonderful / wonderfully woman, and I am thinking serious / seriously of asking her to marry me.
18.   **19.**
What do you think? You're my oldest and dearest friend, and I great / greatly value your opinion. Can
                                               20.
you see me as a married man?

      Please call or write soon. I'm very eager / eagerly to hear from you.
                                    21.

Fond regards,

Jay

II. ADJECTIVES AND ADVERBS

Complete the story, combining the pairs of words in parentheses. Use the correct adjective or adverb forms.

Today was my last day at Ace Computer Company. The day went by _____incredibly fast_____
                                                    1. (incredible / fast)

because I was busy finishing up a project. When I started at Ace, I was _____
                                                     2. (extreme / excited)

about working with people and learning more about computers. I was sure my skills were soon going

to be _____. I know no job is _____, but I found out
        3. (great / improved)   **4.** (absolute / perfect)

_____ that this one was _____. The boss was
      5. (real / quick)   **6.** (total / boring)

_____ , and I don't think he ever liked me. One day I got to work
7. (unreasonable / strict)

_____ , and the boss fired me. At first, I was _____
8. (unusual / late)   **9.** (terrible / upset)

over losing my job. Now I feel nothing but relief!

III. ADJECTIVES AND ADVERBS

Circle the correct adjectives to complete the conversations.

1. A: Sitting at a computer all day can be very <u>tired /(tiring)</u>.
                                              a.

   B: I know what you mean! I get <u>(tired)/ tiring</u> after an hour at the computer.
                                             b.

2. A: Marisa didn't even thank me for my gift. I'm really <u>annoyed / annoying</u> at her.
                                             a.

   B: I'm sure she'll thank you soon. I know she was very <u>pleased / pleasing</u> with it.
                                             b.

3. A: Can you believe how badly our team lost? This loss was really <u>embarrassed / embarrassing</u>!
                                             a.

   B: Yes, it was. But all the players said that they're feeling <u>inspired / inspiring</u> now and are sure
                                             b.

        to win the next game.

4. A: Are you <u>interested / interesting</u> in seeing a movie tonight?
                              a.

   B: Not really. There's a political debate on TV, and I know it will be very

        <u>entertained / entertaining</u> .
                   b.

5. A: The rise in our city's crime rate is truly <u>alarmed / alarming</u> .
                                         a.

   B: You're right. In fact, these days most people are <u>terrified / terrifying</u> of going out at night.
                                             b.

6. A: Of course you're <u>bored / boring</u>! You need to find a hobby.
                             a.

   B: I know, but everything I try turns out to be <u>disappointed / disappointing</u> .
                                             b.

IV. ADJECTIVES: COMPARATIVES AND EQUATIVES

Complete the sentences with the correct comparative form of the adjectives in parentheses. Add than
where necessary.

1. I've lost some weight, so I bought some new clothes I really like. These clothes
    are _____smaller than_____ my clothes from last year, and they're
             a. (small)

    _____ , too.
       b. (nice)

2. Russia is _____ China, but China has a _____
                a. (big)   **b.** (large)
    population.

3. Do you believe it's true that driving in a car is _____ flying in an airplane?
                                                   (dangerous)

4. Let's go to The Palace instead of The Cave. The Palace is _____ , but we

   a. (far)

   can take the car, and it's much _____ .

   b. (lively)

5. Which type of television program do you think is _____ in your country:

   a. (popular)

   soap operas or talk shows? Which do you think is _____ ?

   b. (good)

6. Most small cars get more miles to the gallon than most large cars. That's why small cars are

   usually _____ large cars.

   (economical)

7. I read two novels this month. *Red Silk* has an exciting plot and funny characters. *West Street* has a

   boring plot and dull characters. *Red Silk* is much _____ *West Street*.

   (interesting)

V.   ADJECTIVES: COMPARATIVES AND EQUATIVES

Read the first two sentences. Complete the third sentence with the correct form of be, as . . . as *or* not as
. . . as *and the adjective in parentheses.*

1. Clara can swim almost 1,500 meters without stopping.
   Ed can swim about 1,000 meters without stopping.

   (fit) Ed __isn't as fit as Clara.__

2. The underground railroad system in London opened in 1863.
   The underground railroad system in Budapest opened in 1896.

   (old) The system in Budapest _____

3. The Great Belt Bridge in Denmark is 1,624 meters long.
   The Jiangyin Bridge in China is 1,624 meters long.

   (long) The Great Belt Bridge _____

4. Approximately 478 million people in the world speak Hindi.
   Approximately 413 million people speak Spanish.

   (widely spoken) Spanish _____

5. Our team won three gold medals, two silver medals, and four bronze medals.
   The Nigerian team also went home with three gold medals, two silver medals, and four bronze
   medals.

   (successful) The Nigerian team _____

6. George Washington, the first U.S. president, was 1.88 m tall.
   Abraham Lincoln, the sixteenth president, was 1.93 m tall.

   (tall) Washington _____

VI. ADJECTIVES: SUPERLATIVES

Complete the paragraphs about world geography and other facts. Use the superlative form of the adjectives in the box. Use some adjectives more than once.

common	deep	fast	heavy	high	large	long	sleepy	small

1. Vatican City is only 44 km in area, making it _____the smallest_____ country in the world.

a.

   Russia, on the other hand, is _____ country in the world: over 17 million

b.

   square km.

2. _____ mountain peak on earth is Mount Everest in Nepal; it's

a.

   8,848 m. The Pacific Ocean is two times as large as the Atlantic Ocean; in fact, the Pacific is

   _____ ocean in the world. The Pacific is also _____

b.   c.

   ocean, with a known depth of 11,033 m. The Nile, with an approximate length of 6,690 km, is the

   world's _____ river.

d.

3. _____ city name in the United States is Fairview: There are at least 66

a.

   different U.S. cities called Fairview! The country with _____ official name

b.

   is Libya; Libya's official name has 56 letters!

4. _____ land mammal is the African elephant; it can weigh as much as

a.

   7,000 kg. _____ mammal is the cheetah, which can run at a speed of

b.

   105 km per hour. The koala is _____ animal in the world, sleeping an

c.

   average of 22 hours a day.

VII. ADVERBS: EQUATIVES, COMPARATIVES, SUPERLATIVES

Complete the conversations with the equative, comparative, or superlative form of the adverbs in parentheses. Use as *or* than *where necessary.*

1. **A:** Have you ever driven with Carlos?

   B: No, I haven't. Carlos's father taught me driving and is a really good driver. Does Carlos drive

   _____as well as_____ his father?

a. (well)

   A: No, he's terrible! He drives _____ of anyone I've seen. In traffic,

b. (dangerously)

   he goes _____ everyone else; he passes lots of cars. Then, on

c. (fast)

   the highway, he drives _____ he can. He definitely drives

d. (slow)

   _____ of all our friends.

e. (badly)

2. **A:** Could you invite Laura to the party? You know her _____ I do.
   a. (well)

   B: Sure, I'll invite her, but I don't know her _____ you think.
   b. (well)

   She's a strange person. The _____ you know her, the
   c. (long)

   _____ you understand her.
   d. (little)

   A: Well, she seems to take things _____ most young people. And she
   e. (seriously)

   works _____ of all the students in our class. But I still want her to
   f. (hard)

   come to the party.

VIII. SYNTHESIS

Find and correct the mistake in each sentence.

1. The doctor said the twins were identical, but Gary ^is not as outgoing as Dave.
2. Gary is a little tall than Dave.
3. Dave is heavyer than Gary.
4. Dave is a much more aggressively boy than Gary.
5. Gary is quieter than Dave, but he expresses himself more better.
6. That's why Gary is a better student that Dave.
7. The big the boys get, the more different they become.
8. Dave is starting to become his parents' worsest problem.
9. Dave's teacher says he's not well-behaved as the other students.
10. Also, he isn't working as hardly as he should.
11. Dave has promised he will work hardest from now on.

IX. SYNTHESIS

Circle the letter of the correct answer to complete each sentence.

1. Did you know that the giraffe is _____ mammal in the world?   (A) B   C   D

   (A) the tallest   (C) tall
   (B) taller   (D) tallest

2. The play was great! It was the most _____ show I've ever seen.   A   B   C   D

   (A) moves   (C) move
   (B) moved   (D) moving

3. The Mississippi River _____ the Amazon. The Amazon is longer.   A   B   C   D

   (A) is as long as   (C) isn't as long as
   (B) is longer than   (D) is as short as

4. Be _____ . I just mopped the floor.　　　　　　　　　　**A B C D**

    (A) carefully   (C) more carefully

    (B) the most careful   (D) careful

5. The _____ I try to memorize this poem, the less I remember.　　**A B C D**

    (A) hardly   (C) harder

    (B) hardest   (D) hard

6. Elaine is _____ student in the class.　　　　　　　　　　**A B C D**

    (A) the most hardworking   (C) hardworking

    (B) the more hardworking   (D) hardly working

7. How did you open that jar so _____? I've been trying for the past fifteen　　**A B C D**

    minutes!

    (A) easier   (C) easy

    (B) easily   (D) easiest

8. Have you ever eaten ostrich? It tastes like beef, but it's _____ for you.　　**A B C D**

    (A) best   (C) better

    (B) the best   (D) as good

9. June is never late for work because her apartment is very _____ to the　　**A B C D**

    office.

    (A) close   (C) closer

    (B) closely   (D) the closest

10. This assignment is _____ . Could you help me?　　　　　　**A B C D**

    (A) confused   (C) confuses

    (B) confusing   (D) confuse

11. Gil ran _____ Luis and Hector in all three races.　　　　　**A B C D**

    (A) faster than   (C) the fastest of

    (B) more fast than   (D) fast as

12. The dance performance tonight seemed very _____ .　　　　　**A B C D**

    (A) good   (C) prettily

    (B) well   (D) nicely

13. During the past month, the news has been getting _____ .　　　**A B C D**

    (A) worst   (C) worse and worse

    (B) more and more badly (D) bad, worse, and worst

X. SYNTHESIS

Each sentence has four underlined words or phrases. The four underlined parts of the sentence are marked A, B, C, and D. Circle the letter of the ONE *underlined part that is* NOT CORRECT.

1. We're <u>really</u> <u>exciting</u> today because we<u>'re going</u> to a <u>great</u> concert tonight.
       A   B   C   D
       A (B) C D

2. Yolanda <u>will feel</u> <u>more well</u> if she exercises <u>harder</u> and <u>more regularly</u>.
               A   B   C   D
       A   B C D

3. The <u>competitor fastest</u> will win a <u>beautiful</u> <u>gold medal</u> and <u>a new pair</u> of running shoes.
          A   B   C   D
       A   B C D

4. My <u>older</u> sister is having a party on Friday, and she wants everything to <u>go</u> <u>absolute</u> <u>perfectly</u>.
         A   B
       C   D
       A   B C D

5. <u>The more</u> he <u>practices</u> his French, <u>the more</u> <u>fluent</u> he'll be able to speak.
       A   B   C   D
       A   B C D

6. This year's textbook <u>is</u> much <u>less cheap</u> <u>than</u> last year's book, but it's <u>better</u>.
                     A   B   C   D
       A   B C D

7. Tony has been coming in <u>early</u> than usual, working <u>hard</u> all day, and staying <u>late</u> because he wants a <u>good</u> raise.
                        A   B
       C   D
       A   B C D

8. We enjoyed <u>the most recent</u> Tom Cruise movie, but it was <u>least</u> <u>interesting</u> than some of his <u>older</u> films.
               A   B   C
       D
       A   B C D

9. I've gotten some <u>bad</u> haircuts, but I think this is <u>the</u> <u>worse</u> haircut <u>I've ever gotten</u> in my whole life!
                   A   B   C
       D
       A   B C D

10. The Johnsons have never been to <u>our new house</u> <u>so</u> they'll need <u>very</u> <u>clearly</u> directions.
                                       A   B   C   D
        A   B C D

11. I'm <u>feeling</u> so <u>annoying</u> at Monica that I want to scream <u>as loud as</u> <u>I can</u>.
           A   B   C   D
        A   B C D

12. Donny <u>doesn't read</u> as <u>good</u> as <u>many other</u> children his age because his parents never read to him when he was <u>younger</u>.
                A   B   C
                                     D
        A   B C D

13. Bill Gates is one of <u>the richest</u> people <u>in</u> the world, and he gives <u>extremely</u> <u>generous</u> to charity.
                         A   B   C
        D
        A   B C D

14. Our apartment is <u>conveniently</u> located only <u>a block away</u> from a <u>wonderful</u> shopping center and <u>a</u> best restaurant in the city.
                           A   B   C
                              D
        A   B C D

15. Rick and I play tennis <u>early</u> every Saturday morning, and he <u>usually</u> beats me because he hits the ball <u>forcefully</u> <u>than</u> I do.
                          A   B
                               C   D
        A   B C D

16. If your throat is hurting as <u>bad</u> tomorrow <u>as</u> it <u>is</u> tonight, you'll have to go see your very <u>nice</u> doctor.
                           A   B   C
                         D
        A   B C D

PART VI GERUNDS AND INFINITIVES

I. GERUNDS: SUBJECT AND OBJECT

Complete the sentences with gerunds. Use the verbs in the box.

go	bowl	lose	move	hear	
not go	run	try	stay	~~walk~~	get together

1. ___Walking___ every day is a good habit.

2. I stayed home from work, and I missed an important meeting. _____ to work today
   a.
   was a bad decision. I hope I haven't risked _____ my job.
   b.

3. Fred and some of his friends have organized a bowling team. _____ is Fred's hobby,
   a.
   and he enjoys _____ with his friends at the bowling alley.
   b.

4. Sue likes to start her day off with a five-kilometer run. _____ in shape is important
   a.
   to Sue, and she enjoys _____ more than any other sport.
   b.

5. Fran hates cold weather, so she avoids _____ out in the winter. I wonder if she's
   a.
   ever considered _____ to the tropics.
   b.

6. Do you feel like _____ the new Korean restaurant tonight? I keep
   a.
   _____ really good things about it.
   b.

II. GERUNDS AFTER PREPOSITIONS

Complete the story. Choose the appropriate preposition from the box. (You will use some of the prepositions more than once.) Then add the gerund form of the verb in parentheses.

about	in	of	on	to	with

Keith is thirty-five years old, and he has a dream. What's his dream? Well, he dreams

___of going___ to college. When Keith was younger, he was bored
1. (go)

_____ and he wasn't at all interested _____ his
2. (study)   3. (continue)

education. During his last year of high school, he looked forward _____ and
4. (graduate)

_____ on his own. He was very excited _____ a job
5. (be)   6. (find)

and _____ himself.
7. (support)

When Keith found a small apartment in the city, his parents insisted

_____ him a little money to help him get started. Although Keith
    8. (give)

was opposed _____ his parents' money, he had to admit
    9. (accept)

_____ a little nervous.
    10. (feel)

    Keith worked at a lot of different jobs, and he got used _____ in the city.
    11. (live)

Some years later, he started to realize that being independent wasn't all that great. He succeeded

_____ a lot of good friends, but he was tired _____
    12. (make)   **13. (do)**

the kind of work that was available to him without a college education. More and more often,

he found himself thinking _____ his life. So now, although Keith isn't very
    14. (change)

happy _____ that he made a mistake, he plans _____
    15. (admit)   **16. (enter)**

college next fall. Better late than never!

III. INFINITIVES AFTER CERTAIN VERBS

Use the words in parentheses to complete the conversations. Use an object pronoun where necessary.

1. A: Billy was riding his bike without a helmet.
   B: (I've warned / a million times / wear his helmet.)

    I've warned him a million times to wear his helmet.

2. A: Marla and her assistant sometimes forget about our staff meetings.
   B: (We usually / remind / come to the meetings.)

    _____

3. A: The total on our restaurant bill seemed wrong.
   B: (That's why we / asked / see the menu again.)

    _____

4. A: I thought you didn't mind waiting for a cab.
   B: (I never / expected / wait for an hour, though!)

    _____

5. A: Sarah had a great time on her vacation this year.
   B: (That's why she / has decided / go to Miami next year, too.)

    _____

6. A: We enjoyed meeting John and his wife.
   B: (In fact, we / invited / visit us at our beach house next weekend.)

    _____

IV. INFINITIVES AFTER CERTAIN VERBS

For each conversation, use a verb from the box followed by an infinitive or an object + infinitive.

advise	~~invite~~	need	promise	~~refuse~~	remind	warn	would like

1. **MOTHER:** Do the dishes, please.

   DAUGHTER: No, I won't.

   SUMMARY: The daughter *refused to do the dishes.*

2. **FATHER:** Come in. Make yourself comfortable. Julia will be ready in a minute.

   BOY: Thank you, sir.

   SUMMARY: The father *invited the boy to come in.*

3. **FATHER:** You must be home by 10:00. If you're not, you won't be allowed to go out for two weeks. Do you understand me?

   DAUGHTER: Yes, Dad. I understand.

   SUMMARY: The father _____

4. **MOTHER:** It would make me so happy if you would spend more time with your little sister.

   SON: OK, Mom. I'll try.

   SUMMARY: The mother _____

5. **MOTHER:** Call me as soon as you get there.

   DAUGHTER: OK, Mom. I will.

   SUMMARY: The daughter _____

6. **SON:** Can I use the car tonight?

   MOTHER: I'm sorry. I have to use the car tonight.

   SUMMARY: The mother _____

7. **DAUGHTER:** Mom, please don't forget to sign my report card.

   MOTHER: I won't forget.

   SUMMARY: The daughter _____

8. **DAUGHTER:** I'm so confused, Dad. Should I get a job now or finish school first? What do you think?

   FATHER: I think you should finish high school.

   SUMMARY: The father _____

V. INFINITIVES OF PURPOSE

Read the sentence(s). Then write a new sentence with the same meaning, using an infinitive of purpose.

1. I bought a calculator because I need to balance my checkbook.

    I bought a calculator to balance my checkbook.

2. We avoid eating in restaurants. We don't want to spend a lot of money.

    _____

3. Gerry rides a bicycle because he wants to stay in shape.

    _____

4. We're wearing heavy coats today because we don't want to feel cold.

    _____

5. I stopped by the post office. I needed to buy stamps.

    _____

6. Sylvia uses the Internet all the time. She does research for her clients.

    _____

7. The Jacksons are staying home this weekend. They plan on painting the living room.

    _____

VI. INFINITIVES WITH *TOO* AND *ENOUGH*

Some college students are talking. Complete their conversations with the words in parentheses with the infinitive and too *or* enough.

1. A: Can't you walk any faster?

    B: Sure. What's the problem?

    A: We're not walking ____*fast enough for us to get*____ to the science building on time.
          (fast / us / get)

2. A: Can we get something to eat before class?

    B: No. It's _____ at the cafeteria.
          (late / stop)

3. A: Have you seen the new physics professor?

    B: Yes. I can't believe that guy is a professor. He doesn't look _____
          (old / be)

    a professor.

4. A: Hey, keep your voices down! This is a library, you know. It's _____.
          (noisy / me / concentrate)

    B: Sorry.

5. A: Ugh! This tastes awful!

    B: What do you expect from cafeteria food?

    A: Well, it should at least be _____.
          (good / us / eat)

6. A: Try some of this soup. It's not bad.

   B: Ow! It's _____.
                           (hot / me / eat)

7. A: Do you think we can carry these packages back to the dorm?

   B: Sure. They aren't _____.
                                (heavy / us / carry)

8. A: Do those guys ever stop partying?

   B: I know what you mean. Maybe they're not _____ in college.
                                             (mature / be)

9. A: I'm too tired to study any more tonight.

   B: Let's give it another hour. You've worked _____ now.
                                      (hard / give up)

VII.   GERUNDS AND INFINITIVES

Complete the story with the gerund or infinitive form of the verbs in parentheses.

Kathy is training very hard. She doesn't mind _____working_____ hard because she plans on
                                   1. (work)

_____ for the basketball team. Kathy is used to _____, and she loves it.
  2. (try out)   3. (compete)

Last year she played tennis, but she's decided _____ to basketball because she likes
                                        4. (change)

the idea of _____ a member of a team. Another reason she chose basketball is that she
           5. (be)

wants _____ for a sports scholarship and she thinks she'll have a better chance of
       6. (apply)

_____ one if she proves that she can play basketball really well. Kathy has always
  7. (receive)

been interested in _____ sports medicine because she would like _____
                8. (study)   9. (help)

athletes stay healthy. Unfortunately, she won't be able to afford _____ to college at all
                                                             10. (go)

if she can't persuade someone _____ her a scholarship.
                               11. (give)

VIII.   GERUNDS AND INFINITIVES

Circle the correct form to complete the sentences.

1. I think I'd better call the vet. The dog has stopped to eat / (eating).

2. Please remember to pick up / picking up some milk on your way home.

3. Gary will be home late. He stopped to exercise / exercising at the gym.

4. Why did the phone company send this warning? Did you forget to pay / paying the bill again?

5. I didn't recognize Mr. Rosen at all. I don't remember to meet / meeting him.

IX. GERUNDS AND INFINITIVES

Use each set of words to write two sentences with the same meaning.

1. relax / important
   a. _Relaxing is important._
   b. _It's important to relax._

2. swim / great
   a. _____
   b. _____

3. learn English / not easy
   a. _____
   b. _____

4. meet new people / interesting
   a. _____
   b. _____

X. SYNTHESIS

Find and correct the mistake in each sentence.

1. Have you decided ~~quitting~~ *to quit* smoking? Here are some tips.
2. Don't expect to stopping all at once.
3. Avoid to be with other people who smoke.
4. Remember drinking a lot of water.
5. It's important to getting a lot of rest, too.
6. Don't be nervous about tell people you are quitting.
7. You will get used to be a nonsmoker sooner than you think.

XI. SYNTHESIS

Circle the letter of the correct answer to complete each sentence.

1. We're sorry we're late. We stopped _____ a package.   A   B   C (D)

   (A) mailing   (C) and mail
   (B) mail   (D) to mail

2. You want to know what I'm going to do on my vacation? I plan on _____   A   B   C   D
   anything!

   (A) no do   (C) not doing
   (B) don't do   (D) am not doing

3. Are you sure you should take the day off? Aren't you concerned about _____   **A   B   C   D**

   behind in your work?

   (A) falling   (C) to fall

   (B) fall   (D) fallen

4. Do me favor: On your way home, stop at the drugstore _____ my medicine.   **A   B   C   D**

   (A) for picking up   (C) to pick up

   (B) and picking up   (D) pick up

5. Because he had roommates for such a long time, he isn't used to _____   **A   B   C   D**

   dinner alone.

   (A) had   (C) have

   (B) has   (D) having

6. They don't accept bills on the bus, so remember _____ a lot of change.   **A   B   C   D**

   (A) bring   (C) to bring

   (B) bringing   (D) and bring

7. _____ ignorant, Pete pretended to know more than he really did.   **A   B   C   D**

   (A) To seem not   (C) Not seeming

   (B) In order not to seem   (D) He didn't seem

8. Do you think Tony _____ to school tomorrow? His cough still sounds awful.   **A   B   C   D**

   (A) is well enough to go   (C) is sick enough to go

   (B) isn't too sick for going   (D) is better than going

9. Parents of teenagers can help their children by encouraging them _____   **A   B   C   D**

   about their problems.

   (A) talking   (C) for talking

   (B) talk   (D) to talk

10. The best way to improve your accent is to stop _____ that it's not perfect.   **A   B   C   D**

   (A) to worry   (C) worrying

   (B) be worried   (D) worry

11. Annie doesn't seem very happy about her new baby brother. How long do you   **A   B   C   D**

   think it will take her to get used to _____ an only child anymore?

   (A) being not   (C) doesn't be

   (B) isn't   (D) not being

12. We apologize _____ coming late. We somehow lost track of the time.   **A   B   C   D**

   (A) to   (C) for

   (B) in   (D) with

13. We invited Paolo to come with us on the trip, but he refused _____.   A B C D

(A) going   (C) us going
(B) to go   (D) us to go

XII. SYNTHESIS

Each sentence has four underlined words or phrases. The four underlined parts of the sentence are marked A, B, C, and D. Circle the letter of the ONE underlined part that is NOT CORRECT.

1. It <u>was getting</u> very late and I wanted <u>going</u> to bed, so I <u>asked</u> everyone <u>to leave</u> .   A Ⓑ C D
   A   B   C   D

2. If Sonia <u>doesn't do well</u> on tomorrow's exam, her teacher will insist <u>in</u> <u>giving</u>   A B C D
               A   B   C
   <u>her</u> extra work.
   D

3. We're <u>interested in</u> <u>taking</u> a trip to the Philippines, and our travel agent   A B C D
              A   B
   <u>has recommended</u> <u>we're going</u> in the spring.
            C   D

4. I plan <u>buying</u> a new sofa <u>for</u> the living room, but I <u>don't think</u> we can afford   A B C D
             A   B   C
   <u>to spend</u> money on furniture right now.
        D

5. I'm not <u>enough sick</u> <u>to stay home</u> today, but I'm probably <u>too sick</u> <u>to work well</u> .   A B C D
              A   B   C   D

6. I don't <u>object to work</u> late, because I'm <u>concerned about</u> <u>finishing</u> the project   A B C D
              A   B   C
   <u>on time</u> .
     D

7. <u>Do you think</u> Andy will agree <u>to lend</u> me some money if I promise <u>paying</u> him   A B C D
        A   B   C
   <u>back</u> by Saturday?
     D

8. Many countries are <u>seriously</u> considering <u>introducing</u> <u>stricter</u> fishing and   A B C D
                         A   B   C
   hunting regulations <u>in order save</u> endangered wildlife.
                         D

9. The world of computers <u>has been changing</u> <u>too fast</u> , <u>so</u> some of us <u>to keep up</u> .   A B C D
                              A   B   C   D

10. Wendy went <u>to the</u> office-supply store <u>to buy</u> some folders <u>for help</u> her <u>organize</u>   A B C D
                  A   B   C   D
   her papers.

11. The next time the neighbors <u>ask</u> us <u>to come</u> over for dinner, please <u>don't say</u>   A B C D
                                  A   B   C
   yes without <u>talk</u> to me first.
                D

12. Tom dislikes <u>to go</u> to the dentist, so he put off <u>making</u> an appointment <u>for</u> so   A B C D
                    A   B   C
   long that now he has some serious problems with his <u>teeth</u> .
                                                         D

13. No one <u>reminded me</u> <u>to study</u> for the test, <u>so</u> I forgot <u>bringing</u> my book and   A B C D
              A   B   C   D
   notebook home.

PART VI GERUNDS AND INFINITIVES

FINAL TEST

I. GERUNDS: SUBJECT AND OBJECT

Complete the sentences with the gerund form of the verbs in the box.

allow	cook	feel	make	~~smoke~~	be
argue	discuss	not go	sign up	translate	

1. _____Smoking_____ is a dangerous habit.

2. Dan hates arguments, so he avoids _____ about anything. He doesn't mind
   a.
   _____ politics, though, because he loves a good political discussion.
   b.

3. I admit _____ very angry at people who are late. _____ on time
   a.   **b.**
   is important to me.

4. I didn't go to class today, and the teacher gave a quiz. _____ to school today wasn't
   a.
   very smart of me. I hope the teacher will consider _____ me to take the quiz
   b.
   tomorrow.

5. Rick likes languages, and _____ sounds like interesting work. These days he is
   a.
   considering _____ for a course on translation.
   b.

6. Sharon enjoys _____, but she sometimes resents _____ dinner every
   a.   **b.**
   night of the week.

II. GERUNDS AFTER PREPOSITIONS

Complete the story. Choose the appropriate preposition from the box. (You will use some of the prepositions more than once.) Then add the gerund form of the verb in parentheses.

about	at	in	of	on	to	without

Diane has always dreamt _____of becoming_____ mayor of her city. Her family was
                            1. (become)

opposed _____ her to enter politics at first, but they soon got used
          2. (allow)

_____ Diane do "her own thing." She is very ambitious, but she isn't afraid
  3. (see)

_____. She is accustomed _____ what she thinks
  4. (fail)   **5. (do)**

is best for her and her career, and she insists _____ her views with anyone
                                                  6. (share)

who will listen.

Diane is tired _____ her city fall apart. She is interested
　　　　　　　　　7. (watch)

_____ improvements, and she knows she can do it
　　8. (make)

_____ taxes. She thinks it is time to get rid of the people in city
　　9. (raise)

government who resorted _____ dishonestly to get their jobs.
　　　　　　　　　　　　　　10. (act)

　　　Next week Diane will participate in a public debate. Her opponents and her supporters

can count _____ some new and original ideas. Diane believes
　　　　　　11. (hear)

_____ the truth, and she looks forward _____ the
　　12. (tell)　　　　　　　　　　　　　　　　　　　　13. (challenge)

system. She is very excited _____ her plans. And since she is very good
　　　　　　　　　　　　14. (describe)

_____ in front of a crowd, her supporters are sure that she will succeed
　　15. (speak)

_____ the election.
　　16. (win)

III.　INFINITIVES AFTER CERTAIN VERBS

Use the words in parentheses to complete the conversations. Use an object pronoun where necessary.

1. **A:** We're very busy tonight. I hope you won't mind waiting for a table.
   B: (It's Saturday night, so we expected / have to wait for awhile.)

   　　It's Saturday night, so we expected to have to wait for awhile. _____

2. **A:** Lauren got hurt yesterday because she wasn't wearing her seat belt.
   B: (I remind / all the time / wear her seat belt.)

   _____

3. **A:** Are these overdue library books yours?
   B: (Yes. And the librarian / would like / return them immediately.)

   _____

4. **A:** Did you have trouble returning the computer?
   B: (No. I asked / talk to the manager instead of to a salesperson.)

   _____

5. **A:** Are Jack and Jill new in town?
   B: (Yes, and we've invited / come for dinner tomorrow night.)

   _____

6. **A:** Alan didn't enjoy New York at all.
   B: (That's why I've encouraged / not go / there again.)

   _____

IV. INFINITIVES AFTER CERTAIN VERBS

For each conversation, use a verb from the box followed by an infinitive or an object + infinitive.

ask agree invite promise ~~refuse~~ remind ~~tell~~ warn

1. **MOTHER:** Honey, put your toys away.

   SON: No, Mom. I don't want to.

   SUMMARY: The mother _told her son to put his toys away._

   The son _refused to put his toys away._

2. **SUSAN:** I'm making paella on Saturday night. Do you want to come for dinner?

   STEVE: That sounds great. Thanks.

   SUMMARY: Susan _____

3. **POLICE OFFICER:** Slow down, ma'am. The next time I catch you speeding, I'll give you a ticket.

   WOMAN: I'm sorry, Officer. I won't drive that fast ever again. I promise!

   SUMMARY: The police officer _____

   The woman _____

4. **TANYA:** Could you stop at the store on your way home?

   BURT: Sure. No problem.

   SUMMARY: Tanya _____

   Burt _____

5. **CARL:** Take your medicine at noon. Don't forget.

   PATTY: I've written myself a note.

   SUMMARY: Carl _____

V. INFINITIVES OF PURPOSE

Read the sentence(s). Then write a new sentence with the same meaning, using an infinitive of purpose.

1. Victor bought an exercise bike because he wants to get in shape.

   Victor bought an exercise bike to get in shape.

2. We opened the windows. We wanted to let in some fresh air.

   _____

3. The Garcias are going to the museum on Saturday. They're interested in seeing the Picasso exhibit.

   _____

4. Politicians often appear on TV talk shows. They like to talk about themselves.

    _____

5. I'm going to run into the supermarket. I need to get a few things.

    _____

6. College students use the Internet all the time. They look up information.

    _____

7. Allison walks to work. She saves money that way.

    _____

VI. INFINITIVES WITH *TOO* AND *ENOUGH*

Some friends are talking about women in military combat. Complete their conversations with the words in parentheses with the infinitive and too *or* enough.

1. **A:** Do you think women can carry weapons?

   B: Yes. Women are _____strong enough to carry_____ weapons.
                                    (strong / carry)

2. **A:** What about fighting? Can women fight?

   B: Of course. Women aren't _____.
                                        (delicate / fight)

3. **A:** How would men react to having women in combat? Can they accept women as equals?

   B: I'm not sure. Some men are _____ women as equals.
                                              (afraid / accept)

4. **A:** Would male soldiers follow orders from women?

   B: Some women might not give orders _____ them.
                                                  (strongly / men / obey)

5. **A:** Do you think women can keep up with men?

   B: Sure they can. A lot of women can run _____ with men.
                                                       (fast / keep up)

6. **A:** Does public opinion support women in combat?

   B: I think public opinion is _____ women fight.
                                          (supportive / the government / let)

7. **A:** At what age should women be allowed to join the armed forces?

   B: I don't think either men or women are _____ soldiers until

   they're at least twenty-one.
                                                        (mature / be)

8. **A:** What about women and their emotions?

   B: That's ridiculous! Most women aren't _____ to war.
                                                      (emotional / go)

9. **A:** What do you think about all this, Ben?

   B: To be honest, the issue is _____.
                                           (complicated / me / understand)

VII.   GERUNDS AND INFINITIVES

Complete the story with the gerund or infinitive form of the verbs in parentheses.

Robert is studying and working very hard. He's used to _____working_____ hard because he's had a
                                                          1. (work)

part-time job at a supermarket since he was sixteen. Like many high school students, he doesn't mind

_____ time at a job because he loves the idea of _____ some money.
  2. (spend)   3. (earn)

    Robert would like _____ to college next year. He can afford _____
                       4. (go)   5. (go)

to the state university and has already applied. He hopes _____ a course there this
                                                             6. (take)

summer so that he can get used to being in college. Robert plans on _____ the state
                                                                        7. (attend)

university for two years, but he wants _____ to a famous school in New York for his
                                          8. (transfer)

last two years. He's always dreamt of _____ in a big city, and he thinks he'll have a
                                          9. (live)

better chance of _____ a good job if he moves to New York. But for now, Robert will
                   10. (get)

keep _____ people's groceries into bags. And you won't hear him complain!
       11. (put)

VIII.   GERUNDS AND INFINITIVES

Circle the correct form to complete the sentences.

1. Ines will be here soon. She stopped (to put)/ putting some gas in her car.

2. Hi, this is George. I'm waiting for you at the theater. I guess you forgot to meet / meeting me
   here tonight.

3. I know I wrote a check to the electric company last month, but I don't remember
   to send / sending it.

4. The minute you stop to exercise / exercising, you'll probably gain weight.

5. Tomorrow is your sister's birthday. Did you remember to send / sending her a card?

IX.   GERUNDS AND INFINITIVES

Use each set of words to write two sentences with the same meaning.

1. drive without a license / illegal

   a. _____Driving without a license is illegal._____

   b. _____It's illegal to drive without a license._____

2. talk during a movie / rude

   a. _____

   b. _____

3. listen to music / relaxing

    a. _____

    b. _____

4. take tests / challenging

    a. _____

    b. _____

X. SYNTHESIS

Find and correct the mistake in each sentence.

1. Has Jeff decided ᵗᵒ change jobs?

2. Don't forget to buying subway tokens.

3. I usually avoid to stay out late on weeknights.

4. Remember asking your teacher about the homework assignment.

5. Don't be nervous about speak English.

6. Are you used to live here now?

7. This problem is too hard for doing.

XI. SYNTHESIS

Circle the letter of the correct answer to complete each sentence.

1. I hope I'm not late. I had to stop _____ Carol's birthday cake.   A (B) C D

    (A) picking up   (C) and picked up

    (B) to pick up   (D) pick up

2. Mario isn't afraid _____ some risks to get what he wants.   A B C D

    (A) of taking   (C) takes

    (B) take   (D) to taking

3. Nimisha _____ the top shelf.   A B C D

    (A) isn't too tall to reach   (C) isn't tall enough to reach

    (B) isn't too tall for her to reach   (D) isn't short enough to reach

4. I don't think that restaurant takes credit cards, so remember _____   A B C D
some cash.

    (A) bringing   (C) bring

    (B) and bring   (D) to bring

5. My favorite teacher always encouraged me _____ my best.   A B C D

    (A) doing   (C) to do

    (B) for doing   (D) do

6. We always set two alarm clocks in order _____. That's why we're never late   A B C D
for class.

    (A) not to oversleep   (C) we didn't oversleep
    (B) for not oversleeping   (D) not oversleeping

7. Tomiko never passes a homeless person without _____ about how lucky   A B C D
she is.

    (A) to think   (C) thinking
    (B) think   (D) for her to think

8. Let's run down to the mall _____ if we can find you some new shoes.   A B C D

    (A) and seeing   (C) see
    (B) to see   (D) for seeing

9. Do you want _____ with me tomorrow?   A B C D

    (A) go skating   (C) to go skating
    (B) skating   (D) going skating

10. When people retire, it sometimes takes them a long time to get used to   A B C D
_____ to work every day.

    (A) not going   (C) not to go
    (B) don't go   (D) aren't going

11. The situation there was still dangerous, so they _____ to come.   A B C D

    (A) warned against   (C) didn't warn us
    (B) warned us against   (D) warned us not

12. I'm very nervous about my interview tomorrow. I can't stop _____ about   A B C D
the interview.

    (A) be worried   (C) worry
    (B) to worry   (D) worrying

13. Nothing was damaged, so the judge decided the crime _____ for the man   A B C D
to go to jail.

    (A) was too serious   (C) was serious enough
    (B) wasn't serious enough (D) wasn't too serious

XII. SYNTHESIS

Each sentence has four underlined words or phrases. The four underlined parts of the sentence are marked A, B, C, and D. Circle the letter of the ONE underlined part that is NOT CORRECT.

1. Wendy and her husband are trying <u>to get</u> into the habit <u>of</u> <u>to take</u> a walk
   <u>every night</u> after dinner.   A B Ⓒ D

2. I don't mean <u>to hurt</u> your feelings, but <u>you're not</u> <u>enough old</u> <u>to be</u> out this   A B C D
   late at night.

3. We <u>read</u> an English-language newspaper every day <u>in order no to</u> fall behind <u>on</u>   A B C D
   current events and <u>to improve</u> our reading skills.

4. <u>Voting</u> in a national election is a privilege, and I've always looked <u>forward to</u> <u>be</u>   A B C D
   old enough <u>to have</u> a voice in my country's government.

5. The Dooleys love <u>being</u> outdoors, so they usually <u>decide</u> <u>to go</u> <u>camp</u> on their   A B C D
   vacations.

6. People who <u>start</u> <u>to smoke</u> when they're very young <u>discover</u> that stopping   A B C D
   <u>to smoke</u> is more difficult than they imagined possible.

7. The doctor told me <u>to don't worry</u>, but I<u>'ve been having</u> trouble <u>sleeping</u> since he   A B C D
   told me he plans <u>to operate</u> on my knee next month.

8. I remember <u>to watch</u> cartoons when I was younger, but I dislike <u>watching</u> them   A B C D
   now and I try <u>to encourage</u> my children <u>not to watch</u> them.

9. The guidance counselor has advised Laura <u>against</u> <u>taking</u> too many honors   A B C D
   classes and suggests <u>gets involved</u> in more school activities <u>instead</u>.

10. We enjoy <u>traveling</u>, and we don't mind <u>not to spend</u> much money <u>in order to save</u>   A B C D
    <u>for our trips</u>.

11. Boris used <u>to be</u> a professional tennis player, <u>so</u> he's used <u>to travel</u> a lot and   A B C D
    doesn't mind <u>not being</u> with his family on holidays.

12. When Professor Sato's students seem <u>to be</u> discouraged, he urges them   A B C D
    <u>not to give up</u> and <u>stopping</u> <u>worrying</u> so much about their grades.

13. Mark <u>is</u> only fourteen, <u>so</u> he's still <u>too young</u> <u>for getting</u> his driver's license.   A B C D

PART VII MORE MODALS AND RELATED VERBS AND EXPRESSIONS

I. PREFERENCES: *PREFER, WOULD PREFER, WOULD RATHER*

Complete the conversations with prefer, would prefer, *or* would rather. *Use* prefer *for general preferences; use* would prefer *and* would rather *for specific preferences.*

1. **A:** __Do__ you __prefer__ brushing your teeth before breakfast or after
   _{a.}
   breakfast?

   B: I definitely _____ to brush my teeth after I eat breakfast.
   _{b.}

2. **A:** On our next vacation, _____ you _____ go to the beach or to
   _{a.}
   the mountains?

   B: I _____ not go to the mountains again. We went there last year.
   _{b.}

3. **A:** There are two movies starting at the same time. _____ you _____
   _{a.}
   seeing an action film or a comedy?

   B: You know I _____ to see a comedy any day.
   _{b.}

4. **A:** Table for two? _____ you _____ to sit in the smoking or the
   _{a.}
   nonsmoking section?

   B: Nonsmoking, please. We _____ not smell smoke while we're eating.
   _{b.}

5. **A:** Lola _____ to take oral exams because she doesn't do well on written exams.
   _{a.}

   B: That's interesting. Most language students _____ taking written exams.
   _{b.}

6. **A:** Do you want to have dinner at home tonight?

   B: I _____ go to that new Chinese restaurant if that's OK with you.

7. **A:** _____ you usually _____ walking or biking to school?
   _{a.}

   B: I'm not sure. But today I definitely _____ to bike.
   _{b.}

II. PREFERENCES: *PREFER, WOULD PREFER, WOULD RATHER*

A real-estate agent is talking to a customer. Complete the conversation. Use the words in parentheses plus to *or* than *to make a comparison. If there is a verb, use the correct form.*

AGENT: So you're looking for a place to live. Would you prefer

__renting a house to renting an apartment__ ?
1. (rent a house / rent an apartment)

CUSTOMER: We prefer _____, and we'd rather
2. (an apartment / a house)

_____ .
3. (live in the city / live in the suburbs)

AGENT: OK. Have you decided on a location?

CUSTOMER: Well, we'd rather _____ on the West Side.
4. (move to the East Side / live)

AGENT: Do you have a car? It might be hard to find parking on the East Side.

CUSTOMER: No, we don't have a car. We prefer _____
5. (take public transportation / drive)
in the city.

AGENT: OK. Let's see what we have available.

III. NECESSITY: *HAVE (GOT) TO, DON'T HAVE TO, MUST, MUST NOT, CAN'T*

Complete these rules from a youth hostel. Use have to, don't have to, *or* can't.

1. You _____ have to _____ leave the hostel between 9:00 A.M. and 2:00 P.M. No one is allowed to stay between those hours.

2. You _____ make your bed every morning. Anyone whose bed isn't made will pay an extra charge of $5.00 a day.

3. You _____ make your bed on your last day, but please take the sheets off and leave them next to the bed.

4. You _____ eat or drink in your room. We have a dining room for that.

5. You _____ come in after 11:30 P.M. We lock the doors at exactly 11:30.

6. You _____ leave your passport with us. Just show it to us when you register.

7. You _____ smoke here. No exceptions!

8. You _____ make a reservation ahead of time during the winter. We're not very busy between January and April.

9. You _____ check out by 8:30 A.M. on your last day. Guests who check out late will pay an extra charge.

IV. NECESSITY: *HAVE (GOT) TO, DON'T HAVE TO, MUST, MUST NOT, CAN'T*

Complete the conversations with must, mustn't, *or* don't have to.

1. **A:** Are you going to Chicago tomorrow?
   B: No. The meeting was canceled, so I _____ don't have to _____ go.

2. **A:** Have some more coffee.
   B: No, thanks. It's getting late. I really _____ go home.

3. **A:** What's this switch for?
   B: You _____ touch that! It's very dangerous.

4. **A:** What does that sign mean?
   B: That parking place is reserved for people with handicaps. We _____ park there.

5. **A:** How much does the book for this course cost?
   B: We _____ pay for it. It's included in the class fees.

V. EXPECTATIONS: *BE SUPPOSED TO*

Complete the conversations with the verb in parentheses and a form of be supposed to.

1. **A:** What time are the Smiths expecting us for dinner?

   B: We _____'ve supposed to be_____ there at eight.

(be)

2. **A:** Do you know anything about Block Island?

   B: I've never been there, but my friends have told me about it. It _____

(be)
   really beautiful.

3. **A:** Stop here for a minute. I'm completely out of breath.

   B: But you're a jogger! Joggers _____ in good shape.

(be)

4. **A:** What's wrong?

   B: I'm in trouble. We _____ a writing assignment yesterday, and I

(hand in)
   completely forgot about it.

5. **A:** Why are you carrying an umbrella?

   B: Didn't you hear the weather report? It _____ this afternoon.

(rain)

6. **A:** Why are you so angry with Carol?

   B: She _____ anyone about the party, and she told half the people in

(tell)
   the class.

7. **A:** Why did Julie and Jim's parents punish them?

   B: They _____ home by midnight, but they didn't get in until

(get)
   almost 1:00.

VI. FUTURE POSSIBILITY: *MAY, MIGHT, COULD*

Circle the correct forms to complete the conversation.

A: What <u>may / (will)</u> you do this summer?

1.

B: I'm not sure yet. I <u>may / will</u> go to summer school.

2.

And you? What <u>could / will</u> you do?

3.

A: I <u>maybe / may</u> go to South America. I've been saving my money for a trip, but I

4.

<u>might not / couldn't</u> have enough money to go. If I don't go to South America, I <u>might / must</u>

5.   **6.**

visit some friends in Florida for a couple of weeks. . . . What about tonight?

<u>Might you go / Are you going</u> to Josh's party?

7.

B: Yes, I'm looking forward to it. Do you know what time it <u>could start / 's starting</u>?

8.

A: I'm not sure. <u>Maybe / May be</u> it starts at 6:00.
                        9.

B: That <u>couldn't / might not</u> be. Josh has a meeting at 6:00. I'll go at 8:00.
                  10.

A: I <u>mayn't / may not</u> have my car tonight. Could I get a ride with you?
          11.

VII. ASSUMPTIONS: *MUST, HAVE (GOT) TO, MAY, MIGHT, COULD, CAN'T*

Read the first sentence(s) in each set. Then circle the letter of the information that completes the sentence that follows.

1. "There's the doorbell. That has to be Joan. She promised to be here by 7:30, and   **A   B   Ⓒ**
    she's always on time."

    The speaker is _____.

    (A) expressing a possibility
    (B) expressing necessity
    (C) stating a conclusion

2. "It's almost midnight. Who could be calling at this hour?"   **A   B   C**

    The speaker _____ who's on the phone.

    (A) thinks he knows
    (B) doesn't know
    (C) isn't sure

3. "Bobby has just eaten a cheeseburger, and now he's ordering another one. He must   **A   B   C**
    be really hungry!"

    The speaker is _____.

    (A) stating a conclusion
    (B) expressing a possibility
    (C) making a negative assumption

4. "You couldn't still be hungry. You've just eaten two huge plates of spaghetti!"   **A   B   C**

    The speaker is _____ sure that the other person isn't hungry anymore.

    (A) not at all
    (B) almost 100 percent
    (C) rather

5. "I'm surprised John isn't home yet. He may be working late tonight."   **A   B   C**

    The speaker is _____.

    (A) expressing a possibility
    (B) stating a conclusion
    (C) making a negative assumption

6. "Terry and Wendy might not have heard the news."   **A**   **B**   **C**

   The speaker is _____ that Terry and Wendy haven't heard the news.

   (A) certain

   (B) almost certain

   (C) isn't certain

VIII.   SYNTHESIS

Find and correct the mistake in each sentence.

1. It might ~~rains~~ ^rain^ tomorrow.

2. You don't supposed to arrive late for a wedding.

3. I'm tired, so I wouldn't rather go out tonight.

4. We don't got to rush, because we have plenty of time.

5. Thomas may not to graduate this year.

6. Would you rather going to a movie or to a ballgame?

7. I prefer chicken than fish.

8. Sara doesn't has to work tomorrow.

9. If you want to do well in this class, you must studying very hard.

10. Bob has to take his driving test several times, but he finally passed it.

11. Our teacher was supposed to gives us a quiz yesterday, but he didn't.

IX.   SYNTHESIS

Circle the letter of the correct response.

1. I hope you're not going to miss class again tomorrow.   **A**   **B**   Ⓒ

   (A) I can.

   (B) You mustn't.

   (C) I might have to.

2. Will we have to memorize anything for the exam?   **A**   **B**   **C**

   (A) Yes, you do.

   (B) No, we won't.

   (C) No, we're not.

3. Does Tim prefer playing tennis to playing basketball?   **A**   **B**   **C**

   (A) Playing basketball.

   (B) Yes, he would.

   (C) No, he doesn't.

4. Are we supposed to bring anything to the party?   A   B   C

   (A) I think we should.
   (B) It's supposed to be.
   (C) Yes, we were.

5. Would you like to go out for dinner tonight?   A   B   C

   (A) Yes, I love it.
   (B) I'd rather not.
   (C) Yes, I will.

6. Is there any sandwich bread in the cupboard?   A   B   C

   (A) There might.
   (B) There might have.
   (C) There might be.

7. Tanya isn't eating her carrots.   A   B   C

   (A) She couldn't like them.
   (B) She mayn't like them.
   (C) She must not like them.

X.   SYNTHESIS

Circle the letter of the correct answer to complete each sentence.

1. We're supposed to use a pencil for this test, _____ I only have a pen.   A   B   C   D

   (A) so   (C) but
   (B) because   (D) or

2. More cake? No, thanks. I'd rather _____.   A   B   C   D

   (A) don't   (C) haven't
   (B) no   (D) not

3. I've really _____ leave soon. It's almost midnight.   A   B   C   D

   (A) have got to   (C) have to
   (B) got to   (D) must

4. I didn't mail your card until yesterday, so it _____ arrive in time for your   A   B   C   D
birthday.

   (A) must not   (C) may not
   (B) couldn't   (D) can't

5. _____ you rather buy a new car or a used one?   A   B   C   D

   (A) Would   (C) Will
   (B) Do   (D) Are

6. Eric arrived in time for dinner, but he _____ drive all day to make it in time.   A B C D

   (A) must

   (B) could

   (C) 's got to

   (D) had to

7. The sign says, "Do not enter." That means you _____ go in there.   A B C D

   (A) can't

   (B) couldn't

   (C) don't have to

   (D) might not

8. The Smiths _____ be asleep. It's 9:00, and they never go to sleep before midnight.   A B C D

   (A) might not

   (B) can't

   (C) don't have to

   (D) haven't got to

9. On New Year's Eve, I prefer _____ home to going to parties.   A B C D

   (A) stay

   (B) staying

   (C) to stay

   (D) stayed

10. We _____ put out the trash until Friday, but sometimes the building superintendent lets us put it out early.   A B C D

   (A) don't have to

   (B) couldn't

   (C) aren't supposed to

   (D) mustn't

11. You _____ go grocery shopping. I already did it this morning.   A B C D

   (A) aren't supposed to

   (B) must not

   (C) don't have to

   (D) can't

12. We're not sure how long we'll be away, but it _____ six days.   A B C D

   (A) can be

   (B) must be

   (C) has got to be

   (D) could be

13. When I was in school, students _____ wear shorts to school.   A B C D

   (A) can't

   (B) mustn't

   (C) weren't supposed to

   (D) may not

XI. SYNTHESIS

Each sentence has four underlined words or phrases. The four underlined parts of the sentence are marked A, B, C, and D. Circle the letter of the ONE underlined part that is NOT CORRECT.

1. She's got to leaving the house by six so that she can get to work on time.   A ⓑ C D
      A   B   C   D

2. Henry has been in the hospital for almost a week, so he can be very sick.   A B C D
          A   B   C D

3. I'd love to see a movie tonight, but I'd rather to see a comedy than an action film.   A B C D
      A   B   C   D

4. Tomorrow, all government employees will be supposed to arrive at work one hour earlier than usual.   A B C D
      A   B   C

   hour earlier than usual.
              D

5. She wants <u>to go</u> to the party tomorrow night, <u>but</u> she may <u>got to</u> <u>stay</u> home   **A B C D**

            A   B   C   D
with her little brother.

6. If the weather forecast <u>is</u> correct, we <u>mayn't</u> be able <u>to go</u> to the beach <u>this</u>   **A B C D**

                       A   B   C   D
weekend.

7. Kim <u>must</u> be telling the truth, but I <u>haven't believed</u> anything she's said <u>since</u>   **A B C D**

       A   B   C
she <u>lied</u> to me last week.

     D

8. I like <u>to watch</u> tennis tournaments on TV, but <u>I prefer</u> playing sports <u>than</u> <u>being</u>   **A B C D**

          A   B   C   D
a spectator.

9. <u>When</u> I was a child, I <u>must</u> eat everything on my plate <u>or</u> I <u>wouldn't get</u>   **A B C D**

    A   B   C   D
any dessert.

10. <u>I've got to</u> go to the office because <u>we're supposed</u> <u>to have</u> a meeting, but I   **A B C D**

    A   B   C
would rather <u>to stay</u> home.

                 D

11. You <u>don't have to</u> <u>look at</u> your book while you<u>'re taking</u> an exam because the   **A B C D**

          A   B   C
teacher wants you <u>to come up with</u> the answers without any help.

                       D

12. Wanda and I <u>are</u> <u>supposed to</u> go to a concert last night, <u>but</u> the singer got sick   **A B C D**

               A   B   C
at the last minute and <u>called it off</u>.

                     D

13. The kids <u>were supposed to</u> finish their homework and they <u>had got to</u> put their   **A B C D**

             A   B
things away, but <u>they didn't have to do</u> the dishes or <u>take out</u> the trash.

                   C   D

14. I think I<u>'ll go</u> with Sam tomorrow so that he <u>won't have to</u> <u>drives</u> all that way   **A B C D**

           A   B   C
<u>by himself</u>.

    D

15. We <u>don't mind</u> <u>taking</u> care of your cat <u>while</u> you're away, but we <u>wouldn't rather</u>   **A B C D**

       A   B   C   D
take care of your dog, too.

PART VII MORE MODALS AND RELATED VERBS AND EXPRESSIONS

I. PREFERENCES: *PREFER, WOULD PREFER, WOULD RATHER*

Complete the conversations with prefer, would prefer, *or* would rather. *Use* prefer *for general preferences; use* would prefer *and* would rather *for specific preferences.*

1. **A:** When you go to someone's home, _____do_____ you _____prefer_____ to bring
   a.

   flowers or candy?

   B: Actually, I _____ bringing something a bit more personal—like a pretty candle
   b.

   or a picture frame.

2. **A:** There aren't many empty seats left. _____ you _____ sit in the
   a.

   front or over there on the side?

   B: I'll get a headache if I sit too close to the screen. I _____ to sit on the side.
   b.

3. **A:** _____ you _____ to go to work by bus or by subway?
   a.

   B: I _____ taking the subway to work because it's faster. But on weekends, I
   b.

   _____ the bus.
   c.

4. **A:** _____ you _____ chicken or fish tonight.
   a.

   B: You know I _____ chicken any day. But if you're going to make your famous
   b.

   fried fish, I _____ have fish.
   c.

5. **A:** What do you want to do when we get together tomorrow? _____ you

   _____ see the new exhibit at the museum or go shopping?
   a.

   B: I _____ to go shopping. But if you _____ the exhibit, that's fine, too.
   b.   c.

II. PREFERENCES: *PREFER, WOULD PREFER, WOULD RATHER*

A used-car salesman is talking to a customer. Complete the conversation. Use the words in parentheses plus to *or* than *to make a comparison. If there is a verb, use the correct form.*

SALESMAN: So you're looking for a car. Would you prefer _buying a small car to buying a large car_?
1. (buy a small car / buy a large car)

CUSTOMER: I prefer _____, and I'd rather
2. (small cars / large cars)

_____.
3. (drive an automatic / a stick shift)

SALESMAN: OK. Do you have a specific model in mind?

CUSTOMER: Well, I'd prefer _____.
4. (buy a Japanese car / buy a European car)

SALESMAN: Are you interested in a convertible? I have a beautiful red convertible on the lot.

CUSTOMER: I don't think so. I'd rather _____.
5. (have a safe car / drive a pretty car)

SALESMAN: OK. Let's see if we can find something for you.

III. NECESSITY: *HAVE (GOT) TO, DON'T HAVE TO, MUST, MUST NOT, CAN'T*

Complete the conversation. Use have to, don't have to, *or* can't.

A: What did the doctor say about Bill?

B: He said Bill is OK, but starting today he _____ has to _____ take it easy. He
                                                          1.
_____ rest more and work less.
          2.

A: Is he going to quit his job?

B: Of course not. He _____ stop working. He isn't sick. He just
                              3.
_____ work such long hours.
          4.

A: What is he supposed to do to relax?

B: He _____ exercise more. The doctor said exercising is very important.
            5.

A: I go jogging every morning. He could join me.

B: Well, he _____ jog or play tennis for a while, but walking is OK. In fact,
                    6.
Bill _____ walk at least a mile a day.
        7.

A: When will he be able to play tennis again?

B: I'm not sure. He _____ go back to the doctor until next month. Then the
                            8.
doctor _____ check him again before telling him what he can and can't do.
            9.

IV. NECESSITY: *HAVE (GOT) TO, DON'T HAVE TO, MUST, MUST NOT, CAN'T*

Complete the conversations with must, mustn't, *or* don't have to.

1. **A:** The movie starts at nine o'clock. We'd better go now.

   B: It's only eight o'clock. We _____ don't have to _____ leave so early.

2. **A:** Hi. Come in and sit down for a while.

   B: Thanks, but I really _____ go. I have a lot of errands to run this morning.

3. **A:** What's this note on the refrigerator about?

   B: That's to remind us about the dog. We _____ forget to take him to the vet next week.

4. **A:** Ouch! My knee!

   B: You really _____ tie your shoelaces. You're going to have a bad fall one of these days.

5. **A:** Is Cynthia still in your writing class?

   B: No. She did very well on her placement test, so she _____ take writing this semester.

V. EXPECTATIONS: *BE SUPPOSED TO*

Complete the conversations with the verb in parentheses and a form of be supposed to.

1. **A:** What time does the teacher want us to come to class tomorrow?

   B: We _____'ve supposed to be_____ here an hour early—at ten.
   $\hspace{4cm}$ (be)

2. **A:** I'm thinking of going to Mexico for my vacation.

   B: I've never been there, but I've heard a lot about it. It _____ a
   $\hspace{8.5cm}$ (be)
   fascinating country.

3. **A:** I'm really embarrassed. I don't know how to dance.

   B: But you're an ice skater. Ice skaters _____ dance beautifully.
   $\hspace{5.5cm}$ (be able to)

4. **A:** What should I wear to the Howards' dinner party?

   B: I think men _____ a jacket and tie.
   $\hspace{3.5cm}$ (wear)

5. **A:** You look upset.

   B: I am. I _____ my black dress at the cleaner's, but I totally forgot.
   $\hspace{2.5cm}$ (pick up)
   Now I have nothing to wear tonight.

6. **A:** Why are you wearing such a heavy coat?

   B: Didn't you read the paper this morning? The temperature _____
   $\hspace{9cm}$ (fall)
   drastically this afternoon.

7. **A:** Is Serena angry at you?

   B: Yes, she is. We _____ together last night, but I went to the library
   $\hspace{3.5cm}$ (study)
   with Marty instead.

VI. FUTURE POSSIBILITY: *MAY, MIGHT, COULD*

Circle the correct form to complete the conversation.

A: Our office is moving to a new location.

B: I heard about that. When (will) / may we move?
   $\hspace{3.7cm}$ **1.**

A: It could / couldn't be sometime in the next few months—by the end of the year at the latest.
   $\hspace{0.5cm}$ **2.**

B: That new building on Main Street is almost done. Are we going to / may we move there?
   $\hspace{8.8cm}$ **3.**

A: We couldn't / might not move there—it's just apartments.
   $\hspace{0.9cm}$ **4.**

B: Maybe / May be we'll move to a bigger space. I hope so.
   $\hspace{0.5cm}$ **5.**

A: I heard we'll have a bigger space. But our own offices mayn't / may not be bigger. They
   $\hspace{7.9cm}$ **6.**

   could / couldn't be much smaller, though. I can hardly turn around in my office.
   $\hspace{0.5cm}$ **7.**

B: I don't care about the size of my office—but we have such great views now. In this new place, we

   might / might not even have windows.
   $\hspace{0.5cm}$ **8.**

A: Well, we <u>may / maybe</u> find out more at the meeting tomorrow. But, according to the weather
9.
report, it <u>might / will</u> snow a lot tonight—there's a 60% chance. So we <u>might not / won't</u> be here
10.   11.
tomorrow at all.

VII.   ASSUMPTIONS: *MUST, HAVE (GOT) TO, MAY, MIGHT, COULD, CAN'T*

*Read the first sentence(s) in each set. Then circle the letter of the information that
completes the sentence that follows.*

1. "The boss has been yelling at people all morning. He's got to be in a really bad   A (B) C
   mood."

   The speaker is _____.

   (A) expressing a necessity
   (B) stating a conclusion
   (C) expressing a possibility

2. "Terry has been working twelve hours a day all week. She must be exhausted!"   A   B   C

   The speaker is _____.

   (A) stating a conclusion
   (B) expressing a necessity
   (C) expressing a possibility

3. "Juan can't be in Puerto Rico. I saw him about an hour ago."   A   B   C

   The speaker is _____ sure that Juan isn't in Puerto Rico.

   (A) not at all
   (B) rather
   (C) almost 100 percent

4. "It could get very cold today, so don't forget to wear gloves and a warm hat."   A   B   C

   The speaker is _____.

   (A) making a negative assumption
   (B) expressing a possibility
   (C) stating a conclusion

5. "A letter for me? Who could it be from?"   A   B   C

   The speaker _____ who the letter is from.

   (A) thinks she knows
   (B) isn't sure
   (C) doesn't know

6. "If you go to Hollywood, you may see a movie star or two."

   The speaker is _____ .

   (A) expressing a possibility
   (B) giving permission
   (C) stating a conclusion

A   B   C

VIII. SYNTHESIS

Find and correct the mistake in each sentence.

   1. We're ~~supposing~~ to be at the restaurant at 7:30. *(supposed)*
   2. I really must to finish this letter this morning.
   3. Oksana knows how to drive, but she rather not.
   4. What time does he has to go to work today?
   5. Do you prefer eat a big lunch or a big dinner?
   6. The weather is supposed to be beautiful, but it rained all weekend.
   7. I don't think Mr. Sato is here today, but he maybe.
   8. Mike mayn't come if he can't get off work early.
   9. Do you got to do a lot of homework tonight?
   10. May the children be hiding under the bed?
   11. Our neighbors prefer using public transportation than driving.

IX. SYNTHESIS

Circle the letter of the correct response.

   1. Will we have to take a final exam for this class?

   (A) Yes, you do.
   (B) No, we won't.
   (C) Yes, you have.

A   (B)   C

   2. Would you like to go bowling this weekend?

   (A) No, I'd prefer not.
   (B) Yes, I do.
   (C) I'd rather not.

A   B   C

   3. Was I supposed to help clean up after the party?

   (A) Yes, you were.
   (B) I think you should.
   (C) No, you aren't. Don't worry about it.

A   B   C

4. Do we have to go to the supermarket today?   **A   B   C**

     (A) We might have.

     (B) We might be.

     (C) We might.

5. Would the children rather have ice cream than cookies?   **A   B   C**

     (A) Yes, I think they would.

     (B) No, they wouldn't rather.

     (C) No, they don't.

6. That huge oak tree in the park fell over.   **A   B   C**

     (A) That can't be true!

     (B) That doesn't have to be true!

     (C) That hasn't got to be true!

7. I'd prefer going to a museum. How about you?   **A   B   C**

     (A) I do, too.

     (B) So would I.

     (C) So had I.

X. SYNTHESIS

Circle the letter of the correct answer to complete each sentence.

1. No one has told the teacher that Salah left the program, so she _____ think   **A   B   Ⓒ   D**
he's still in our class.

     (A) can   (C) must

     (B) maybe   (D) couldn't

2. There's a sign in the school hallway that says, "No smoking." That means you   **A   B   C   D**
_____ smoke there.

     (A) couldn't   (C) might not

     (B) don't have to   (D) can't

3. The economy _____ supposed to improve over the next two years.   **A   B   C   D**

     (A) will   (C) is

     (B) is going to   (D) has been

4. Ines finished her homework last night, but she _____ stay up until midnight   **A   B   C   D**
to get it all done.

     (A) must   (C) has got to

     (B) had to   (D) could

5. You've really _____ call your parents. They'll be very worried if they don't
hear from you soon.

    (A) have to   (C) got to

    (B) must   (D) have got to

A B C D

6. The package isn't here yet—_____ it arrive tomorrow?

    (A) I may not   (C) could

    (B) may   (D) must not

A B C D

7. You _____ forget to take your medicine every day. If you forget,
you could become seriously ill.

    (A) couldn't   (C) aren't supposed to

    (B) mustn't   (D) don't have to

A B C D

8. Does Mr. Chang prefer _____ to his grandchildren in English or in
Cantonese?

    (A) speaks   (C) speak

    (B) spoken   (D) speaking

A B C D

9. Everyone _____ to hand in their test about half an hour from now.

    (A) had   (C) got

    (B) has   (D) must

A B C D

10. Luis _____ call me back over an hour ago, but I haven't heard from
him yet.

    (A) was supposed to   (C) has got to

    (B) must   (D) might

A B C D

11. Do you really think Alex and Tina will get married next year? Well, you know
them well, so you _____ right.

    (A) are   (C) could be

    (B) can be   (D) were

A B C D

12. That show _____ be on TV tonight. I've checked the whole TV guide,
and it's not listed anywhere.

    (A) doesn't have to   (C) must not

    (B) may not   (D) hasn't got to

A B C D

13. _____ you and your sister rather be in touch by phone or by e-mail?

    (A) Do   (C) Will

    (B) Would   (D) Are

A B C D

XI. SYNTHESIS

Each sentence has four underlined words or phrases. The four underlined parts of the sentence are marked A, B, C, and D. Circle the letter of the ONE *underlined part that is* NOT CORRECT.

1. Please <u>tell</u> the teacher I <u>maybe</u> late tomorrow because I <u>have to</u> <u>run</u> an errand   A Ⓑ C D

A   B   C   D

before class.

2. You <u>mustn't</u> eat too much before <u>exercising</u> because you <u>might</u> <u>getting</u> sick.   A B C D

A   B   C   D

3. Julio enjoys good food, but he<u>'d rather</u> <u>cook</u> his own meals <u>to</u> <u>eat</u> in restaurants.   A B C D

A   B   C D

4. My teacher <u>told me</u> that I <u>will be</u> supposed to <u>memorize</u> this poem and <u>recite</u>   A B C D

A   B   C   D

it in front of the class tomorrow.

5. Rick <u>may</u> not <u>know</u> much about computers, because he doesn't even know how   A B C D

A   B

<u>to turn</u> <u>one on</u>.

C   D

6. If Mike still has a bad cold, he <u>could</u> not <u>be able to</u> <u>go</u> to work <u>tomorrow</u>.   A B C D

A   B   C   D

7. Do you <u>think</u> Yolanda <u>would</u> rather <u>works</u> for a small company <u>or</u> for a large one?   A B C D

A   B   C   D

8. We<u>'ve never got</u> <u>to wait</u> so long for a table, so the restaurant <u>must</u> <u>be</u> really   A B C D

A   B   C   D

busy tonight.

9. When <u>renting</u> a car, you're <u>suppose to</u> <u>fill</u> the gas tank before you <u>return</u>   A B C D

A   B   C   D

the car to the rental company.

10. It's <u>surprising</u> that Jack <u>prefers</u> watching old movies <u>than</u> <u>seeing</u> newer films.   A B C D

A   B   C   D

11. I <u>wouldn't mind</u> <u>going</u> shopping with you today, but I <u>wouldn't rather</u> <u>go</u> to   A B C D

A   B   C   D

the busy mall.

12. The Parkers <u>had to</u> <u>drive</u> to the city this morning, <u>and</u> they <u>mayn't</u> be home yet.   A B C D

A   B   C   D

13. We're not sure if Sue <u>will come</u> to class tonight, <u>but</u> she <u>might</u> <u>will be</u> in class.   A B C D

A   B   C   D

14. Ken <u>must</u> <u>take care of</u> his sister last Saturday night, so he <u>wasn't</u> able to <u>join</u>   A B C D

A   B   C   D

his friends at the school dance.

15. Tara's parents want her <u>to go</u> to college in New York, but she<u>'d rather</u> <u>no</u> <u>go</u>   A B C D

A   B   C D

so far away from home.

PART VIII NOUNS AND ARTICLES

DIAGNOSTIC TEST

I. NOUNS AND QUANTIFIERS

Find and capitalize the proper nouns.

1. **A:** My mother went to J̶apan last month.

    B: Really? My mom and dad were in asia last month, too.

2. **A:** When is ramadan this year?

    B: I think it starts in october.

3. **A:** I like alicia bernstein.

    B: I do too. She's a really good english teacher.

4. **A:** Are you busy saturday?

    B: I'll be out of town. I'm going to st. louis for the weekend.

5. **A:** When did europeans first come to america?

    B: Most historians think it was a long time before columbus.

II. NOUNS AND QUANTIFIERS

Circle the correct words to complete the conversations.

1. **A:** I need to buy some gift /(gifts) for my nephew's birthday.

a.

    B: How much /(How many) gifts do you want to buy for him?

b.

2. **A:** The electricity / electricities just went out in all the houses on the block.

a.

    B: The power company will turn it / them on again soon.

b.

3. **A:** Do you think we'll get into trouble if we get to class few / a few minutes late?

a.

    B: Take it easy. There's / There are still a lot of time / times .

b.   **c.**

4. **A:** Could we open some window / windows? It's / They've been closed since we left for vacation.

a.   **b.**

    B: You're right. We need a little / a few fresh air in here.

c.

5. **A:** There's / There are a lot of chocolate / chocolates in this cake.

a.   **b.**

    B: Mmm, that's why it's so delicious. I hope you left some / any cake for me.

c.

6. **A:** Is there any / many pizza left?

a.

    B: There's only a little / a few pizza left, but we still have a lot of / much hamburgers.

b.   **c.**

7. A: I've sent Paul several / much notes, but he's never replied.

a.

   B: Well, I heard a little / a few news about Paul yesterday. He's moving to Costa Rica.

b.

8. A: There isn't a little / much bread left. And we need some meat for sandwiches. Would you

a.

     go to the store?

   B: Sure. How much / How many meat do you want? And I'd like some / any tomato on my

b.   c.

     sandwich, so I'll get a tomato, too.

III. ARTICLES: INDEFINITE AND DEFINITE

Complete the story with a, an, some, *or* the.

Once there was _____*a*_____ poor peddler. _____ peddler had

                                 1.   2.

_____ donkey that carried his goods. One day, _____ peddler bought

        3.   4.

_____ salt at the market. He loaded _____ salt on _____

        5.   6.   7.

donkey and started home. On the way, they crossed _____ stream. _____

                                                8.   9.

donkey fell into _____ stream, and _____ salt melted away. When

               10.   11.

_____ donkey stood up, he felt that his load was much lighter. _____

     12.   13.

peddler returned to _____ market and bought _____ sponges and

                  14.   15.

_____ cake for his wife.

     16.

   When they crossed _____ stream again, _____ donkey lay down,

                                  17.   18.

hoping to melt his heavy load. But _____ sponges soaked up water, and his load

                                         19.

became even heavier.

IV. ARTICLES: INDEFINITE AND DEFINITE

Complete the conversations with a, an, *or* the.

1. A: Where's Kathy?

   B: I think she's in _____*the*_____ kitchen. She was going to make herself

                                   a.

     _____ cup of tea.

        b.

2. A: Why are you looking for _____ new apartment?

                                    a.

   B: Because we need _____ bigger kitchen. This one's too small to cook in.

                           b.

3. A: I found some coins, some cookies, and _____ key under the sofa.

                                         a.

   B: Let me see _____ key. Maybe it's the one I lost.

                   b.

4. **A:** Can you help me? I need to get into this room, and I can't open _____ door.
⠀⠀⠀⠀⠀⠀⠀⠀⠀⠀⠀⠀⠀⠀⠀⠀⠀⠀⠀⠀⠀⠀⠀⠀⠀⠀⠀⠀⠀⠀⠀⠀**a.**

⠀⠀⠀**B:** That's because you're using _____ wrong key.
⠀⠀⠀⠀⠀⠀⠀⠀⠀⠀⠀⠀⠀⠀⠀⠀⠀⠀⠀⠀⠀⠀⠀⠀⠀**b.**

5. **A:** I'm _____ accountant. What do you do?
⠀⠀⠀⠀⠀⠀⠀⠀⠀⠀**a.**

⠀⠀⠀**B:** I'm _____ bus driver.
⠀⠀⠀⠀⠀⠀⠀⠀⠀⠀**b.**

6. **A:** Thanks for _____ scarf. It's really beautiful.
⠀⠀⠀⠀⠀⠀⠀⠀⠀⠀⠀⠀⠀⠀⠀**a.**

⠀⠀⠀**B:** You're welcome. I thought it was _____ prettiest one in the store.
⠀⠀⠀⠀⠀⠀⠀⠀⠀⠀⠀⠀⠀⠀⠀⠀⠀⠀⠀⠀⠀⠀⠀⠀⠀⠀⠀⠀⠀⠀⠀⠀⠀**b.**

V.⠀ARTICLES: INDEFINITE AND DEFINITE

Complete the sentences. Use no article (Ø) for general statements. Use the *for specific statements. Capitalize the first letter where necessary.*

1. _____Ø_____ ~~d~~Doctors go to school for many years.

2. I found _____ new video games you wanted.

3. Don listens to _____ classical music because it relaxes him.

4. _____ milk is a good source of calcium.

5. _____ water in this stream is polluted.

6. _____ pilots of World Air are very experienced.

7. Ira really enjoys _____ cartoons.

8. Who drank _____ milk? I wanted some.

9. _____ food in this restaurant is excellent.

VI.⠀ARTICLES: INDEFINITE AND DEFINITE

Complete the conversations with no article (Ø) or some.

1. **A:** Are Ted and Sally _____Ø_____ teachers?

⠀⠀⠀**B:** Yes, they are. Ted teaches math, and Sally teaches biology.

2. **A:** Are those _____ peaches?
⠀⠀⠀⠀⠀⠀⠀⠀⠀⠀⠀⠀⠀⠀⠀⠀**a.**

⠀⠀⠀**B:** No, they're _____ nectarines.
⠀⠀⠀⠀⠀⠀⠀⠀⠀⠀⠀⠀⠀⠀**b.**

3. **A:** I never eat any desserts; _____ desserts are too sweet for my taste.
⠀⠀⠀⠀⠀⠀⠀⠀⠀⠀⠀⠀⠀⠀⠀⠀⠀⠀⠀⠀⠀⠀⠀⠀⠀⠀**a.**

⠀⠀⠀**B:** Really? _____ desserts are too sweet for me, but others are fine.
⠀⠀⠀⠀⠀⠀⠀⠀⠀⠀⠀⠀⠀⠀**b.**

4. **A:** I see some oak trees.

⠀⠀⠀**B:** Those aren't _____ oak trees. I have an oak tree in my yard, and it looks very

⠀⠀⠀⠀different.

VII. SYNTHESIS

Find and correct the mistakes in the note. There are eleven mistakes. The first mistake is already corrected.

Dear Nita,

We arrived in M̶iami yesterday. We're going to the beach soon, but I have a few time to write this note. Our Hotel room is beautiful. It's a nicest place we've ever stayed in. A pool is lovely, too. We swam in it yesterday, and the water were just the right temperature. After that, we had lunch here in hotel, and we met the man from Centerville. We didn't know him, but he was sitting near our table so we started talking. He's the pilot, and he travels all over world. I know we're going to meet a great deal of interesting people here.

I must run. I'll call you soon.

Love,

Midge

VIII. SYNTHESIS

Circle the letter of the correct answer to complete each sentence. (Ø means "no article.")

1. You must be hungry. Can I make you _____ sandwich?   (A)   B   C

   (A) a
   (B) Ø
   (C) an

2. The Sorbonne is _____ university in France. It's very famous.   A   B   C

   (A) an
   (B) the
   (C) a

3. Have _____ rice. It's delicious.   A   B   C

   (A) a
   (B) some
   (C) little

4. Could I borrow _____ dollars? I'll pay you back on Friday.   A   B   C

   (A) a few
   (B) few
   (C) a little

5. That actor is not very popular. He has _____ fans.   A   B   C

   (A) few
   (B) any
   (C) little

6. The oatmeal doesn't taste very good because we didn't use _____ milk.   **A**   **B**   **C**

   (A) some
   (B) enough
   (C) many

7. Mrs. Noone is _____ acting teacher. She gives private lessons to young   **A**   **B**   **C**
   students who dream of being stars.

   (A) a
   (B) the
   (C) an

8. Look at all those ants! Oh, no! They're not ants. They're _____.   **A**   **B**   **C**

   (A) some termites
   (B) termites
   (C) the termites

9. _____ new assistant is very efficient. I'm glad we hired him.   **A**   **B**   **C**

   (A) A
   (B) Ø
   (C) The

10. Teachers in _____ countries of the world don't receive very high salaries.   **A**   **B**   **C**

    (A) much
    (B) a great deal of
    (C) many

11. I put your mail on your desk. You received _____ mail today.   **A**   **B**   **C**

    (A) a great deal of
    (B) a few
    (C) several

IX. SYNTHESIS

Each sentence has four underlined words or phrases. The four underlined parts of the sentence are marked A, B, C, and D. Circle the letter of the ONE underlined part that is NOT CORRECT.

1. <u>The</u> president of <u>the company</u> is looking for <u>a</u> assistant, and Friday is <u>the last</u>   **A**   **B**   Ⓒ   **D**
      A   **B**   **C**   **D**
   day to apply.

2. They grow <u>a lot of</u> corn in <u>the United States</u> because of the <u>weathers</u> in <u>many</u>   **A**   **B**   **C**   **D**
            A   **B**   **C**   **D**
   parts of the country.

3. <u>My cousin Tito</u> is going to buy <u>his girlfriend, Lisa</u>, <u>an</u> expensive jewelry for her   **A**   **B**   **C**   **D**
          A   **B**   **C**
   <u>birthday</u> next month.
      D

4. People in <u>the United States</u> and <u>Canada</u> celebrate <u>Thanksgiving</u> in the <u>Fall</u>.
    A · B · C · D   A B C D

5. Many people <u>agree</u> that <u>the chocolate</u> is <u>the most</u> delicious food in <u>the world</u>.
    A · B · C · D   A B C D

6. Matt didn't have <u>many informations</u> before he started <u>the assignment</u>, but he's
    A · B   A B C D

done <u>a great deal of</u> research and now he knows <u>a lot of</u> facts about elephants.
    C · D

7. Mrs. Cohen has decided to move to <u>an island</u> in <u>the mediterranean</u> because she
    A · B   A B C D

hates <u>the cold</u> and wants to live in <u>a</u> warm climate.
    C · D

8. We heard <u>a few</u> news about the earthquake in <u>Mexico</u> but not <u>many</u> details,
    A · B · C   A B C D

so we're trying to get more <u>information</u>.
    D

9. If you want to save <u>money</u>, <u>a</u> best way to buy <u>tickets</u> is to go out to <u>the</u> stadium.
    A · B · C · D   A B C D

10. <u>The next time</u> I have <u>an</u> extra money, I think I'll buy <u>Maggie</u> a new <u>winter</u> coat.
    A · B · C · D   A B C D

11. <u>Much</u> of <u>the families</u> on our street plant beautiful <u>gardens</u> every <u>April</u>.
    A · B · C · D   A B C D

PART VIII NOUNS AND ARTICLES

I. NOUNS AND QUANTIFIERS

Find and capitalize the proper nouns.

1. **A:** My husband travels to ~~S~~an ~~F~~rancisco every month.

   B: Really? I've heard that california is a beautiful state.

2. **A:** My birthday is on friday this year.

   B: Why don't we have dinner at the new italian restaurant?

3. **A:** Which course does professor hugo teach?

   B: I think she teaches russian.

4. **A:** What are you doing for christmas?

   B: I'm going to the philippines to visit my family.

5. **A:** Where did eskimos come from originally?

   B: They probably came from asia.

II. NOUNS AND QUANTIFIERS

Circle the correct words to complete the conversations.

1. **A:** I've been studying English for six years.

   B: That's (a long time) / some long times.

2. **A:** I need some luggage / luggages for my trip.

a.

   B: How much / How many do you plan to buy?

b.

3. **A:** Come into the pool. The water / waters is / are just great.

a.   b.

   B: No, thanks. It's / They're too cold for me.

c.

4. **A:** Do you have enough fresh soil / soils for your garden?

a.

   B: I think so. I'm only planting corn / corns and some bean / beans this year.

b.   c.

5. **A:** There's / There are a lot of mistakes in this essay. I don't think you should hand it in yet.

a.

   B: Thanks for the advice / advices. I appreciate it / them. Could you help me proofread my

b.   c.

   paper?

6. **A:** <u>How much / How many</u> salt did you put in this soup?
        a.

    B: I'm not sure. It has <u>a lot of / much</u> olives. Maybe the olives made it so salty. Will it help if
                              b.

    I add <u>a / some</u> potato or two?
          c.

7. **A:** Have you read this terrible article? The journalist didn't do <u>enough / a lot</u> research.
                                                                          a.

    B: You're right. The article contains <u>little / few</u> facts and too <u>much / many</u> opinions.
                                               b.   **c.**

8. **A:** Have you gotten <u>much / many</u> mail from your family recently?
                           a.

    B: Yes, I received <u>a few / a little</u> news yesterday. Everything is fine, and they have <u>much / many</u>
                           b.   **c.**

    hope for the future.

III. ARTICLES: INDEFINITE AND DEFINITE

Complete the story with a, an, some, *or* the.

Aster and Mayumi, two of my classmates, used to be enemies. Several years ago, they both worked for

_____*a*_____ big company. Aster was _____ salesperson for _____
        1.   **2.**   **3.**

company and Mayumi was _____ secretary. One day, Aster didn't come to work because
                              4.

she had _____ bad cold. While she was out, she got _____ phone
         5.   **6.**

messages from _____ important customer, and Mayumi forgot to give her
                    7.

_____ messages. Because of that, Aster lost _____ customer, and
      8.   **9.**

_____ president of _____ company was very upset with her.
      10.   **11.**

    Aster couldn't forget Mayumi's mistake, and they had _____ nasty arguments.
                                                               12.

Later, Aster got _____ better job and left _____ company.
                      13.   **14.**

_____ next year, _____ two women ran into each other in
      15.   **16.**

_____ English department at Berlini's Language School. They were signing up for
      17.

_____ English class. They soon found out they were going to be in _____
      18.   **19.**

same class. They were able to laugh about their problem, and now they are good friends.

IV. ARTICLES: INDEFINITE AND DEFINITE

Complete the conversations with a, an, *or* the.

1. **A:** Have you seen my backpack?

    B: I think it's in _____*the*_____ kitchen.

2. A: I'd like to find _____ apartment that has _____ dining room.
   _a._   _b._

   B: My apartment doesn't have _____ dining room, but _____ living
                                    _c._   _d._

   room is very large.

3. A: There's _____ green glove on the front seat of the car.
                 _a._

   B: It's mine. See? Here's _____ other one.
                                _b._

4. A: Excuse me. Is there _____ bus going to Mill Springs from here?
                            _a._

   B: I'm not sure, better ask _____ ticket agent. He's over there.
                                  _b._

5. A: Is Jim _____ accountant?

   B: Yes, he is. He's had his own accounting firm for over ten years.

6. A: _____ weather is beautiful. Let's go for a walk.
         _a._

   B: Good idea. How about going down to _____ fish market on Ocean Street?
                                            _b._

   I think it's called Snappy's.

V.   ARTICLES: INDEFINITE AND DEFINITE

Complete the sentences. Use no article (∅) for general statements. Use the *for specific statements.*
Capitalize the first letter where necessary.

1. _____∅_____ P̸ilots have to be healthy.

2. We drank all _____ orange juice. I hope you didn't want any.

3. _____ cartoons on this channel are too violent for children to watch.

4. _____ water is necessary for life.

5. _____ doctors in this clinic are very good.

6. _____ music in this movie is annoying, isn't it?

7. _____ video games have become incredibly expensive.

8. _____ air pollution in this city seems to be getting worse and worse.

9. Lee is thinking of studying _____ journalism.

VI.   ARTICLES: INDEFINITE AND DEFINITE

Complete the conversations with no article (∅) or some.

1. A: Jan and Tim are _____∅_____ photographers.

   B: I know. And they're very talented.

2. A: I'm going to get a cat, because _____ cats are always such good company.
                                          _a._

   B: In my experience, _____ cats are good company but other cats aren't interested
                           _b._

   in people at all.

3. A: Are those _____ bananas?
                             a.

   B: No, they're _____ plantains.
                           b.

4. A: I usually like _____ spy novels, but this one is too confusing.

   B: I won't borrow it, then.

VII.   SYNTHESIS

Find and correct the mistakes in the note. There are eleven mistakes. The first mistake is already corrected.

Dear Lydia,

I started school this ᵂ̶Ŵeek, so I'm very busy. Woodrow University is a good school, but our instructors give a great deal of homeworks. I'm taking russian, Math, and English this semester. I also have a part-time job, in the evenings and on saturday, so I have few time to study.

     I'm living in a same apartment as last year, but I have two new roommates: Ruth and Sumalee. They're the nursing students. Our apartment is crowded, but we have an good arrangement. Ruth studies in a kitchen, I study in my bedroom, and Sumalee studies in the living room.

     English class starts in five minutes, so I have to go. I don't get many mail these days, so please write soon.

Love,

Anita

VIII.   SYNTHESIS

Circle the letter of the correct answer to complete each sentence.

1. _____ French Impressionist exhibit at the museum is very exciting.   **A** **B** Ⓒ

  (A) Some
  (B) Ø
  (C) The

2. The weather is nice here most of the year, but it can be very hot in _____.   **A** **B** **C**

  (A) a summer
  (B) the summer
  (C) Summer

3. Could you lend me _____ sugar? I'd like to bake Allen a birthday cake.   **A** **B** **C**

  (A) a little
  (B) a few
  (C) few

4. These apples look good. Oh, wait! They're not apples. They're _____.   A   B   C

   (A) the pears
   (B) some pears
   (C) pears

5. _____ archeology lecture was very interesting. Thanks for inviting me.   A   B   C

   (A) The
   (B) A
   (C) An

6. After the earthquake, everything seemed dark. People who lost their homes had   A   B   C

   _____ hope for the future.

   (A) a little
   (B) little
   (C) few

7. This classroom still needs a great deal of _____.   A   B   C

   (A) chair
   (B) chairs
   (C) furniture

8. We had a bad storm last night. _____ kept me awake all night long.   A   B   C

   (A) Thunders
   (B) The thunder
   (C) The thunders

9. Researchers in _____ parts of the world are working to find a cure for cancer.   A   B   C

   (A) many
   (B) a great deal of
   (C) much

10. No, this isn't my coat. _____ orange one over there is mine.   A   B   C

   (A) An
   (B) The
   (C) Ø

11. If you give someone a gift in Japan, don't wrap it in white paper because _____   A   B   C

   white is associated with death.

   (A) the
   (B) a
   (C) Ø

IX. SYNTHESIS

Each sentence has four underlined words or phrases. The four underlined parts of the sentence are marked A, B, C, and D. Circle the letter of the ONE part that is NOT CORRECT.

1. Jake called me <u>much</u> times yesterday, but I was out <u>much</u> of <u>the day</u>, so he left   (A) B C D

A   B   C

<u>a few</u> messages on my answering machine.

D

2. From December 26 to January 1, <u>many</u> people of <u>African</u> ancestry in   A B C D

A   B

<u>the United States</u> celebrate the holiday of <u>kwanzaa</u>.

C   D

3. <u>Applesauce</u> is <u>a</u> best food for <u>a</u> stomachache, so I'll buy you <u>some</u> applesauce.   A B C D

A   B   C   D

4. Before Mr. Sullivan retired and moved to <u>the Caribbean</u>, he was <u>the</u> president of   A B C D

A   B

<u>an</u> university in <u>California</u>.

C   D

5. About <u>a month</u> ago, Javier decided <u>to change</u> his major to economics because   A B C D

A   B

he thinks <u>they're</u> interesting and because he's always been good at <u>mathematics</u>.

C   D

6. My classmates and I had <u>a few</u> trouble with Unit 37, but <u>the grammar</u> in   A B C D

A   B

Unit 38 was <u>the easiest</u> <u>in the</u> entire book.

C   D

7. If you like <u>a good food</u>, you're going to love <u>the food</u> at <u>the new</u> seafood   A B C D

A   B   C

restaurant on <u>Main Street</u>.

D

8. We don't have <u>enough</u> time, but we can make it to <u>the 8:00 show</u> if we leave   A B C D

A   B

<u>the</u> house in less than half <u>an hour</u>.

C   D

9. <u>The</u> school counselor has <u>a great deal</u> of advice but only <u>a little of</u> information,   A B C D

A   B   C

so we're probably just wasting <u>a lot of</u> time talking to him.

D

10. To be healthy, <u>people</u> should get <u>enough</u> sleep, exercise <u>several</u> times a week,   A B C D

A   B   C

and eat <u>a great deal of</u> vegetables and fruits.

D

11. <u>The police</u> found out today that <u>the</u> information that they have about   A B C D

A   B

<u>the suspected kidnappers</u> <u>are</u> false.

C   D

NOTES

NOTES

NOTES

NOTES

NOTES

NOTES